DIMENSIONS
OF DETENTE

edited by
Della W. Sheldon

DIMENSIONS
OF DETENTE

PRAEGER PUBLISHERS
Praeger Special Studies

New York • London • Sydney • Toronto

0726839

40830

Library of Congress Cataloging in Publication Data

Main entry under title:

Dimensions of detente.

  Includes index.
  1. United States--Foreign relations--Russia--
Addresses, essays, lectures. 2. Russia--Foreign
relations--United States--Addresses, essays, lectures.
3. Detente--Addresses, essays, lectures. 4. United
States-- Foreign relations--1969-1974--Addresses, essays,
lectures. 5. United States--Foreign relations--1974-
1977--Addresses, essays, lectures. I. Sheldon, Della W.
E183.8.R9D55   327.73'047   78-6041
ISBN 0-03-044246-X

PRAEGER SPECIAL STUDIES
385 Madison Avenue, New York, N.Y., 10017, U.S.A.

Published in the United States of America in 1978
by Praeger Publishers,
A Division of Holt, Rinehart and Winston, CBS, Inc.

89 038 987654321

Preface

Harnessing the ideological great power rivalry between the United States and the Soviet Union to avoid nuclear war and halting or reversing the arms race are the overriding priorities in world politics today. Because of their crucial importance, the controversy over what detente* portends for these issues has occupied a prominent place in domestic and international political debates for over two decades. The intensity of the dispute has heightened in the face of attempts to implement detente, or peaceful coexistence, as the basis of day-to-day U.S.-Soviet relations. At issue in the volatile exchange of critical and supportive views—in the United States, the Soviet Union, and elsewhere—are serious and fundamental questions upon whose answers may depend the survival or destruction not only of the United States and the Soviet Union but of other nations and peoples as well. U.S.-Soviet relations, of course, occupy center stage in any discussion of detente. Central to that relationship is the necessity for fostering at least a minimal level of trust and cooperation to make possible the negotiations, compromises, and political agreements necessary to defuse the menacing arms race between the superpowers.

Beyond immediate U.S.-Soviet relations loom the problems of nuclear proliferation, the energy crisis, world trade, the international economy, and the growing militancy of the developing countries over the inequities they perceive in the disparity between North-South standards of living and terms of trade. If the United States and the Soviet Union are to fill constructively the leadership roles assigned them by their power, they must first stabilize their own relations and competition. In the past, the worldwide rivalry, activism, and interventionism of the United States and the Soviet Union not only set the tone for international politics but also created a dangerous milieu conducive to overreactions, miscalculations, and risky confrontations. The Cuban missile crisis is a classic example of the dangers inherent in such a milieu.

Implicit in the examination of the quest for detente and attempts to implement it in practice are the issues of change and uncertainty. Any changes in the relationship between the United States and the Soviet Union have an immediate and strong impact on international politics. The most

---

*"Detente" is the term used by U.S. foreign policy makers to denote a relaxing of tensions between the superpowers. The Soviet leaders use the term "peaceful coexistence" to describe their efforts to improve relations between capitalist and communist nations. For an analysis of "peaceful coexistence," see Chapter 1, "The Road to Detente."

positive legacy of detente one could envision—beyond survival—would be as a symbolic model for renouncing or limiting the use of force in the settlement of disputes. The nuclear era has made many modes of national and international conduct obsolete and the search for innovative approaches imperative. There is scarcely any part of international politics to which the lessons and benefits of detente could not apply—from the problems created by the growing gap between the northern industrial and southern developing countries; to the Middle Eastern embroglio; to relations with Europe, Japan, Latin America, and Africa; and toward the People's Republic of China (PRC) and its pivotal role between the United States and the Soviet Union.

Until 1972, the intermix of distrust and fear of the other's intentions and consideration of the consequences of a false step had resulted in virtual *immobilisme* in dealing creatively and constructively with the threat of nuclear war. Agreement on the principle of detente, or peaceful coexistence, as the basis for relationships between the United States and the Soviet Union was the first, tentative step away from this paralysis. Will detente falter on the shoals in attempts to implement it in practice, or will it at least partially overcome very real obstacles and controversies to create a more stable pattern of relations between the rival nuclear powers in particular and the international community in general? Does detente presage an era of productive big power negotiations and compromise, or an era of "hot peace" that may degenerate into World War III at any time? How is the transformation from implacable confrontation to limited cooperation and continuing rivalry to be realized in practice? Given the legacy of the cold war, suspicions and antagonism are easily revived or fanned, and relations could quickly degenerate. It is generally conceded that the cold war has ended, but what is to take its place? The underlying policies characteristic of that period linger on—a remaining commitment to the "containment of communism" still confronts the "expansion of communism"—as shown by the U.S. reaction to Soviet support of Angola and the introduction of Cuban troops.

If the phasing out of the cold war and the beginnings of a concerted effort to achieve detente can be attributed to the U.S.-Soviet confrontation over Cuba, it was a different set of opportunities that made agreement possible in 1972. Increasing alarm at the growing intensity of the Sino-Soviet dispute and the possibility of a direct confrontation with the United States over Vietnam strengthened the Soviet Union's long-term quest for U.S. acceptance of peaceful coexistence as the basis for relations between the two nations. As a result of Henry Kissinger's secret diplomacy and the much-heralded "ping-pong" diplomacy, Sino-U.S. relations were visibly and rapidly improving. Improvement of U.S.-Soviet relations would not only strengthen the Soviet Union in its stance vis-à-vis its communist rival, the PRC but would also enable it to come to terms, however limited, with one of its two adversaries. Also, with the escalation of the war in Vietnam to include

U.S. bombing of North Vietnam and the mining of the Haiphong Harbor (which contained Soviet ships), the Soviet Union was confronted not with an imminent attack upon a socialist state (as it had believed to be the case in Cuba), but an actual, sustained, and escalating attack on a socialist ally. An agreement with the United States might help end the war in Vietnam and at the same time rescue the Soviet Union from the awkward dilemma of failing to "decisively rebuff" imperialist aggression against a socialist state.

From its perspective, the United States saw similar security-enhancing opportunities in these circumstances. It could use its improving relations with the PRC as a lever to reach an agreement with the Soviet Union, not only to improve U.S.-Soviet relations but also to encourage the Soviet Union to pressure North Vietnam to negotiate an end to the protracted war in Vietnam, which was causing domestic turmoil and increasingly alienating the allies of the United States. It was primarily this amalgam of perceived opportunities and fears that made possible the agreements reached at the Moscow Summit in 1972.

The 1972 Moscow Summit marked the formal beginning of an attempt to transform the cold war relationship between the United States and Soviet Union into one characterized by attempts to reduce the risk of war between them and to reach agreements on limited cooperation in other areas, most importantly to halt the spiraling arms race. The major agreements were on political, military, and commercial relations. The formal acceptance and public proclamation of the agreements were lauded in both nations as the beginning of a new era in U.S.-Soviet relations.

The renunciation of war as a means of settling international disputes between the nuclear superpowers was dictated by the obvious price of doing otherwise—the devastation potential created by the development of the "ultimate" weapon and its delivery systems. The language of the agreements was sparse and vague: Competitive coexistence represented the lowest common denominator agreement possible between two distrustful rivals. Although there may have appeared to be additional increments of security or "guarantees" realizable from a more specific agreement, for example, on handling conflicts in the gray area of the Third World, the overriding priority was to establish all possible safeguards against a nuclear war between the two nuclear powers. Beyond the limitations of the possible, it was necessary, perhaps even desirable, to allow sufficient flexibility to meet unforeseen events and to provide for leeway to work out in practice methods of resolving the many conflicts of interest that inevitably arise between all nations, and great powers in particular.

There is also a need for a realistic awareness and acceptance of both the possibilities and the limits of detente. Such recognition would not only reduce disillusionment and cries of "foul play" that result from overoptimistic expectations or inflation of the results that realistically can be expected from detente but it would also focus efforts on the possible rather than utopian or "final" solutions. There is, at present, no "hot" war between the United States and the Soviet Union, as well as some evidence of cooperation and even occasional collaboration. However imperfectly, however unevenly the urge to detente has progressed, it has been a major factor in the avoidance of nuclear war thus far. One cannot fail to note that in those instances where a military conflict or political crisis threatened to escalate into a direct confrontation, there have been prompt, pragmatic, and cautious efforts to reduce tensions sufficiently to avoid such an eventuality. Cuba, the Berlin crisis of 1958–61, the Yom Kippur War of 1973, Vietnam in 1969–72, and Angola are cases in point.

There is no assurance, obviously, that this will always be the case. Therefore, in addition to efforts to improve relations, there must be consideration of and preparation for instances where one side behaves in an irrational manner, or its leaders are so lacking in political skills or information as to miscalculate grossly the risks and alternatives involved. What if the Soviet Union had reacted to the U.S. bombing of Hanoi or the mining of Haiphong Harbor by commiting Soviet troops to the defense of its socialist ally North Vietnam? What if U.S.-Soviet communications had broken down during the 1973 Arab-Israeli War when President Richard Nixon ordered a strategic air command (SAC) alert because it was feared that the Soviet Union was preparing to commit combat troops to Egypt? What if either nation's leaders perceive its existence or international prestige to be so seriously threatened that they are willing to risk war, as for example, in Cuba?

The danger of nuclear war remains ever-present until a realistic procedure for the resolution of crises is agreed upon, created, and *used*. The international anarchy resulting from the sovereignty of the great powers prevents the arbitrary establishment of binding settlement procedures, and the United Nations has been rendered impotent in settlement of great power disputes. The present fragile network of agreements and the increased communications are the important first steps in dealing with these "worst case" scenarios as well as less dramatic state-to-state conflicts.

A monograph on detente has yet to appear. While such a treatise is beyond the scope and intent of this volume, an attempt has been made to analyze the political, military, and economic dimensions of detente in order to increase general knowledge and understanding of an issue that is of vital import to the security and welfare of all nations and peoples. Although the issues involved are complex and often technical in nature, every effort has been made to present them in a manner comprehensible to anyone interested in knowing more about detente and its implications. Finally, an attempt has been made to raise thoughtful and provocative questions about the theoretical rationale, implications, and legitimate concerns surrounding the issue of detente.

In the first chapter, "The Road to Detente," Della W. Sheldon provides a broad overview of detente by tracing the origins of peaceful coexistence in the early days of the Soviet Republic and then contrasting it with contemporary policy. The major components of the policy—capitalist-socialist relations, the probability of war, the transition to socialism, and the Soviet world view—are then analyzed to show their import for U.S.-Soviet relations and international relations.

"Detente and U.S. Foreign Policy Making" (Chapter 2), by Fred Warner Neal, analyzes the Nixon-Kissinger foreign policy that began in 1969 to break the rigid mold in which U.S. foreign policy had been encased for nearly 30 years. The policy, as Nixon and Kissinger envisioned it, was to try to evolve a network of mutually advantageous relationships that would induce both the United States and the Soviet Union to avoid confrontation and to "link" them into continued collaboration to keep the danger of thermonuclear war at a minimum.

In "Detente and the Sino-Soviet-U.S. Triangle" (Chapter 3), Thomas W. Robinson analyzes the triangular and interacting nature of detente by examining the U.S.-Soviet, Sino-Soviet, and U.S.-Sino relationships with the policies of the third state as a "factor" in those relations.

Chapter 4, "Detente and U.S.-Soviet Relations in the Middle East During the Nixon Years (1969–74)" by Robert O. Freedman, analyzes the extent to which detente was actually present in the U.S.-Soviet relationship in the Middle East during the 1969–74 period. Particular attention is devoted to the question of whether Soviet actions during this period could be said to have been aimed at, or had the effect of, increasing or reducing tensions between the superpowers.

Arthur Jay Klinghoffer analyzes "Oil Politics and U.S.-Soviet Relations in the Middle East" (Chapter 5) for their implications for U.S.-Soviet relations in the area and their impact on the broader detente relationship. Several aspects of Soviet oil policies in the Middle East are explored, as well as the growing dependence of the United States on Middle East oil. The article concludes with an examination of five broad problem areas that could result in a U.S.-Soviet military confrontation over oil rights in the Middle East.

"East-West Commercial Contacts and Changes in Soviet Management" by Alice C. Gorlin (Chapter 6) analyzes the impact of commercial negotiations between U.S. and Soviet economic officials to determine the results, if any, of increased U.S.-Soviet contacts, and speculates on possible future changes in the Soviet economic system as a result of these contacts. Particular attention is devoted to the questions of transferability of managerial practices from the West's capitalist economies to the state-owned and centralized system and the insights gained by U.S. businessmen on these questions as a result of their negotiations with their Soviet counterparts.

In "Detente and the Defense of Europe" (Chapter 7), Elliot R. Goodman contends that, despite detente, the Soviet Union has proceeded unabated with a buildup of military forces in the heart of Europe, and that because of this the North Atlantic Treaty Organization (NATO) is as necessary as ever. Foreseeing only marginal increases in NATO's defense spending, he concludes that NATO force improvements must come from a more rational arms procurement policy for NATO (particularly from more standardization or interoperability of arms and equipment), greater rationality in the use of defense funds, and political leadership in both these areas and in healing of some of the "self-inflicted" wounds stemming from political divisions within NATO.

In Chapter 8, Jacob W. Kipp analyzes "Detente Politics and the U.S.-USSR Military Balance" by examining three major U.S. attitudes on the issue—which he characterizes as "alarmist," "realist," and "complacent"—and their divergence from the Soviet view, with its linkage of detente, the Soviet-U.S. military balance, and the ideological struggle in a global context. He warns of the danger of treating arms control issues in isolation from the general framework of U.S.-Soviet relations, and emphasizes the necessity of securing a SALT II agreement to preclude another escalation in the arms race.

Contents

1 The Road to Detente

Della W. Sheldon

INTRODUCTION

Detente did not suddenly emerge as a result of the negotiations concluded at the 1972 Moscow summit meeting between Richard Nixon and Leonid Brezhnev. The Soviet policy of peaceful coexistence or detente, as it is referred to in the West has been an integral part of Soviet theory and strategy, and therefore of U.S.-Soviet relations, since the early days of the Soviet Republic[1] and the oft-proposed basis of U.S.-Soviet relations since 1956.

With the advent of "detente" between the Soviet Union and the United States in 1972, the continuing debate over the relationship between Marxist-Leninist ideology and Soviet foreign policy was joined by a second set of questions about the "true" nature of peaceful coexistence, or detente, and what it portends for U.S.-Soviet relations and national security. How much is style? How much is substance? And to what extent do style and substance interact in the conduct of foreign policy? Is peaceful coexistence primarily concerned with the protection of the national interests and security of the Soviet Union through improvements in its relations with the capitalist West? Or is the goal of peaceful coexistence the realization of "international socialism"?* Is there any correlation between Khrushchev's and Brezhnev's repeated statements on coexistence and the USSR's conduct in international affairs? The answer is "yes," on all counts.

The affirmative response to the questions posed above creates an apparent paradox: How can the Soviet leaders simultaneously employ the policy of

---

*The terms "international socialism," "international communism," "world socialism," and "world communism" have been used interchangeably in conformity with Soviet usage. It should be noted that the Soviet leaders have yet to define precisely what *they* mean by these terms, that is, whether they imply political dominance of the international system or the adoption of socialism by all the nations of the world.

1

coexistence to enhance the Soviet Union's national security *and* to expand socialism—which inevitably brings it into conflict with the United States? On the other hand, is not acceptance of the long-term coexistence of the socialist and capitalist systems an implicit renunication of the goal of achieving international socialism? Does the USSR's commitment to peaceful coexistence mean abandonment of its goal of international socialism? If not, how are competition and cooperation between the two political systems related to the achievement of world socialism? The answers to these complex questions lie in the Soviet leaders' complex and subtle definition of coexistence as a dual and internationally interacting strategy designed both to avoid war with the United States and to expand the power and influence of socialism. The relative emphasis placed upon Soviet national security or support of revolutionary change in the international status quo depends upon an analysis of the "objective conditions" and "correlation of forces" between the two systems present in a given situation or epoch. This dual nature of coexistence was the major impediment to its acceptance by Western leaders, the greatest source of U.S.-Soviet conflict in 1956–72, and has been the major irritant in post-1972 relations.

In the Soviet conceptualization, the policy of coexistence has as its primary goal the avoidance of war and the preservation of the security of the Soviet Union and its socialist allies through reduction of the areas of tension and conflict between the Soviet Union and the United States. (Because of the intensity of the hostility and rivalry between the Soviet Union and the People's Republic of China, references to the "socialist system" or "fraternal allies" do not include the People's Republic of China.) The secondary function of the policy is to provide ideological clothing for the Soviet Union's attempts to expand its influence and power wherever possible, most particularly in the Third World countries.* Much evidence of the correlation between professed dedication to the principles of coexistence and the Soviet Union's foreign policy behavior exists in the pragmatic agreements concluded with the United States and other Western countries and in its championship of the Third World countries' aspirations for political and economic independence.

Peaceful coexistence is, at the same time, the foundation of Soviet political strategy and the major goal of that strategy. Coexistence, thus is, both a defensive and an offensive strategy. The two pillars of this multifaceted and interacting policy are to be found in the renunciation of the "inevitability" of war between the capitalist and socialist systems (the avoidance of war) and the Soviet Union's commitment to support national libera-

---

*The term "Third World" refers to the newly independent and nonaligned countries of Asia and Africa. It does not include the traditionally neutral European countries, such as Switzerland, Norway, Austria, or Finland. Furthermore, "Third World" is used as an abstract designation that is not intended to obscure the political, economic, and historic diversity among them.

tion movements and wars of national liberation (to expand the influence and power of socialism). Detente with the capitalist West and support of liberation movements in the Third World delineate the dual parameters of the policy of coexistence. Through the interaction of these two major components of coexistence, the Soviet leaders have attempted to accomplish a dialectical unity of opposites—security and expansion—in their quest for the realization of their ideological goal of the victory of socialism over capitalism. Peaceful but competitive relations with the Western nations are envisioned as facilitating the unfolding of the international class struggle that will eventually usher in the age of world socialism.

What, specifically, is peaceful coexistence? When, why, and how did the policy emerge? What is its relationship to detente? What impact has it had on U.S.-Soviet relations? What will be its role in future U.S.-Soviet interaction? Any attempt to analyze in so brief a space the complex trends in contemporary Soviet foreign policy is fraught with the dangers of oversimplification and incompleteness, but the importance of U.S.-Soviet relations and their impact on international politics and the implications that the policy of coexistence has as a partial guide to foreign policy making and interpretation of often highly ambiguous actions (by both the Soviet Union and the United States) warrant such risks.

To place detente in context, the origins of the policy of coexistence in the Leninist-Stalinist period are briefly traced as background for a more detailed examination of the contemporary concept of coexistence. The method employed was to analyze the policy statements of Soviet leaders and theoreticians to determine how *they* conceptualize peaceful coexistence, and then to elaborate upon some of the components of the policy, both theoretical and practical, that created obstacles to its acceptance in principle by Western nations prior to 1972 and that complicate attempts to implement it in practice in the post-1972 period.

THE ORIGINS OF PEACEFUL COEXISTENCE

To trace the origins of peaceful coexistence, it is necessary to begin with a brief synopsis of Karl Marx's and V.I. Lenin's analyses of capitalist-proletariat relations. Marx dealt with the antagonisms between the proletariat and the capitalists primarily at the national level: Because of continued oppression and impoverishment, the workers would eventually rise and overthrow their capitalist taskmasters and form a classless society under the guidance of the dictatorship of the proletariat. (Marx considered it possible that in countries with strong parliamentary systems, such as Great Britain and the United States, the working class might come to power through the parliamentary process.) In his analysis, capitalism would ultimately collapse as a result of a series of internal proletarian revolutions in individual countries.

An important contribution to Marxist theory was Lenin's emphasis on the international dimension of the class struggle and intercapitalist conflict. In *Imperialism: The Highest Stage of Capitalism*, he propounded that intercapitalist wars were inevitable so long as imperialism existed because of the capitalist competition to divide the world into "spheres of influence" for access to raw materials, markets, and investments—of which World War I was an example.[2] Lenin concluded that imperialism and war were inherent in the capitalist system. In Lenin's internationalized schema, the imperialist nations filled the role of the capitalists in Marx's analysis of capitalist-proletarian relations, and the colonial areas were analogous to the national working class: The imperialists and the colonies were the capitalists and the proletariat writ international.[3]

War was still viewed as resulting from class conflict, but in the age of "finance capital and monopolies" the entire world was transformed into an arena of conflict characterized by internecine capitalist competition and subjugation of nonindustrialized countries. In Lenin's analysis, intercapitalist rivalry and war would be the agent's of the downfall of capitalism.

Lenin laid the theoretical basis for capitalist-socialist relations at the Seventh All-Russian Congress in 1919 (held during the Allied intervention) when he emphasized "the fundamental antagonism between the capitalist and socialist systems," and warned that Soviet Russia must expect, and strengthen itself for, future interventions by the West.[4] This anticipation of future Western aggression against the Bolshevik state resulted in an extension of Lenin's theory of imperialism to include the inevitability of capitalist-socialist conflict because of the hostility of the capitalist nations toward the new Soviet state. Lenin declared:

> We are not living merely in a state, but in a system of states; and it is inconceivable that the Soviet republic should continue to exist for a long period side by side with imperialist states. Ultimately one or the other must conquer. Until this end occurs a number of terrible clashes between the Soviet Republic and bourgeois states is inevitable.[5]

The emphases were clear and strong. He anticipated a long-term period of conflict between the two systems in which war would be inevitable:

> The experience in history of revolutions, of great conflicts, teaches us that wars, a series of wars, are inevitable. The existence of a Soviet Republic alongside capitalist countries—a Soviet Republic surrounded by capitalist countries—is so impermissible a thing for capitalism that the capitalists will seize any opportunity to begin war again.[6]

The inevitability of war between the two systems thus became an article of faith in Soviet statements and policies: "Only after we overthrow, completely defeat, and expropriate the bourgeoise *in the entire world*, and not only in one country, will wars become impossible."[7]

Lenin's analysis of the international situation in December 1921 noted "a certain equilibrium" in international relations that necessitated "coexistence between the lone socialist state and the hostile capitalist world surrounding it." The Bolsheviks must maintain constant vigilance and preparedness, however, because ". . . we are always a hair's breadth away from intervention."[8]

At the Fourteenth Congress in December 1925, Joseph V. Stalin formalized peaceful coexistence as the necessary policy for a weak and isolated Soviet Union during a "whole period of respite," declaring that there existed a "certain temporary balance of power" between the bourgeois world and the proletarian world that had "determined" the present period of "peaceful coexistence."[9] In a series of statements in 1925–28, Stalin reiterated the Soviet Union's position on peaceful coexistence and capitalist stability, explaining the Soviet Union's policy with his theories of "respite" and the "ebb and flow" in the tide of revolution.[10] These interrelated theories simultaneously served to account for the lack of further revolutionary eruptions in Europe and as a justification for the theory of "socialism in one country" proclaimed in 1924. All forces, internal and external, must be rallied to strengthen and defend the USSR,[11] to prepare for the eventual world revolution by building socialism in one country.

Although the capitalist world was, of course, immeasurably stronger than the Soviet Union, capitalism was viewed as torn by internal divisions and conflicts, and therein lay the hope for the salvation of the new Soviet state: ". . . we have been able to hold out, and have been able to defeat the Entente powers . . . only because there was no unity among those powers. We have so far been victorious only because of the most profound discord among the imperialist powers. . . "[12] It therefore behooved the Soviet Republic to follow Lenin's advice to exploit the contradictions among the capitalists* to increase Soviet security:

The more powerful enemy can be conquered only by exerting the utmost effort, and by *necessarily*, thoroughly, carefully, attentively and skillfully taking advantage of every, even the smallest "rift" among the enemies, of every antagonism of interest among the bourgeoisie of the various countries and among the various groups and types of bourgeoisie within the various countries. . . .[13]

Neither Lenin nor Stalin expected that future proletarian revolutions

---

*In addition to the major contradictions between the socialist and capitalist systems and between the proletariat and the bouregeoisie in capitalist countries, the bourgeois world was considered to be rent by conflict between the status quo and revisionist powers over the spoils of World War I and between the imperialist states and their colonies.

would occur peacefully; because of capitalist strength and hostility, the transition to socialism would require war or revolutionary violence. Lenin warned in *State and Revolution* that "The replacement of the bourgeois by the proletarian state is impossible without violent revolution."[14] The emphasis on the necessity for violence in the transition to socialism continued under Stalin: ". . . the transition from capitalism to socialism and the liberation of the working class from the yoke of capitalism cannot be affected by slow changes, by reforms, but only by a qualitative change in the capitalist system, by revolution."[15] The conclusion was that capitalist-socialist relations would continue to be marked by conflict and war, and that revolutionary violence would be necessary to give birth to future communist regimes, but it was *possible* that the Soviet Union could temporarily forestall war with the capitalists through the policy of peaceful coexistence.

In the Leninist-Stalinist era, the soviet leaders, despite their emphasis upon the contradictions within capitalism, viewed the West essentially as a monolithic and hostile system with which genuine, long-term cooperation was impossible. Lenin's *Imperialism*, World War I, and the subsequent Allied intervention all had engendered the belief that capitalist aggression was inevitable so long as capitalism existed. Adoption of the policy of coexistence was an act of pragmatism, a desperate maneuver to prolong the period of "respite" until the Soviet Union was sufficiently strengthened to defend itself against a renewed capitalist onslaught.

In essence, the Leninist-Stalinist strategy of peaceful coexistence was defensive and short term—*defensive* to forestall the "inevitable" collision between the Soviet Republic and the capitalist countries and short term in that it would continue only until the capitalists once again committed aggression against the Soviet Union. In sum, the Leninist-Stalinist policy of peaceful coexistence was adopted in an effort to secure an intermission between wars. The policies of "coexistence" and "socialism in one country" did not signify an abandonment of the Bolsheviks' commitment to the achievement of international communism, merely its postponement.

The primary goal during this period was to ensure the survival of the Soviet state. The strategy was to call for a hiatus in revolutionary activities of foreign communists through the Comintern, to exploit the perceived internal and external contradictions in capitalism, and to attempt to postpone hostilities between the USSR and the capitalist countries through the development of traditional diplomatic and trade relations. In practice, this meant a temporary accommodation with the capitalists in state-to-state relations.

COEXISTENCE IN THE NUCLEAR AGE

The contemporary concept of coexistence[16] can be defined as a fundamental, long-term strategy to avoid war between the capitalist and socialist systems in order to (1) protect the construction of communism in the Soviet Union and socialism in the rest of the system, (2) expand the power of socialism and the influence of its ideas, and (3) alter the international balance of power, or "correlation of forces," in favor of socialism through victories in the ideological and economic competition with capitalism.

In essence, there have been two distinct concepts of coexistence: an early one that was applicable "when there was one Socialist country coexisting with the world capitalist system" and the contemporary one developed when "two world systems—the Socialist and the capitalist system"— coexisted in the world: "It is only natural that this second phase should be governed by other objective laws than the first."[17] The advantages and objectives have changed, too:

> Previously . . . the advantages of peaceful coexistence were used above all for consolidating the Soviet state, for gaining at least a temporary respite. . . . Today (it) provides a real opportunity to save mankind from the terrible menace of thermo-nuclear war. . . furnishes the conditions for building socialism (in the socialist system) . . . and paralyzes the aggressive, counter-revolutionary actions of imperialism . . . thereby creating a favorable atmosphere for the growth of the revolutionary and national-liberation movements.[18]

There are also implicitly two geopolitical wings of coexistence: pursuit of detente and acceptance of the status quo in Europe by the Western nations and advocacy of sociopolitical change in the Third World to enhance the international position of socialism at the expense of the capitalists. These interacting components of coexistence are symbolized by the dual parameters of renunciation of force in relations with the United States—the "noninevitability of war" thesis—and support of "just" or "holy" wars of national liberation in the Third World.

The Soviet Union's emergence from World War II as one of the two superpowers and the formation of the socialist system were exhilarating experiences for the formerly isolated and beleaguered Soviet communists. These factors, plus the post-World War II reemergence of capitalist-socialist hostility, necessitated a reappraisal and modification of Marxist-Leninist strategy and tactics so that they would correspond to a vastly changed international situation that contained prospects of both a "flow tide" of revolution and "the most destructive war in history."

The catalysts for the change in the concept of peaceful coexistence from a defensive to a defensive *and* offensive policy were the development of nuclear weapons and the formation of the socialist system in the late 1940s and an expanded world view (including abandonment of the "two-camp" or "monolithic capitalism" doctrine) that enabled changes in relations with the West and the newly independent and colonial areas. The USSR was no longer a beleaguered socialist outpost in hostile capitalist terrain, but one of the two nuclear superpowers, head of the socialist system, and a rival model of political and economic development. The thesis of "capitalist encircle-ment" was therefore jettisoned in favor of that of a growing, dynamic, and ultimately triumphant "socialist system." In the new Soviet scenario, it was the capitalists who eventually would be "encircled" by the progressively triumphant socialist system.

In terms of devotion to the principles of Lenin, at the Twentieth Party Congress in 1956, Khrushchev proclaimed peaceful coexistence to be the "fundamental principle of Soviet foreign policy," and dwelled upon the im-proved possibilities for peaceful transition to socialism via the parliamentary process. The Soviet Union was now confident that it could win the competi-tion with capitalism without the "export of revolution." Most important, war—capitalist-socialist war or intercapitalist war—was no longer a "fatalistic inevitability" because of the strength of the "world camp of socialism" and the "peace forces" opposed to war.[19] The proclamation of the "noninevita-bility of war" thesis was the keystone of the updated doctrine of coexistence.

Together, these modifications of Marxist-Leninist doctrine greatly moderated the element of violence traditionally associated with capitalist-socialist relations and the establishment of communist regimes, thus paving the way for improved relations with leaders of both Western capitalism and Third World countries and peoples. These changes were the ideological clothing for the practical changes in policy dictated by superpower rivalry in the nuclear era. Far more important than considerations of ideological tidi-ness were the practical applications of the noninevitability of war doctrine. At one stroke, the United States and the Soviet Union were removed from the nuclear collision course upon which the doctrine of inevitable war had placed them. Granted, this semantic abandonment of the inevitability of war still had to be worked out in practice, but inasmuch as foreign policy leaders' perception of what is "inevitable" and what is "avoidable" affects their selec-tion of both goals and strategy, it was an important modification. If war could be avoided, then it followed that serious negotiations and agreements with the capitalists were possible to eliminate the "hot beds of war" and on arms limitations.

The contemporary doctrine of peaceful coexistence, introduced at the Twentieth Party Congress in 1956 and reiterated at subsequent party con-gresses and international conferences by Khrushchev and Brezhnev, reflects a modification of the traditional Soviet world view and important new conclu-sions about the nature of international and capitalist-socialist relations in the nuclear age. The Leninist-Stalinist view of capitalism as monolithic and in-herently hostile gave way to an analysis of capitalist-socialist relations that separated ideological rivalry from state-to-state relations.[20] The ideological struggle between the two systems will continue unabated until one or the other is victorious, but this does not preclude improving relations, cooperating in their common goal of avoiding war and concluding trade and other agreements.

The Soviet leaders assert that the change in doctrine was made possible by the alterations in the "correlation of forces" including political, economic, and social, as well as military, power between the systems that enables the Soviet Union to deter capitalist aggression. The purpose of these announcements and subsequent statements on peaceful coexistence was to amend Marxist-Leninist ideology to correspond with the realities and opportunities of the nuclear era—the necessity for avoiding nuclear war, the potential for improving relations between the Soviet Union and the Western nations in the post-Stalin era, and the opportunities the Soviet leaders glimpsed in the Third World for the expansion of socialism and its influence.

Long-term coexistence with capitalism is now necessary because of the danger of nuclear war and possible because of the change in the balance of forces between the two systems. The socialist system is viewed as growing and dynamic, whereas the capitalist system is judged to be stagnant and decaying—the "last exploiting system." While capitalism will stagger on for some time, [21] perhaps even experiencing periods of growth in various countries,[22] its eventual eclipse or demise is considered to be inevitable. The current epoch is therefore characterized as one of transition from capitalism to socialism and peaceful coexistence is considered the best strategy for facilitating that transition.

The might of the Soviet Union and the United States is sufficient to result in their mutual destruction.* As Soviet leaders from Khrushchev to Brezhnev have frequently reiterated, the choice is either "peaceful coexistence or the most destructive war in history."[23] The possibility of nuclear annihilation of much of contemporary civilization and growing economic and political interdependence make peace and peaceful coexistence far more than "merely a truce between world wars."[24]

Khrushchev defined peaceful coexistence as the renunciation of war as a means of resolving the basic antagonism and controversial issues between the two systems.[25] Regular communication, serious negotiations, and binding agreements between the ideological rivals are mandatory if war—whether through design, accident, or escalation—is to be avoided. Existing political issues and tensions between the two systems must be resolved through negotiation and compromise, and future relations must be based upon mutually acceptable principles to enable peaceful resolution of the international and interstate problems that inevitably arise in the contemporary international system. Only if some "rules of the game" are developed can

---

*It is ironically appropriate that this mutual destructive capability is commonly referred to by the acronym MAD.

the competition between the systems be continued without resulting in war or a direct confrontation as a result of the escalation of a conflict involving their respective client states, for example, in the Middle East, Vietnam, and Angola. Also, to capitalize upon the opportunities the Soviet leaders perceived in the Third World countries, a means had to be found to permit expansion of Soviet influence and socialism that would not result in war with the defenders of the *status quo,* that is, the Western nations under the leadership of the nuclear-armed United States.

Instead of war, Khrushchev proposed that the two systems engage in peaceful political and economic competition to demonstrate before the nations of the world which is the better system: "Watching the progress of this competition, anyone can judge which is the better system, and we believe that in the long run all the peoples will embark on the path of struggle for the building of socialist societies."[26] It was contended that in the interim, the Soviet Union, together with the "peace-loving peoples" of the Third World and the working classes in the West, could restrain and isolate the "imperialist groupings" that are striving to "unleash military aggression" against the socialist system and to inflict reaction and "neocolonialism"[27] upon the Third World countries. In other words, Soviet might would be deployed to protect the security of the socialist system and to act as a deterrent to Western "interference" with the Third World countries' pursuit of their political and economic goals. This altruistic extension of the shield of Soviet protection contained an implicit inducement for Third World states to turn to the USSR for assistance if they ran afoul of the Western powers.

Just as Lenin had found it necessary to extend Marx's analysis in the light of World War I, Khrushchev had found it necessary to reinterpret Lenin, because again objective conditions had changed radically. The Soviet Union in 1956 faced a policy dilemma very similar to that of the early years of the Bolshevik state. In 1924, the choice had been between "socialism and one country" and fomenting world revolution, that is, between protection of Soviet national security and militant advocacy of "world communism." The Soviet Union then had little choice but to protect its national security until "capitalist stability" ended and another "flow tide" of revolution swept in. In the post-Stalin era, the choice was between considerations of national security and the opportunities perceived for the expansion of socialism and its international role. The Soviet Union, equipped with a nuclear arsenal and augmented by a ring of fraternal allies in the socialist system and the moral force of the "peace-loving peoples," chose to pursue both goals in its quest for victory over capitalism. Adoption of both options was explicitly set forth by a member of the Soviet leadership in a restatement of the Soviet position on coexistence in 1960 : "Two historical tasks are being carried out in the struggle for triumph of the policy of peaceful coexistance: the rallying and mobilization of the forces against the preparation and unleashing of a new war, and the winning of the masses to the side of the ideas of socialism."[28]

Coexistence, although long term, is not permanent. Its primary goal is to prevent world war, and it will end with the triumph of socialism over capitalism: "Coexistence . . . is a historical category. It has a beginning and is effective for as long as there exist on earth two socio-economic systems; in other words, until the old formation, capitalism, is replaced by the new— Socialism."[29] Soviet leaders warn that coexistence should not be distorted to mean that it is the "permanent coexistence of the Socialist and capitalist systems" inasmuch as this would impede social progress and mankind's advance to socialism.[30] In dialectical terms, the conflict between capitalism and socialism is viewed as beneficial and progressive because it facilitates the emergence of the new, higher form of social and political organization, socialism. Ideological rivalry between the two sociopolitical systems is the motor force that propels society from one stage of development to the next.

The international interaction of the dual pillars of peaceful coexistence was explicitly outlined at the Moscow Conference in late 1960:

> In the conditions of peaceful coexistence favorable possibilities are created for developing the class struggle in the capitalist countries and the national liberation movement of the peoples of the colonial and dependent countries. The successes of the revolutionary class and national-liberation struggle, in turn, help strengthen peaceful coexistence.[31]

Peaceful coexistence is viewed both as a means of avoiding war and intensifying the national and international class struggle against the capitalist system that will facilitate the predicted victory of socialism over capitalism. It intensifies, not limits, ideological warfare:

> The policy of peaceful coexistence is a particular form of class warfare in the international arena. It not only does not restrain revolutionary warfare but helps to boost it. The principle of peaceful coexistence does not and cannot extend to class warfare within the capitalist countries, to ideological warfare, to the war of oppressed peoples against their enslavers.[32]

In the parlance of Marxism-Leninism, the goal of coexistence is the avoidance of war and the expansion of socialism by championing the cause of the Third World countries against the West. The strategy is ideological warfare and economic competition between the two systems to demonstrate before the nations and peoples of the world which is superior; cooperation and negotiation with the Western nations to resolve existing and future sources of tension; support of nationalist movements to alienate them from the West and win them over to socialism; and encouragement of working-class activity in the capitalist nations to deepen the class struggle and gain support for the Soviet Union's "peace policy." The tactics require accenting the cooperative or competitive facet of coexistence as circumstances dictate.

Quest for Detente with the Capitalist West

Khrushchev led the exploration of opportunities for improving relations with the West with his 1956 proposals for the conclusion of nonaggression or treaties of friendship and cooperation, arms limitations, increased trade, and expansion of business and cultural contacts.[33] He argued that agreements in these areas would greatly diminish the conflicts between the United States and the USSR and reduce international tensions.*

Despite a promising beginning, the path to agreement proved to be a long and perilous one. The "spirit of Camp David" of 1959 gave way in the early 1960s under the impact of the second Berlin crisis, Khrushchev's militant assertion of Soviet support, "without reservation," of wars of national liberation (such as those in Algeria, Vietnam, and Cuba), which he described as being "just" or "holy" wars, [35] and the growing involvement of the United States in Vietman. The result was a dramatic illustration of the dangers inherent in the policy of cooperative but competitive relations between rival superpowers.

As the post-Stalinist Soviet leadership conceptualized it, Soviet foreign policy would progress along the dual lines of coexistence and expansion, with the socialist system steadily gaining in power and influence as the West was relentlessly weakened by the demise of colonialism. In actuality, the two nations moved ineluctably toward confrontation as a result of the Soviet Union's championship of a socialist regime in a U.S. sphere of interest—and the U.S. determination to defend that interest. The result was not the hoped-for geopolitical coup for the Soviet Union, but the fearsome "missile crisis" over Cuba in late 1962; not coexistence, but confrontation.

During 1955–59, the years of the "spirit of Geneva" and the "spirit of Camp David," the leitmotivs in U.S.-Soviet relations were the necessity for avoiding war, through negotiation, compromise, and cooperation and the co-responsibility of the nuclear powers for maintaining peace. With the continuing stalemate over Berlin in 1958–61 and the U-2 incident and the disrupted Paris Summit of 1960, U.S.-Soviet relations seriously deterio-

---

*The policy of peaceful coexistance has always emphasized improved economic relations because of the importance of Western trade for strengthening the Soviet Union and building socialism and communism. At the Twenty-first Party Congress in 1959, the economic aspects of peaceful coexistance received particular stress:

The economic program of peaceful construction in the USSR in 1959–65 opens up broad prospects for the development of Soviet foreign trade with all countries. We can at least double the volume of foreign trade.

We offer the capitalist countries peaceful competition, and our offer goes beyond the seven-year plan. We are drawing up a long-term plan for USSR development covering 15 years. This plan, too, is based on the principles of peaceful development and peaceful economic competition.[34]

rated. The era of good feelings and optimistic hopes gave way to consternation and increasing militancy.

The major components of the missile crisis emerged in 1960–61[36]—the culmination of Khrushchev's elaboration upon the Soviet Union's position on support of wars of liberation, Castro's announcement in April 1961 that Cuba was a "socialist state," and the election of President John Kennedy in the United States. Adding to the Cuban drama was Khrushchev's need for tangible foreign policy successes to quell the People's Republic of China's (PRC) growing criticism of the Soviet Union's policy of accommodation with the United States, as well as President Kennedy's political sensitivity and vulnerability following the aborted Bay of Pigs invasion, his meeting with Khrushchev in Vienna, and his growing alarm over events in Vietnam, Germany, and Africa.

These same considerations, plus the gains the Soviet Union glimpsed in the emergence of a revolutionary regime in Latin America, apparently prompted Khrushchev to elaborate upon the Soviet leadership's views on the nature of war and the necessity for avoiding it, with certain reservations. In his speech of June 20, 1960, Khrushchev admonished that general war, that is, world war, must be avoided; local war also must be avoided since "it may grow into a world war."[37] Khrushchev was also responding to the PRC's charges in a series of articles in April 1960 that peaceful coexistance was a "revisionist" policy. Wars of liberation were another matter. It was the international duty of socialists "to prevent or decisively rebuff the interference in the affairs of the people of any country who have risen in revolution."[38] The emphasis on the competitive pillar of coexistence, Khrushchev's elaboration upon the Soviet Union's duty to support wars of liberation, and the Kennedy administration's growing alarm at Soviet intentions all paralleled the Soviet Union's deepening involvement in Cuba.

The Soviet Union's emplacement of offensive missiles in Cuba undoubtedly resulted from an amalgam of considerations, but a strong motivation was its ideological commitment to the defense of a newly established socialist regime* against imperialist attack (which the Soviet leaders apparently sincerely believed to be forthcoming) and considerations of international prestige. The real issue for both the United States and the Soviet Union were their national security and international prestige. The United States and the USSR, like all great powers, have a special interest in those areas that have strong geopolitical importance to them, for example, Eastern Europe and Latin America. Any intervention of another power in such special areas inevitably precipitates a crisis. What the United States was ready to wage war to prevent, and what the Soviet Union was willing to gamble for, was a perceived change in the international balance of power, or correlation of forces.

---

*Following Castro's April 1961 declaration that Cuba was a "Socialist state," Cuba rapidly evolved from a "popular liberation movement"[39] to a socialist state by mid-April 1962.[40]

The ideological commitments of the Soviet Union, the policy positions the Soviet leaders had taken in 1960–62, pressures from the PRC, and the U.S.-sponsored Bay of Pigs invasion all had converged to leave the Soviet Union little apparent choice but to defend the newly established socialist regime in Cuba. To have done otherwise would have incurred an incalcuable loss of prestige and credibility for the Soviet Union in the eyes of other socialist states and the Third World states, which the Soviet Union desired to win over to the cause of socialism.

That similar considerations of prestige and international rivalry were involved in U.S. insistence that the Soviet Union remove the missiles from Cuba was evident in President Kennedy's retrospective remarks on the missile crisis: ". . . this was an effort to materially change the balance of power . . . not that (the Soviet Union) was . . . intending to fire (the missiles). . . . But it would have politically changed the balance of power. It would have appeared to, and appearances contribute to reality."[41]

The results of the Cuban crisis were a victory for neither side. Perhaps Khrushchev best summarized the situation in his report to the Supreme Soviet in December 1962: "Which triumphed? Who won? In this connection it can be said that it was reason, the cause of peace and security of peoples, that won."[42] The lesson that Khrushchev drew from the Cuban crisis was that "Not one problem of the revolutionary movement of the working class, of the national-liberation movement, can now be considered in isolation from the struggle for peace, for preventing thermonuclear war."[43] Khrushchev's thesis of peace and co-responsibility found a positive response in President Kennedy's speech at American University in June 1963:

> Both the United States and its allies, and the Soviet Union and its allies, have a mutually deep interest in a just and genuine peace and in halting the arms race. . . Let us not be blind to our differences, but let us also direct attention to our common interests and to the means by which those differences can be resolved.[44]

The crisis was the most severe in the cold war era, but in retrospect it proved to mark a turning point in U.S.-Soviet relations. The course of events in Cuba had firmly impressed upon the leaders of both nations that avoidance of war between them took precedence over all else. Peace had won, but would it next time? Given the role that personalities, irrationality, chance, and policy momentum play in international politics, it is utopian to assume that reason, security, and peace will prevail unless concerted efforts are made to assure that they will. Sobered by the prospect of a nuclear confrontation, both nations moved with renewed urgency in the quest for agreements to reduce the probability of a war between them, beginning with the Nuclear Test Ban Treaty of 1963. Unfortunately, this momentum was interrupted by the assassination of President Kennedy later in the year and Khrushchev's ouster in late 1964. Nevertheless, the realistic recognition of the imperative need to avoid war served as impetus for the patient quest for detente through a steady series of agreements, despite the strain on U.S.-Soviet relations of growing U.S. involvement in Vietnam and the successive crises in the Middle East. Symbolizing this two-tier relationship was the Glassboro Summit of June 1967 on ABM deployment, which indicated that diplomatic efforts to reach agreement on limited cooperation and arms control continued. . . . the Middle Eastern and Vietnam conflicts notwithstanding.

Sixteen long, tumultuous years after Khrushchev proclaimed peaceful coexistence to be the "fundamental principle" of Soviet foreign policy in 1956, the foundation of detente was laid with the signing of the U.S.-Soviet agreement on "Basic Principles" in Moscow in 1972. The agreement stated that the two nations would

> . . . proceed from the common determination that in the nuclear age there is no alternative to conducting their mutual relations on the basis of peaceful coexistence. . . .
>
> Both sides recognize that the effort to obtain unilateral advantage at the expense of the other, directly or indirectly, are inconsistent with these objectives. The prerequisites for maintaining and strengthening peaceful relations between the USSR and the U.S.A. are the recognition of the security interests of the parties, based on the principle of equality, and the renunciation of the use or threat of force.[45]

To this foundation was soon added the Vladivostok arms control agreement of 1974[46] and the Helsinki agreement on European security in August 1975, which legitimized the geopolitical status quo in Europe.[47]

Speaking of these agreements at the Twenty-fifth Party Congress in February 1976, Brezhnev characterized them as having laid ". . . a solid political and legal basis for the development of mutually advantageous cooperation between the USSR and US on the principles of peaceful coexistence.[48] Together, these agreements on coexistence, arms limitations, and permanent borders in Europe mapped out a "code of conduct" between the Soviet Union and the United States.[49]

The relaxation of tensions accompanying these agreements enhances Soviet security and national interests through Western acceptance of the "renunciation of force" agreement, diminishment of the "hot beds of war" in Europe, and potential arms limitations and troop reductions that would permit the Soviet Union to devote more of its resources to the development of its economy. This would hasten the realization of communism in the Soviet Union and the building of socialism in the rest of the system, which, in turn, would enhance the Soviet Union's ability to serve as the model for political and economic development in the Third World countries and, presumably, enable it to win the economic competition with the West more quickly.*

Adjusting the International Correlation of Forces

The offensive, or expansionist, wing of coexistence focuses on national liberation movements in the developing Third World countries. The Soviet Union continues to compete with the capitalist system through political, economic, and military support of national liberation movements in an attempt to win the political allegiance of these countries. As Brezhnev stated in his remarks on Angola at the Twenty-fifth Party Congress: "Our Party supports and will continue to support peoples who are fighting for their freedom."[50] Moreover, force might have to be used in defense of socialist regimes and "just" wars or liberation "The C.P.S.U. and the entire Soviet people . . . consider it their duty to support the sacred struggle of oppressed peoples and their just wars of liberation against imperialism.[51] Both these qualifications of renunciation of force were to have great impact on Soviet foreign policy and U.S.-Soviet relations.

The Soviet Union's commitment to the defense of socialist regimes outside its geopolitical core embroiled it in the Cuban missile crisis of 1962. Soviet support of wars of national liberation in Vietnam and Angola heightened Western skepticism about the sincerity of the Soviet leaders' commitment to and definition of "peaceful coexistence" between the two systems. In addition, there is the everpresent danger of escalation of "local" or "brushfire" wars into direct confrontation between the Soviet Union and the United States because of their championship of opposing belligerents. U.S.-Soviet involvement in these conflicts clearly points up the dangers inherent in the dualism of the Soviet Union's doctrine of coexistence: Support of national liberation movements is both the hinge that joins the two geopolitical wings of coexistence and the greatest source of past and potential conflict between the United States and the Soviet Union. It is this frankly expressed intent to continue its advocacy of revolutionary change in the Third World while negotiating agreements with the West to reduce the probability of war that has drawn the strongest fire from U.S. critics of detente. They deny that the Soviet commitment to peace is genuine, charging instead that detente is a ruse to lull the Western nations into a false sense of security while the Soviet Union surges ahead of the United States.

---

*Khrushchev's optimistic claims of the USSR's ability to surpass the United States in per capita production (by 1970) and the early transition to communism (perhaps as early as 1980) have become a dead letter owing to the decline of the rapid Soviet growth rate of the 1950s and because the USSR continued to be plagued by drops in agricultural production, which necessitated heavy grain purchases abroad in the 1960s and 1970s.

The Soviet leaders' recognition of the risks involved is tempered by their view that support of the "progressive" forces in such causes not only enables the Soviet Union to increase its own power and influence but also to fulfill its historic mission to usher in the age of world socialism: "An analysis of new present-day social phenomena shows that the present stage is characterized by growing possibilities for the further advancement of revolutionary and progressive forces.[52] This has remained their basic view despite numerous disappointments and setbacks in their relations with nationalist regimes in the Third World, for example, in Algeria and Egypt. The hypothesis that events in the Third World would flow from acceptance of Soviet political and economic support, to progressive reforms, to adoption of socialism was a major assumption in the Soviet Union's schema for the expansion of socialism—one that has been disproven by the many frustrations and dangers that the Soviet Union has encountered in, and as a result of, its relations with Third World countries.

The Soviet leaders' commitment to the revolutionary role assigned it by the Leninist tradition publicly commits the Soviet Union to support liberation movements and wars of liberation regardless of any short-term setbacks this may cause in its relations with the Western nations. At the practical level, the Soviet leaders are confident that the USSR's power and the desire of both nations to avoid world war are sufficient to contain any resulting conflicts at the "local" level. And, indeed, their experiences in Korea, Cuba, Vietnam, and the Middle East have thus far borne out this assumption. In addition, they can point to very concrete gains in the international political position of the USSR. The former international pariah now plays a major role in Asia and Africa, and often finds itself among a comfortable majority of communist and developing nations capable of opposing U.S. positions in the United Nations. The USSR also has succeeded in firmly establishing itself as both an alternate model of economic development and as an alternate source of trade and aid in the developing countries. It has gained acceptance of its legitimacy and an admixture of fear and respect as one of the two most powerful nations on earth.

The basic paradox of the Soviet policy of coexistence lies in the Soviet leaders' attempts to retain Western acceptance and support of a policy that simultaneously advocates cooperation with the Western nations to avoid war and intensification of ideological warfare to bring about capitalism's eclipse. Although Soviet policies are often more moderate than Soviet rhetoric, the explicit duality of the Soviet concept of coexistence was, for many years, an insurmountable obstacle to Western acceptance of the policy. It required the Cuban confrontation, the recurring wars in the Middle East, and the crisis of Vietnam to persuade leaders of both nations that an agreement on "rules of the road" between the two nations, however limited and ambiguous, was preferable to lurching from crisis to crisis. Given the global scope of the interests of the two nations and their rivalry for supremacy, it is inevitable that there will be conflicts in their relations and indirect confrontations resulting from the interaction of their client states. Acceptance of the policy of coexistence does not eliminate such encounters and conflicts, but it does provide for consultation and cooperation to prevent such situations from escalating into direct conflicts. The "code of conduct," however imprecise, introduces an expectation of certain types of behavior in conflicts of interest, and provides a basis for negotiation and resolution of crises.

The events in Angola sparked an intense debate over what detente means in practice. Does it mean that the two nations will continue to become embroiled in conflicts because of their support of opposing sides, as in the Middle East and Vietnam? Or does it mean that they will, in the language of the "Basic Principles," cooperate to resolve existing conflicts and to avoid future ones and forgo seeking unilateral advantage at each other's expense? Was Soviet support of a national liberation movement in Angola a violation of detente? U.S. foreign policy makers strongly answered in the affirmative. Secretary of State Henry Kissinger charged that Soviet arms aid to the Popular Movement for the Liberation of Angola (MPLA) was a violation of the rules of conduct between the two nations agreed upon in Moscow in 1972: ". . . we consider those actions irresponsible, inconsistent with the principles that govern the conduct between our nations, and the introduction of Cuban surrogate forces a very dangerous precedent.[53]

In the Soviet view, as Brezhnev reiterated, the USSR was merely continuing its long-term support of "peoples who are fighting for their freedom." From the U.S. perspective, this was a violation of the agreement to abstain from taking "unilateral advantage" of each other. At the Twenty-fifth Party Congress a month later, Brezhnev piously disavowed any "unilateral advantage" by asserting that ". . . the Soviet Union seeks no advantages for itself, is not hunting for concessions, does not seek political domination, does not ask for military bases. We act as we are bidden by our revolutionary conscience and our communist conviction.[54]

Again, the duality inherent in the Soviet definition of coexistence is evident. The Soviet leaders will exercise "restraint" in their dealings with the United States to avoid or minimize the impact of those situations that might lead to war between the two states. In all other situations, but particularly in those instances where U.S. "security interests" are not clearly involved, the Soviet Union considers itself free, indeed compelled by its revolutionary commitment, to continue its offensive against the capitalist nations. Coexistence, "restraint," and renunciation of "unilateral advantage" were accepted as the basis of U.S.-Soviet relations at the 1972 Moscow Summit. What these abstract principles mean in practice will have to be defined in the crucible of day-to-day encounters. Clearly, the Soviet leaders reject the interpretation, whether by Western leaders or their fraternal rival,

China, that detente implies the USSR's acceptance of the international status quo.

The thesis of avoidance of world war is the keystone of the Soviet policy of coexistence. Support for national liberation movements and wars of national liberation is the connecting link between the defensive goal of protecting Soviet national security through detente with the West and the offensive goal of extending socialism and its influence. Through political, economic, and military support of national liberation movements and wars of liberation, for example, in Algeria, Vietnam, and Angola, the Soviet Union seeks to "liberate" these areas from political and economic dependence upon the Western nations, thus destroying capitalism's colonial "hinterland." Soviet support of the nationalist aspirations of these countries has facilitated the Soviet Union's penetration of areas from which it had previously been excluded, and has permitted it to follow skillfully Lenin's advice to exploit the differences between the capitalists and the colonial peoples.

Soviet support of Third World political and economic objectives is designed to direct their resentment of traditional Western imperialism toward U.S. "neocolonialism," to demonstrate the effectiveness and superiority of the Soviet model of political and economic development, to increase Soviet influence and prestige internationally, and to win new converts to the socialist system. In the Soviet view, winning the political allegiance of the Third World countries would facilitate the transition from capitalism to socialism by creating a major change in the correlation of forces between the two systems, that is, by giving the socialist system an over-whelming preponderance of power vis-à-vis the capitalist system. In the future, the socialist system would then be able to dictate the course of international events as the capitalists had done when *they* were the dominant political power.

The dilemma created by the two geopolitical wings of coexistence is much in evidence here. The Soviet Union is willing, often even eager, to cooperate with the West to avoid war, achieve security in Europe, and reduce the arms burden; but in the Third World countries, which they regard as the prime arena of competition, they are all-out rivals for primacy. These latter efforts are in contravention of the agreement in the "Basic Principles" of 1972 that "efforts to obtain unilateral advantage" are inconsistent with "development of normal relations" and "preventing the development of situations capable of causing a dangerous exacerbation of their relations,[55] and have been a continuous source of conflict. Western leaders protest that the Soviet Union has a responsibility to decrease, rather than increase, areas of tension that might, by accident or escalation, transform local wars into major ones. The Soviet commitment to support the "progressive" change in the international status quo or the correlation of forces between the two systems and U.S. defense of the status quo, embodied in its long-term commitment to the "containment of communism," have produced the major crises of the post-World War II period.

CONCLUSION

The USSR's pursuit of these dual objectives—avoidance of war with the West and expansion of socialism—is rationalized by a complex, dualistic, and internationally interacting strategy that acknowledges and warns against the danger of war, while at the same time actively competing with its capitalist rivals for supremacy. The Soviet Union, forced by "objective conditions," that is, the realities of the nuclear era, to seek a modus vivendi with its rival superpower, also seeks to function as the vanguard of revolutionary change in the international system. Considerations of national security obviously must, and do, receive primacy, but support of national liberation movements remains an essential component of the Soviet Union's challenge to capitalism for dominance of the international system.

The contradictory aspects of this two-pronged pursuit of detente with the Western nations and revolutionary change in the international status quo have been repeatedly pointed out by both Western leaders and the Soviet Union's fraternal "ally," the People's Republic of China.[56] Western leaders recognized the necessity for, and in 1972 agreed to, the "renunciation of force" facet of peaceful coexistence, but have balked at acceptance of the Soviet definition of coexistence as including "crawling peg" alterations in the existing international power configuration. To the leaders of the PRC, the Soviet Union's recognition of the necessity for making concessions to and agreements with the capitalist nations constituted a betrayal of the cause of international communism.[57] (Although the PRC continues its charges that the United States and USSR are seeking to establish a superpower "duopoly" or "condominimum," its argument obviously lacks the moral force and impact that it carried before the PRC entered upon its own path to agreement with U.S. imperialists through the "ping-pong" diplomacy of 1972. Ironically, the PRC is now under attack by its former staunch ally, Albania, for abandonment of the "liberation movements" in Asia, Africa, and Latin America.[58])

The paradox of the Soviet position lies in the attempt to achieve transitional relationships with both the capitalist nations and the national leaders in the Third World countries, each of which requires a different approach.* The Soviet position on the "non-inevitability" of war and support for wars of

---

*These relationships are "transitional" because, in the Soviet view, ultimately both the Third World and Western countries must either adopt socialism or be under the influence of international socialism. Ultimately, these countries must be led by the working class, the prerequisite to the achievement of socialism.

liberation delineates the dual parameters of a policy which seeks to dialecti-
cally combine two apparently contradictory policy objectives into one international strategy. In its negotiations with the Western nations, the Soviet
Union primarily sought to enhance its security by securing Western acceptance of the existing socialist system and agreements on European security
and disarmament, that is, recognition of the status quo in the West. In the
Third World countries, the Soviet Union has posed as the champion of
nationalism and as a model for political and economic development to increase Soviet influence, alienate the developing countries from the West,
and to expand socialism. In these efforts, the Soviet goal is to alter the
international status quo.

The intricacies of trying to establish viable relations with nations that, it
is predicted, will ultimately be vanquished by socialism's advent are amply
illustrated by the Soviet leaders' prolonged wrestling with this thorny issue;
by Western leaders' skepticism of the Soviet Union's pursuit of agreement
on the renunciation of force *and* support of wars of national liberation and
defense of new socialist regimes, such as Cuba; and finally, by the Chinese
leaders' charges that peaceful coexistence with the West means sacrifice of
the revolutionary cause upon the altar of improved Soviet relations with the
Western nations.

The contemporary Soviet leaders postulate the victory of socialism on a
world scale, not as a fruit of war but as a result of the inherent superiority and
attractiveness of the Soviet system and mode of production. The emergence
of each new socialist state is viewed as a victory for the socialist system in its
ideological rivalry with capitalism and a step closer to world socialism. The
interests of the Soviet Union once again have been internationalized and
identified with the expansionism of socialism abroad as in 1917–24. There is
nothing new or surprising in this identification of national and international
goals; communists have wrestled with the question of national versus international goals since before World War I. What is new is that the power and
influence of the Soviet Union now make pursuit of both its national and
international goals possible—goals that it believes can be realized without
world war with the capitalists.

The Soviet Union is no longer dependent upon revolutions abroad; on
the contrary, it is now sufficiently powerful to deter capitalist aggression
against the socialist system, to act as a "shield" for the nationalist aspirations
of the developing countries and as a beacon to the working class in the
capitalist West. In communist theory, when history takes its "inevitable"
course and the "transition from capitalism to socialism" occurs, world war
will "become impossible"* because the "root cause" of international tension,

---

*This leaves unresolved the questions raised by the possibility of intersocialist war, with
which neither the Soviet nor the Chinese leaders have attempted to deal theoretically. Accord-

the antagonism between capitalism and socialism, will no longer exist. In the interim, intercapitalist wars, with their dangerous propensity to involve the Soviet Union, can be deterred by the might of the Soviet Union and the "peace-loving" peoples.

In comparison with the Leninist-Stalinist concept of coexistence, the contemporary version is considerably more sophisticated and complex. The Leninist-Stalinist concept of coexistence was short term, defensive, and relatively precise: War was an integral characteristic of capitalism and, because of capitalist hostility toward communism, a collision between the two systems was probably inevitable. The Soviet Union must therefore forgo advocacy of revolutions abroad for the time being, and concentrate upon building its strength in preparation for the next capitalist attack. Because of the strength of capitalism and its opposition to communism, new communist regimes would undoubtedly emerge only as a result of war or revolutionary violence. Capitalism was expected eventually to collapse as a result of its inherent contradictions and internecine warfare.

The contemporary strategy of coexistence is more ambiguous. It is defensive and offensive, and it envisions both peaceful and nonpeaceful change, both cooperation and competition. Intercapitalist and capitalist-socialist wars are still possible, but because of the changes that the Soviet leaders perceive in the "correlation of forces" in favor of the socialist system, they now consider it possible for the Soviet Union to deter the capitalists from unleashing wars in either category. The growing strength of the USSR and socialism and the end of the West's colonial empires have given the Soviet leaders confidence that world war can be avoided, but war will not become truly "impossible" until the transition from capitalism to socialism has been completed.[59]

Also, the basic nature of capitalism has not changed,[60] nor has its hostility towards communism, despite limited cooperation in such areas as the Middle East, European security, and arms limitations. Capitalism remains a threat because of its power and the very nature of its system; however, the "realistic" leaders of both systems recognize the irrationality of world war as a means of achieving political objectives, and they are therefore compelled by necessity to cooperate to avoid it. Neither capitalism nor socialism, as it now exists, can survive a nuclear holocaust.

Furthermore, the transition from capitalism to socialism can now be achieved either peacefully or nonpeacefully. The strength and "power of attraction" of socialism offer increased opportunities for the realization of

---

ing to Marxism-Leninism, war is an extension of the internal class struggle in capitalist states; inasmuch as classes do not exist in socialist states, there can be no war between them, theoretically speaking.

socialism via the parliamentary process, as events in Chile and Italy indicate, or behind the shield of Soviet deterrence of Western interference.

Finally, instead of collapsing as a result of its internal contradictions and warfare, capitalism is now envisioned as being gradually reduced to eventual political impotence as a result of its defeat in the ideological and economic competition with socialism.

If the contemporary concept of coexistence is more sophisticated—as the exigencies of the nuclear age requires—it also provides a less clear-cut guide to action. During the cold war era, the two tightly drawn camps were implacably opposed to each other, and each move by either the U.S. or the USSR was unhesitatingly viewed and reacted to as hostile or threatening. The slow move toward detente that began in 1963—the positive legacy of the Cuban missile crisis—has been characterized by an admixture of competitive-cooperative U.S.-Soviet relations that are both more flexible and more complex because of the increase in the number of probable outcomes in each situation. This is a distinct advantage for the USSR, for it gives the Soviet leaders optimum flexibility in their attempts to maximize both the Soviet Union's national security and opportunities for advancement of the cause of socialism. Which of the two pillars of coexistence, security or expansion, receives priority at a given time depends upon the Soviet leaders' assessment of the "objective conditions" and of the relative balance of power between the two competing systems.

The implications of the tactical flexibility inherent in the contemporary policy of coexistence have been a continual source of criticism and controversy among Western policy makers, and understandably so. They are confronted with the delicate and risk-laden responsibility for conducting relations with a nation that has agreed to cooperate to avoid war but that continues its support of revolutionary movements, which frequently brings it into indirect conflict with the United States. They must negotiate to halt or reverse the arms race, while each side continues to maintain its military power at unprecedented levels. They must seek to avoid situations that contain a risk that the two nations might become directly involved, and strive to prevent tensions from heightening in existing controversies. And, all the while, they must seek to construct a U.S. foreign policy offensive to meet the ideological challenge laid down by the Soviet Union.

How is it possible to improve or relax state-to-state relations when the cooperative-competitive policy of coexistence, by its very nature, contributes to confusion and distrust? Are Soviet initiatives and agreements an olive branch or a Trojan horse? These questions and suspicions comprise the shadow that the offensive wing of coexistence casts over the Soviet Union's efforts to secure Western cooperation in improved arms limitations, trade relations, and other areas of mutual concern.

The 1972 agreement on "Basic Principles" contained an implicit acceptance of each nation's spheres of interest in its "recognition of the security interests of the parties," but the major source of conflicts between them lie outside these spheres, in the "gray area" of their rivalry in the developing countries. The development of a "code of conduct" covering the two nations' interaction in these areas is a necessary next step in order to clarify the renunciation of "unilateral advantage" agreement and to avoid future Angolas, which cast a pall over detente and even threaten its continuance.

The 1972 U.S.-Soviet agreement on peaceful coexistence as the basis for relations between them marked the formal commitment of the two nations to detente. The road to securing this agreement in principle is strewn with the debris of the advances and setbacks that have characterized U.S.-Soviet relations since Khrushchev declared peaceful coexistence to be "the fundamental principle of Soviet foreign policy" in 1956. The steps necessary to transform, detente from a concept into a concrete reality undoubtedly will prove to be equally protracted and arduous. Whether the path of detente proves to be relatively smooth and straight or, more likely, uneven and strewn with obstacles, it is one that must be traveled. As Khrushchev emphasized at the Twentieth Party Congress in 1956: "Indeed, there are only two ways: either peaceful coexistence or the most destructive war in history. There is no third way."[61]

NOTES

1. See, for instance, Franklyn Griffiths, "Origins of Peaceful Coexistence: A Historical Note," *Survey*, no. 50 (January 1964): 195–207.

2. V.I. Lenin, *Imperialism: The Highest Stage of Capitalism* (New York: International Publishers, 1969), pp. 9–10, 119.

3. Ibid., pp. 124–25.

4. V.I. Lenin, "Report to the Seventh All-Russian Congress of Soviets of Workers', Peasants', Red Army, and Cossack Deputies," December 5, 1919, cited in Alvin Z. Rubinstein, ed., *The Foreign Policy of the Soviet Union*, 3rd ed. (New York: Random House, 1972), p. 62.

5. V.I. Lenin, Speech to the Eighth Congress of the Communist Party in 1919, in *Selected Works*, vol. 8 (New York: International Publishers, 1943), p. 10.

6. V.I. Lenin, *On Peaceful Coexistence* (Moscow: Foreign Languages Publishing House, n.d.), p. 135.

7. V.I. Lenin, "Military Program of the Proletarian Revolution," *Sochineniya (Works)*, vol. 13, p. 67, cited in Jan Librach, *The Rise of the Soviet Empire* (New York: Praeger 1965), p. 16. Elsewhere Lenin stated that " . . . the victory of the socialist revolution can be regarded as final only when the proletariat has triumphed at least in several of the advanced countries." V.I. Lenin, *Sochinenia (Works)*, 4th ed. (Moscow: Institute of Marx-Engels-Lenin, 1950), vol. 30, p. 185; cited in Alvin Z. Rubinstein, ed., *The Foreign Policy of the Soviet Union*, 3rd ed. (New York: Random House, 1972), p. 62.

8. V.I. Lenin, "Report to the Congress of Soviets," December 23, 1921, cited in Myron Rush, ed., *The International Situation and Soviet Foreign Policy: Reports of Soviet Leaders* (Columbus, Ohio: Merrill, 1970), pp. 28–31.

9. J. V. Stalin, Fourteenth Party Congress, December 1925, cited in Alvin Z. Rubinstein, ed., *The Foreign Policy of the Soviet Union*, 3rd ed. (New York: Random House, 1972), p. 11.

10. Joseph Stalin, *Foundations of Leninism* (New York: International Publishers, 1970), pp. 92–93.

11. *Resolutions of the Sixth Congress*, vol. 8, no. 84 (New York: International Publishers, 1930), p. 1950.

12. Lenin, *On Peaceful Coexistence*, pp. 97–98, 123.

13. V.I. Lenin, *"Left-Wing" Communism, An Infantile Disorder* (New York, International Publishers, 1969), p. 53.

14. V.I. Lenin, *State and Revolution* (New York: International Publishers, 1932), p. 20.

15. J.V. Stalin, *Leninism: Selected Writings*, pp. 424–26, cited in Michael P. Gehlen, *The Politics of Coexistence* (Bloomington, Ind.: Indiana University Press, 1967), p. 30.

16. Khrushchev's elaboration of the concept of peaceful coexistence remained the official line of the current Soviet leadership despite his removal from office in 1964. See in particular the reports of the Twenty-third Party Congress in 1966, which asserted that the CPSU is "guided by the line laid down by the 20th and 22nd Party Congresses." *Current Soviet Policies*, vol. 5 (Columbus, Ohio: American Association for the Advancement of Slavic Studies, 1973), p. 4; and the Twenty-fourth Congress, "Peace Program" (Moscow: Novosti Press Agency Publishing House, 1971), pp. 4, 37–39.

17. A. Sovetov, "Co-existence and Progress," *International Affairs* (Moscow) 8 (January 1962): 13.

18. G. Starushenko, "The National-Liberation Movement and the Struggle for Peace," *International Affairs* (Moscow) no. 9 (October 1963): 3–4. See also Khrushchev's speech of January 17, 1963 to the German Party Congress in which he remarked that coexistence now had "an essentially new content." *Pravda* and *Izvestia*, January 17, 1963, English translation in *Current Digest of the Soviet Press* 15, no. 3, (February 20, 1963), p. 17 (hereafter cited as *CDSP*).

19. Khrushchev's report to the Central Committee at the Twentieth Party Congress, cited in Leo Gruliow, ed., *Current Soviet Policies*, vol. 2 (New York: Praeger, 1953), pp. 36–38. Lenin and Stalin had considered war among capitalists to be inevitable. During the Leninist-Stalinist period, the theory of inevitable capitalist-socialist conflict had been added. At the Nineteenth Party Congress (Gruliow, *Current Soviet Policies*, vol. 1, pp. 7–8), Stalin had strongly implied that capitalist-socialist wars were no longer likely because of their great danger. In 1956, Khrushchev declared that neither capitalist-socialist nor intercapitalist wars were any longer inevitable. Khrushchev's announcements on peaceful coexistence, separate roads to socialism, and peaceful transition basically were restatements of existing Marxist-Leninist theory. The proclamation on the "noninevitability of war" was an original contribution to Marxism-Leninism.

20. Leo Gruliow, ed. *Current Soviet Policies*, vol. 2 (New York: Praeger, 1957) p. 37; and Georgi Arbatov, head of the Institute of the USA of the Academy of Sciences, *Izvestia*, September 4, 1975, English translation in *CDSP* 27, no. 36 (October 1, 1975) p. 3.

21. At the Twentieth Party Congress, Khrushchev presented a comparison of Western and Soviet industrial output to show the disparity in economic growth rates. He contended that the collapse of the West was being temporarily forestalled by military expenditures, foreign economic expansion, renewal of capitals equipment, and exploitation of the working class and the underdeveloped countries. Gruliow, *Current Soviet Policies*, vol. 2, pp. 29–31.

22. Ibid., p. 6.

23. Ibid., p. 36.

24. N.S. Khrushchev, "O mire i mirom sosushchestvovanni" (On peace and peaceful coexistence), *Kommunist*, no. 17 (1964); 3–5.

25. N. S. Khrushchev, "On Peaceful Coexistence," *Foreign Affairs* 38, no. 1 (October 1959): 3–4.

26. Ibid., p. 6.

27. V. Bogoslovsky, "The Essence of Collective Colonialism," *International Affairs* (Moscow), no. 12 (December 1960): 19–24.

28. B. Ponomarev, "Peaceful Coexistence Is a Vital Necessity," *Pravda*, August 12, 1960, English translation in *CDSP* 12, no. 32 (September 7, 1960), p. 5.

29. Sovetov, "Co-existence and Progress," p. 13.

30. Ibid.

31. "Statement of Conference of World Communist Parties," *Pravda* and *Izvestia*, December 2, 1960, English translation in *CDSP* 12, no. 48 (December 28, 1960), p. 9. See also Twenty-second Party Congress, *Current Soviet Policies*, vol. 4 (New York: Columbia University Press, 1962), p. 14.

32. Boris Ponomarev, "V. I. Lenin—The Great Leader of the Revolutionary Epoch," *Kommunist*, no. 18 (December 1969): 24

33. Twentieth Party Congress, *Current Soviet Policies*, vol. 2, pp. 35–36.

34. Leo Gruliow, ed., *Current Soviet Policies*, vol. 3 (New York: Columbia University Press, 1960), p. 61.

35. See Myron Rush, ed., *The International Situation and Soviet Foreign Policy* (Columbus, Ohio: Merrill, 1970), pp. 237–38; and Khrushchev's speech at the German Party Congress, English translation in *CDSP* 15 no. 4 (January 17, 1963): 17.

36. For other interpretations and analyses of the Cuban missile crisis, see Arnold Horelick, "The Cuban Missile Crisis," *World Politics* 16 (1964): 363–89; David L. Larson, *The "Cuban Crisis" of 1962: Selected Documents and Chronology* (Boston: Houghton Mifflin, 1963); Abram Chayes, *The Cuban Missile Crisis: International Crises and the Role of Law* (New York: Oxford University Press, 1974); and Andrés Suárez, *Cuba: Castroism and Communism* (Cambridge, Mass.: MIT Press, 1967).

37. Speech to the Rumanian Party Congress. English translation in *CDSP* 12, no. 25 (July 20, 1960): 6.

38. "Statement of Conference of Representatives of Communist and Workers' Parties," *Pravda*, December 6, 1960, and *Izvestia*, December 7, 1960, English translation in *CDSP* 12, no. 49 (January 4, 1961): 6.

39. *Pravda*, January 3, 1959. English translation in *CDSP* 11, no. 1 (February 11, 1959): 30.

40. *New York Times*, April 15, 1962. Cuba was acknowledged to be "building socialism" in the annual May Day greetings to the fraternal parties.

41. *Washington Post*, December 18, 1962.

42. N. S. Khrushchev, *To Avert War, Our Prime Task* (Moscow: Foreign Languages Publishing House, 1963), p. 45.

43. Khrushchev's speech at the German Party Congess, *Pravda* and *Izvestia*, January 17, 1963. English translation in *CDSP* 15, no. 4 (February 20, 1963): 16.

44. Address by President John F. Kennedy, Washington, D.C., "Toward a Strategy of Peace," June 10, 1963, U.S. Department of State, *Bulletin* 49, no. 1253, p. 4; *New York Times*, June 11, 1963.

45. "Basic Principles of Relations Between the Union of Soviet Socialist Republics and the United States of America," *Pravda* and *Izvestia*, May 30, 1972, English translation in *CDSP* 24, no. 22 (June 28, 1972): 22.

46. "Soviet-American Meeting in Vladivostok," English translation in *CDSP* 26, no. 47, (December 18, 1974): 1–6.

47. "Conference on Security and Cooperation in Europe: Final Act," U.S. Department of State, *Bulletin* 73, no. 1888 (September 1, 1975): 323–48.

48. Twenty-fifth Party Congress, *Pravda* and *Izvestia*, February 25, 1976, English translation in *CDSP* 28, no. 8 (March 24, 1976): 9–10.

49. G. Trofimenko, "From Confrontation to Coexistence," *International Affairs* (Moscow), no. 10 (October 1975): 38.

50. Ibid., p. 7.

51. Twenty-second Party Congress, *Current Soviet Policies*, vol. 4, p. 14. See also Khrushchev's speech at the German Party Congress in January 1963 English translation in *(CDSP* 15, no. 3 (February 13, 1963): 19) characterizing such wars as "holy wars and his January 6, 1961 "Report on the World Meeting of the Communist Parties," cited in Rush, *The International Situation and Soviet Foreign Policy*, p. 238. Strong statements on Soviet support for wars of liberation emerged in the aftermath of the Sino-Soviet confrontation at the meeting of communist parties in November 1960, and they continue today. See, for instance, Brezhnev's remarks on Angola at the Twenty-fifth Party Congress in February 1976, English translation in *CDSP* 28, no. 8 (March 24, 1976): 7.

52. Mikhail Suslov. "Leninism and the Revolutionary Transformation of the World," *Kommunist*, no. 15 (October 1969): 34.

53. The Secretary of State, Press Conference, April 22, 1976 (Washington, D.C.: U.S. Department of State), p. 1.

54. Twenty-fifth Party Congress, English translation in *CDSP* 28, no. 8 (March 24, 1976): 7.

55. "Basic Principles," p. 22.

56. The Sino-Soviet dispute, which began at the 1960 World Meeting of Communist Parties and escalated to public exchanges following the Partial Test Ban Treaty of 1963, dealt a severe blow to Khrushchev's and Brezhnev's desire to maintain the unity of the socialist system in the ideological offensive against capitalism. For the Soviet version of the dispute, see O. B. Borisov and B. T. Koloskov, *Soviet-Chinese Relations, 1945–73* (Moscow: Progress Publishers, 1975).

57. See, for instance, "The Proletarian Revolution and Khrushchev's Revisionism," *Peking Review*, no. 14 (April 3, 1964): 5–22.

58. *New York Times*, July 14, 1977.

59. See Lenin's quoted remarks on page 5, footnote 8.

60. F. Ryzhenko, "Peaceful Coexistence and the Class Struggle," *Pravda*, August 22, 1973 , English translation in *CDSP* 25, no. 34 (September 19, 1973): 5–6.

61. Twentieth Party Congress, *Current Soviet Policies*, vol. 2, p. 37.

2 Detente and U.S. Foreign Policymaking

Fred Warner Neal

Almost certainly, the movement away from the cold war was the greatest legacy of the Nixon-Kissinger foreign policy. Equally certain, it has been the most controversial. Nor is it surprising that this is so. The cold war had become a way of life for the United States. Numerous and powerful individuals and organizations had a stake in it—political, monetary, intellectual, and emotional. A sharp break away from such a deeply entrenched set of beliefs and institutions was certain to produce a sharp reaction. Also, the most serious and complex issues of national security were involved. And, by no means least, the Nixon-Kissinger policy of detente was something new under the sun—the seeking of a network of treaties, agreements, and understandings with a powerful and sometimes difficult adversary requiring at least a modicum of trust that had heretofore not existed.

There is little point in belaboring a definition of detente. As used here, it simply refers to the policy of actively seeking to improve relations with the Soviet Union. As Henry Kissinger, its chief architect, characterized it, detente "is a continuing process, not a final condition that has been or can be realized at any one specific point in time."[1] The idea behind it is essentially that, despite conflicting interests and a continuing adversary relationship, the overriding interest of both the United States and the Soviet Union is to agree on rules of the road for coexistence in order to avoid blowing each other—to say nothing of a good deal of the rest of the world—to smithereens. The policy, as Kissinger envisaged it, was to try to evolve a network of mutually advantageous relationships that would induce both countries to avoid confrontation and tie them into continued collaboration to keep the danger of thermonuclear war at a minimum.

The detente concept was, of course, broader than this, being conceived of as the prerequisite underpinning of a stable and peaceful world based on the realities of power. "There can be no peaceful international order," Kissinger declared, "without a constructive relationship between the United

States and the Soviet Union. There will be no international stability unless both the Soviet Union and the United States conduct themselves with restraint and unless they use their enormous power for the benefit of mankind."[2]

The U.S. policy of detente by no means either assumed or promised such a stable, peaceful international order. The assumption was that there was no alternative to trying. The promise was to make the effort.

In the short run, at least, the new policy failed, partly because of the difficulty of the task, partly because of faulty execution, and partly because of domestic circumstances. Yet it also had outstanding successes, which may be one reason it came under such heavy attack. One success outweighs all else: The detente effort broke the rigid mold in which U.S. foreign policy had been encased for nearly 30 years. A new departure was made. Continued efforts are now more possible, and, if they are pursued resolutely, more likely to succeed than would have been the case had not the Kissinger policy opened the way. Study of the past, present, and future of detente can throw light not only on superpower relations but also on the uses of balance of power, the implications of moralism as a basis for foreign policy, and the dependence of foreign policy on domestic politics and attitudes.

The policy of detente can be understood only against the backdrop of the cold war and U.S. involvement in Vietnam. This is not the place to debate the origins of the cold war. Suffice it to say that while the revisionist approach is refreshing, its purveyors, no less than the traditionalists, distort what seems to have been the reality. The cold war involved serious misperceptions on both sides.[3]

The Soviet Union may have hoped for limited cooperation with the United States after World War II, but was not prepared to risk very much to achieve it. In addition, Stalin's views were unquestionably conditioned by rebuffs, actual and imagined, from the capitalist countries in the interwar period. Enormously weakened by the war, the Soviet Union felt exposed and endangered before the awesome power of the United States, which, with bases surrounding the giant periphery of the USSR, commanded absolutely the seas and the skies. Moreover, the United States alone possessed atomic bombs. Given the ideologically inspired belief in the inevitability of both war and capitalist hostility, it should not have been surprising that the Kremlin interpreted as inimical positions that a less paranoiac view of the world might have seen as benign—and that it acted accordingly.

U.S. misperceptions were at least as great as those of the Soviet Union, and some of them less explicable. There were four major misperceptions that formed the basis of the U.S. cold war posture: first, the idea that the Soviet Union, by its very existence, posed a threat of military aggression, and that its *cordon sanitaire*-in-reverse in Eastern Europe presaged inexorable expansion; second, that the USSR controlled communists everywhere; third, that revolutionary activity anywhere was the work of communists inspired, if not directed, by Moscow; and, fourth, that the United States could indefinitely maintain military superiority over the Soviet Union, and that to safeguard itself it had to have a global military posture.

The result was a withering of diplomacy, an unprecedented arms race, and a zero-sum view of the world on both sides. In the United States, there arose an anticommunist, and antiSoviet, ideology nearly as rigid and all-encompassing as the communist ideology in the Soviet Union. When Stalin, shortly before his death, switched Soviet foreign policy from its long defensive stance to a global (albeit nonmilitary) offensive against the United States, it looked as if the cold war might heat up dangerously.[4] By 1954, both sides had thermonuclear weapons, giving the context a literally lethal potential, and not only for the two adversaries.

The Soviet Union was first to recognize this. Khrushchev, at the Twentieth Party Congress in 1956, made a fundamental break with basic tenets of Marxism-Leninism, which, from the Soviet side, had blocked any serious efforts toward a different approach. While he emphasized the great new strength of communism, Khrushchev made it clear that he was also influenced by the thermonuclear situation, which, he indicated, had changed the nature of the world. As a result, he advocated a new type of peaceful coexistence, not short run and tactical like Lenin's coexistence, but a long-run, strategic goal. Peaceful competition with capitalism, he held, would in the end bring victory to communism. But in the long interim, it was necessary, in the interests of communism, to make sure that there was no thermonuclear war. This meant, above all, meaningful agreements with the United States, where, he said, there was also evidence that this necessity had been perceived. It was obvious that an additional reason for Khrushchev's position was the need to devote more resources to the civilian economy, which he pledged to expand.[5]

The new Soviet position implied no surcease in the war of ideas and, of course, no compromise on basic Soviet national interests. Moreover, Khrushchev emphasized, the USSR would continue to support "wars of national liberation" and come to the aid of socialist regimes once established. Two additional caveats were implied: First, the Soviet Union must be treated by the United States as an equal power; and, second, communism must be accorded the status of a legitimate world system, like capitalism. Because the United States was aggressively opposing communism and saw combating revolutionary wars in its national interest, the Soviet ideological departure was virtually ignored here and had, at the time, little impact on the cold war. It was, however, a shift of momentous significance, providing the basis for a new Soviet view of international relations.

Until after the departure of John Foster Dulles, there was little response from Washington to the shift in the Soviet position. Then, in 1959,

President Dwight Eisenhower, as if suddenly aware of a new situation, invited Khrushchev to Camp David. The immediate problem was Berlin, and, after a tour of the United States, Khrushchev left, apparently believing that the president was prepared to compromise at the upcoming summit conference in Paris. If there ever was any chance of agreement, the still mysterious U-2 affair on the eve of the conference spoiled it.[6] When the Kennedys came to power, prepared not only to continue the cold war but to do it with vigor, things were right back where they were earlier. If the meeting of the two leaders in Vienna startled Kennedy, it frustrated Khrushchev, who found no sign of treatment of the Soviet Union on the basis of equality or recognition of the legitimacy of communism. One may surmise that this frustration accounted in part for Khruschev's shoe-pounding at the United Nations and also for his drastic action with the missiles in Cuba. Whatever other motives the Kremlin may have had in regard to Cuba, it seems clear that emplacement of the missiles manifested a Soviet resolve to protect socialist regimes wherever they existed, and also a desire to impress upon the United States that the USSR could no longer be ignored as a "military inferior."

After risking Armageddon in Cuba, both sides drew back in horror, and it may have been that the cold war could have been ended then and there. Certainly Kennedy gave evidence of a new approach in his speeches at the University of Washington and at American University, and Khrushchev gave in to the U.S. position in the nuclear test ban treaty of 1963. But soon thereafter Kennedy was assassinated, Khrushchev was ousted, and the United States plunged into the maelstrom of Vietnam. Efforts at cooperation continued in the Johnson administration, resulting in the nonproliferation treaty, an airlines agreement, extension of consular representation, and the beginnings of strategic arms limitation talks (SALT) negotiations in 1969. Washington's preoccupation with Vietnam, however, plus the uncertainty of authority in Moscow, precluded anything of significant scope from resulting. The newly emerged Soviet leader, Leonid Brezhnev, spoke vigorously about the need to implement coexistence,[7] but the election of Richard Nixon in 1968 seemed to offer little hope of a change in U.S. policy.

Nor was there anything in the background of Henry A. Kissinger to suggest he would provide an underpinning for a bold, new approach to the Soviet Union. Influenced first by William Yandell Eliott and then by Nelson Rockefeller, it is hardly surprising that he embraced most of the widely held underlying cold war assumptions. But ideology did not really interest Kissinger, and he was never a hard-line cold warrior. As his reputation became more firmly established, his public utterances became more independent and more heuristic in their approach to foreign policy. It would appear that it was this pragmatism more than anything else that the president and his national security adviser had in common.

It did not take much pragmatism in 1969 to see that, besides ending the Vietnam war, U.S. foreign policy badly needed not only a major overhaul but a new direction. The United States was seriously overextended, its alliances were rickety, the unprecedented stagflation was worsening, the dollar was in disarray; and there was a sharp decline in foreign trade. At home, there were widespread disorders and disaffection among the populace. In addition, constant expansion of the arms race posed an ever-greater danger of thermonuclear war. Clearly, something had to be done.

Detente did not spring fullblown out of the mind of Henry Kissinger. Rather it evolved—indeed, was almost a by-product—out of a complex set of circumstances. Both Nixon and Kissinger realized that the only way out of the foreign policy cul-de-sac was to change U.S. relationships with the Soviet Union,[8] as well as with the People's Republic of China (PRC). Nixon, in particular, had thoughts about a new approach to China, even before taking office.[9] Now, advised by Kissinger, he came to realize that the split between the two communist giants was deep and serious. Still, the immediate problem was Vietnam, where increasingly the question became not how to win but how to get out without seeming to have lost.

The situation was almost made to order for a student of balance of power politics and Metternich,[10] and Kissinger rose to the occasion. What he did was to fashion an approach calculated to take advantage of the Sino-Soviet conflict, ease cold war tensions with Moscow and Peking, and, in the process, gracefully extricate U.S. forces from Vietnam.

The first step was the Nixon Doctrine, aimed at limiting U.S. overseas military involvement. Kissinger then laid the groundwork for an overall approach to Moscow while dealing with the SALT negotiations already in progress. He also discovered that Moscow was increasingly worried that the United States and China might come to terms. Nothing could have pleased Kissinger more. It took only the ping-pong diplomacy signals from Peking to start him on his secret mission to China. The plan was to offer to patch up relations with China and, using the bait of trade opportunities and a possible tough line toward Moscow, to get the Chinese leaders to persuade the North Vietnamese to end the war on what Washington regarded as reasonable terms. Then he would jet to Moscow with the same kind of proposition, but with the expectation that the Soviet leaders, out of fear of a U.S.–PRC rapprochement, would be more willing to play ball than they had indicated. Trade advantages would, it was believed, make the communist powers more amenable and, at the same time, give the wobbly U.S. economy a shot in the arm.[11]

In one way, this Nixon-Kissinger gambit was eminently successful, but not quite in the way anticipated. Kissinger found China's leaders both willing and eager to improve relations, but when the president arrived in Peking it became apparent that they had very limited influence with Hanoi.

Further, although Peking badly wanted trade with the United States, it was clear that not much would be forthcoming very soon because of internal economic and political problems. And China's adamant position on Taiwan stood as a barrier to much more than the sort of abnormal normalization of relations that resulted.

In Moscow things were much different. Soviet eagerness to deal with Nixon was indicated by the nonreaction to the bombing of Hanoi and the mining of Haiphong Harbor on the eve of the presidential visit. The Soviet leaders proved both willing and able to urge a settlement on North Vietnam. They were ready to trade with the United States in large volume and, basically, on its terms. (The resulting trade agreement, for example, provided that exports to the Soviet Union not only would be cleared by a U.S. government board but also would not be sold directly or indirectly in competition with American products.) Additionally, they made substantial compromises on SALT and professed satisfaction with a German settlement less favorable than they had hoped for.[12]

The Soviet position reflected not only fear of U.S.–PRC collusion. The U.S. approach was, indeed, just what Moscow had been waiting for. The Soviet leaders were ready for a big breakthrough, for an overall settlement of differences that would end the cold war and usher in a new era of U.S.-Soviet relations. They called it *razryadka*—detente.[13] Their motives were fairly clear. They, too, had problems—different but more severe than those of the United States—with the guns and butter correlation. Their economy could profit enormously by U.S. trade to help it computerize and to open vast new resources in the East. They also shuddered at the danger of a thermonuclear war. They too, had troubles with allies. And, not least of all, there was China.[14]

The sweep of the "Declaration of Principles" proposed by Brezhnev took the visiting Americans by surprise. It envisaged much more than an easing of tensions. Explicitly, the Declaration was a call for general collaboration. Implicitly, it met the Soviet sina qua non for meaningful coexistence: recognition of the Soviet Union as an equal power and of communism as a legitimate system. In effect, it proclaimed an end to the cold war. At first, Nixon was hesitant, but, after discussions with Kissinger and making some changes in language, he signed it, as well as agreements on SALT, trade, and other matters.[15]

For Kissinger, also, it was a big breakthrough. In addition to the anticipated help with Vietnam, the new relationship could, he felt, lead to a comparatively stable and peaceful world in which U.S. security would be increased and its international role enhanced. Essential U.S. military superiority was not affected, but the danger of thermonuclear war would be greatly lessened and in the future armaments could be substantially reduced. The Soviet Union would be "linked" into such a cooperative arrangement, both by eagerness to prevent a U.S. accord with China and also by a network of mutually advantageous agreements, first and foremost that providing for a massive expansion of trade. If the Soviet Union really wanted to cooperate with the United States, the United States would not only meet it half way, but make it worth its while. Meanwhile, the United States would keep its guard up, seek to strengthen its alliances, and ensure that the Soviet leaders did not take advantage.[16]

Such was the Nixon-Kissinger vision of detente. As a vision, surely there was nothing wrong with it. It was based, as Kissinger said, on the necessity for maintaining "peace in the world as it is" in order to move to a "world of the future."[17] Its implementation into actual foreign policy was something else, however. As a working arrangement between the two countries, and as a stabilizing influence in the world, it initially showed every sign of succeeding. Already the German agreements, which had been worked out in an atmosphere of evolving detente, had reduced tensions in Europe. The conferences on European security and on reduction of conventional weapons showed promise. As a part of the detente complex, SALT I banned the ABM, and the partial limitations of the Interim Agreement constituted a necessary first step toward actual arms reduction. Moreover, the USSR, whatever its role in encouraging the Arabs, was cooperative politically and restrained militarily in the Middle East—at least as Kissinger saw it.[18]

Kissinger had told the Soviet leaders that "we cannot have the atmosphere of detente without the substance," adding that, "It is equally clear that the substance of detente will disappear in an atmosphere of hostility."[19] The atmosphere improved almost at once. Moscow stopped its ideologically based attacks on the United States and President Nixon ceased to engage in the militant anticommunist rhetoric of his predecessors. The Voice of America, no longer jammed in the USSR, changed its previous strident, hostile tone and content.[20] Additionally, the U.S. Navy quietly canceled the provocative "show the flag" movements that U.S. warships had been making in the Black Sea; Soviet flotillas, which had made one foray into the Caribbean, now stayed out. Concomitantly, U.S. businessmen in considerable numbers went to Moscow in response to the new trade agreement, which called for most-favored-nation (MFN) treatment of the Soviet Union and multibillion dollar credits from the Export-Import Bank.

Despite this very real beginning, it is now apparent that detente began to falter almost as soon as it began. If the trouble was initially a matter of atmosphere, the more the atmosphere eroded the more impediments to achieving substance appeared. The difficulties lay most importantly in the U.S. political scene, but also in certain differences between the Soviet and the Kissinger concepts of detente. A third factor was doubtless the power and uncompromising positions of the military establishments and their civilian supporters in both countries.

The revolution in U.S. foreign policy—and the Declaration of Principles signified nothing less—was almost entirely a revolution from above. There was no alternative to this. Cold war images were deeply engraved in Americans' consciousness, reinforced over a long period by repeated, solemn warnings from our "best and brightest"; by editorials, columns, and press and TV news; by scholarly books and articles; by novels, plays, and even comic strips. Many powerful organizations and individuals could envisage no alternative to the cold war. Politicians could be permanently submerged if they exposed themselves to charges of being "soft on communism." U.S. professional diplomacy was both timid and rigid. Left to the normal political and bureaucratic channels, detente would have never been born at all. No one but Nixon, with his Eagle Scout anticommunist credentials and his reputation as a hard-line cold warrior, could have brought it about. Kissinger may have been the architect of the grand design, and even of the details, but a Nixon in the White House was absolutely essential.

But President Nixon provided little leadership of public opinion. He tried to explain his position: He had come to the conclusion after taking office, Nixon wrote in 1972, that "one of the most dangerous elements in the world" was the "policy paralysis" afflicting U.S. relations with the Soviet Union and the PRC. He saw, he said, that rigid hostility to the communist powers was working against the interests of the United States. He had also discovered that the USSR and the PRC were now looking for ways to live with the noncommunist world, that they had "accepted the idea that their best interests would be better served by negotiations than by confrontation." And, he added: "We held the same view concerning the best way of serving American interest."[21]

Nixon's authority as Mr. Conservative Republican was sufficient to keep the right wing of his party silent, if perplexed. His proposals for a larger military budget, detente or no detente, served to appease the Joint Chiefs of Staff and their claques in Congress and elsewhere. And large sections of big business, interested in trade with the USSR as well as a more stable international climate, supported the new policy with unexpected enthusiasm. (A joint U.S.-Soviet Trade and Economic Council, comprising many large U.S. corporations, was promptly formed to assist in working out trade deals.)

But this was not enough. Such a sudden and dramatic shift in a long-established, emotionally involved policy had to be actively sold to the U.S. public. It was not so much that there was a large public constituency opposed to detente as it was that there was no large public constituency for it. As a consequence, what the opponents of detente had to say—and, increasingly, they said it at every opportunity—fell on ears accustomed to hearing these views. And Nixon really never took it upon himself to combat them. Partly, perhaps, he had reservations himself; after all, ideas enunciated during a lifetime of politics are tenacious. Further, Nixon, as well as Kissinger, invariably emphasized the restraints detente put on the Soviet Union without devoting much attention to those placed upon the United States. Certainly, the oft-repeated charge that Nixon and Kissinger built up hopes too high is without substance. Nixon did on one occasion write that if the principles of the Moscow Declaration "are proved [in practice], then the world will be on the way . . . to a generation or more of lasting peace." Most statements by either him or Kissinger, however, stressed the persistence of the adversary relationship and urged caution about expecting too much.[22]

Nevertheless, it may well be the case that if Nixon had remained in the White House, especially if he had been unfettered by the Watergate scandals, he could have carried it off. As it was, Nixon's credibility began to erode soon after he returned from the Moscow summit; and even before he was forced to resign, critics of detente were using Nixon's authorship of the policy to disparage it. Kissinger, who never had had real political clout of his own in any event, became preoccupied with the Middle East, and soon his credibility also came under attack.

The detente policy, in large part because it was initiated by a Republican administration, received scant support from the liberals in the Democratic party, many of whom traditionally had a cold war orientation in any event. Except for Senator Fulbright, its chief political supporters were among liberal Republicans, who are not the most prominent segment of their party. The left, generally, tending to be wary of power politics, was suspicious. And much of the news media were skeptical when not negative.

The attack on detente was not long in coming. Its spearhead was Senator Jackson, first in his criticism of SALT I and then in his opposition to legislation necessary to implement the trade agreement with the Soviet Union. In the latter effort, he was joined by the U.S. Jewish community, although who was leading whom is in some doubt. George Meany, who has an esoteric foreign policy all his own, soon arrayed the not inconsiderable clout of the AFL-CIO on the attackers' side.

The anti-Soviet attitude of many U.S. Jews, begun as a result of Moscow's support for the Arabs, increased as the USSR cracked down on Jewish "dissidents" and denied many of them visas to emigrate to Israel. There had already been discussions on this point between Kissinger, himself a Jew, and leaders of U.S. Jewish organizations. Kissinger broached the matter informally in Moscow, strongly urging freer emigration to encourage support for detente in the United States. But Kissinger realized that it was a highly delicate topic and that he must avoid even the appearance of trying to dictate to the Soviet Union on its internal policies. His "quiet diplomacy" resulted in a dramatic upturn in the number of Soviet Jews permitted to leave the country between 1971 and 1973. In 1970, for example, there were 992 exit visas issued to Soviet Jews; in 1971, 13,700; in 1972, 29,800; and in 1973, 33,524. Also, Kissinger was given unofficial assurances that there would be further increases.[23]

Senator Jackson and U.S. Jewish leaders, however, were not satisfied. They quickly seized on Kissinger's concept of linkage and turned it against him. The original idea was that one of the advantages of increased U.S.-Soviet trade was that it would help guarantee Soviet cooperation. The Jackson amendment to the trade act in effect made increased trade dependent on changes in Soviet emigration practices. This was an altogether different kind of linkage than Kissinger had envisaged, and one that he was convinced could not succeed.

The whole trade act fiasco illustrated much about the domestic restraints under which U.S. foreign policy makers labor, especially when trying to reach agreements with the Soviet Union. First, there was a Pavlovian response in Congress to combined cold war and Jewish pressures to support the Jackson amendment—so great that there never was any possibility of combatting it, despite significant business opposition. Second, the amendment itself, either because it reflected Senator Jackson's anti-detente position or because its sponsors did not want it to appear "too Jewish," made extension of MFN privileges to the Soviet Union—that is, withdrawing the trade discrimination against the USSR—dependent not on an increase in Jewish emigration but on completely free emigration for everybody. It is virtually certain that the Soviet Union would not have accepted such a congressional mandate even if it had been confined to Jewish emigration; there was never any chance whatsoever that Moscow would remove all emigration barriers. It is hard to believe that Jackson did not know it.

The Soviet leaders earlier had advised Kissinger that they would not implement the trade agreement—which stipulated extension of MFN status to the USSR—if the Jackson amendment were part of the package. Almost as if to make sure they did not, Senator Adlai Stevenson, Jr., secured passage of another amendment, severely limiting export-import loans to the Soviet Union and indirectly tying them to free emigration.

Kissinger, seeing his number one linkage going down the drain, frantically tried to save things by soliciting unofficial assurances from Moscow that increases in Jewish emigration would continue. But Jackson, possibly with presidential ambitions in mind, outsmarted him, stole the show at a public White House ceremony, and proclaimed the whole affair a great victory for his position. The Soviet Union promptly announced that it would not implement the trade agreement. Detente had suffered its first major setback. So, incidentally, did Jewish emigration.

Encouraged by this evidence of lack of political support, opponents of detente took heart and strengthened their attacks. Their position was further enhanced by the fact that an unelected president, Gerald Ford, was in the White House. Ford lacked either the political will or ability, or both, to lead forcefully. In his efforts to secure the Republican presidential nomination, he was running against the more or less cold war position of the right wing of his own party, dominated by Ronald Reagan. The campaign began almost as soon as Ford took office, and he concluded early that exposing himself in defense of detente would bring his defeat at the nominating convention. At Kissinger's urging, the president declined to meet with Aleksandr Solzhenitsyn, who was campaigning against detente up and down the country. But the outcry over this was such that he pointedly eschewed further use of the word "detente."

The combination of conflict within the Republican party and the anti-detente sentiment resounding in Congress and the press trapped Ford on the issue of the Final Act of the Conference on Security and Cooperation in Europe, signed at Helsinki.[24] This had been envisioned as one of the pillars of detente. Its most significant part was originally considered to be the pledge not to change national borders in Europe by force—a sort of substitute for a peace treaty 30 years after World War II. The Western powers succeeded in inserting into the Helsinki Agreement the so-called "third basket" on human rights aimed largely at Moscow. Despite this, right-wing critics of detente, resurrecting the controversy over the wartime agreements three decades earlier, denounced the agreement as a sellout of Eastern Europe to the Soviet Union. Ford thus felt unable to hail Helsinki as an accomplishment. He was not able to utilize politically the inclusion of the "third basket" as an anti-Soviet device, however, because this would have indicated agreement with his critics about the overall detente policy, which he was unable to repudiate.

Ford's own administration was divided, and he proved unable to control it, at least that powerful part quartered in the Pentagon. With SALT II talks in progress, Secretary of Defense Schlesinger in late 1974 announced what amounted to a more hard-line strategic warfare doctrine and declared the United States would not forgo the option of first use of nuclear weapons. The SALT II negotiations were further complicated when the Pentagon, over Kissinger's objection, produced the strategic cruise missile as a bargaining chip against the Soviet Backfire bomber. As a result, the Vladivostok agreement Ford had signed in 1974, providing for the first time equality in certain aspects of U.S. and Soviet nuclear weaponry, was never translated into treaty form.[25]

Although Ford ultimately fired Schlesinger and kept Kissinger, he never did really go to bat for his secretary of state on the issues. In the end, Kissinger saw himself, and the administration's foreign policy, virtually repudiated by the Republican party at the 1976 nominating convention.

Finally, differences between the U.S. and the Soviet concept of detente do exist, and they are important. But they have been exaggerated out of all proportion. The problem has been not so much the differences as the failure to face up to them. The differences were reflected in regard to armaments, the Middle East, and Angola. Even though Kissinger apparently believed that linkage would be sufficient to keep the Soviet Union in line in all these areas, it is not clear how far the Soviet Union really got out of line, as far as detente is concerned. At least, there is no agreement about it.

The equality implicit in detente means to Moscow full military equality with the United States. As of mid-1977, the Soviet leaders did not think they had it,[26] Paul Nitze and General Keegan to the contrary notwithstanding.* While the admitted Soviet military buildup may have been disquieting, the problem of asymmetry in weapons and the difficulties of defining "equality" and "strategic superiority" are such that it was at least as easy to accept as to refute the Soviet view. Additionally, of course, the United States is not the only potential enemy the Kremlin feels it has to guard against.

Except for the cruise missile-Backfire dispute, Moscow appeared more willing than many anticipated to accept limitations proposed by the United States. Kissinger once said that in SALT I the Soviet leaders had made all the compromises.[27] The USSR insisted that it was U.S. reluctance to accept "real equality" that was at issue, pointing out that U.S. armaments programs had not been exactly standing still.

The crux of the problem is that the value of detente will ultimately be determined by whether there is a mutual limitation and reduction of armaments, but that meaningful limitations and reductions can be achieved, if at all, only in the context of detente. If the United States was still "ahead" of the Soviet Union overall, there was no question that the USSR had made giant strides toward catching up, and in some categories of weapons had surpassed it. Those in both countries who feared that the other side would never settle for equality urged continued expansion of their respective arsenals.[28] Thus the ongoing armaments development in both countries made detente more difficult, although it did not by itself necessarily violate the perimeters of detente.

One clear precept of detente is that neither side will seek unilateral advantage, at the expense of the other, especially in areas of high priority interest to either. In the core interest areas of both sides—Latin America and Western Europe for the United States and Eastern Europe for the Soviet Union—this has worked fairly well. In gray areas, where both sides have important but less than clear core interests—the outstanding example being the Middle East—Kissinger thought detente worked fairly well also.[29] Where Kissinger felt detente went off the tracks was in Angola.

Since many Americans do not share Kissinger's view about the Middle East, and at least some do not share it about Angola, a brief word needs to be said about both.

Keeping in mind that detente was born while the United States was

---

*Keegan, who recently retired as Chief of Air Force Intelligence, and Nitze, a former high Defense Department official and SALT negotiator, are prominent among those claiming the Soviet Union has achieved strategic superiority.

mining Haiphong Harbor and bombing the daylights out of Hanoi, it is not too surprising that the USSR did not feel that detente barred continued support to the Arabs. If there was Soviet pressure on the Israelis, it was still primarily Kissinger who in 1973 prevailed upon them not to encircle and destroy the Egyptian Third Army, because Kissinger felt this would contribute to the negotiating positions he had in mind for his follow-up diplomacy.[30] And as Kissinger proceeded to take the ball away from Moscow in the Middle East, the Kremlin was disapproving but did not try to impede him.

One problem with detente and the Middle East is the same as that which arose in connection with Angola: In neither case did Kissinger use the detente mechanism of diplomatic discourse with the USSR. In the Middle East, this doubtless was because he felt his own one-man shuttle diplomacy would work, and the USSR did not make an issue of it. Africa he simply ignored, partially, perhaps, because even Kissinger found it difficult to be in more than two places at one time. One result was that the Soviet Union never was given reason to consider Angola a particular U.S. interest. While the United States was indirectly supporting the Portuguese in their futile effort to hang on to their colony, it was well known that the USSR was extending low-level aid to the People's Movement for the Liberation of Angola (MPLA). Even after the abrupt Portuguese withdrawal, there was no evidence of a massive increase in Soviet assistance until the United States itself, as well as South Africa, intervened on behalf of the MPLA's opponents, the Union for the Total Independence of Angola (UNITA) and the National Front for the Liberation of Angola (FNLA). It was only then that the State Department began to suggest that Soviet support of the MPLA was a "violation of detente."[31] Whether advance discussions between Kissinger and the Soviet leaders could have prevented Angola from sprouting into the issue it became, one cannot know. But they might have. At least such discussions would have made clear the importance each side attached to developments in that area.

That Angola became such a problem illustrates some of the ambiguities of the U.S.-Soviet cooperative adversary relationship. Soviet leaders have stressed over and over again that detente does not mean they will not support national liberation movements. An attempt to implement this position in a U.S. core interest area, say, Latin America, would clearly destroy detente. But what about areas where the United States has no apparent interest? Kissinger *seemed* to be saying that detente meant no interventions of any kind "in any area of the world."[32] But he was not always clear. He declared, on the one hand, that "there are many crises in the world where the United States cannot and should not intervene," but in Angola, he asserted, "we face a blatant challenge. . . ." Why a challenge? Because it was an important interest of the United States? "That," Kissinger said, "begs the principal question."[33] What the principal question *was* was not spelled out.

There was also some confusion over linkage. Earlier, Kissinger had asserted that Soviet disregard of the restrictions he felt detente placed on the USSR would imperil "its entire relationship with the United States."[34] "For us detente is indivisible."[35] But after Angola, where he insisted the USSR had been guilty of violating detente, ambiguity still prevailed. In January 1976, Kissinger told the Senate Finance Committee that because of Angola the administration would not press Congress to change the trade act.[36] Four days later, in San Francisco, he argued against reacting by hardening the U.S. position on SALT and further limiting grain sales to the USSR because "these arrangements benefit us as well as the Soviet Union and are part of the long-term strategy for dealing with the Soviet Union."[37]

The election itself was followed by what can only be described as an all-out offensive against detente that rapidly gathered momentum. Opponents focused on two issues: human rights and the claims that the Soviet Union had, was seeking, or was about to achieve—depending upon to whom one listened—strategic superiority. They comprised two diverse but overlapping U.S. groups: one emphasized moral principle, the other military strength. What the latter group sought was clear: larger military outlays and a public awareness of the Soviet Union as a dangerous military threat. It centered around such organizations as the American Security Council and the newer Committee on the Present Danger, and the still newer Coalition for a Democratic Majority.[38] The more amorphous moral principles group held that the United States should not seek a detente relationship with Moscow unless the Soviet Union adopted U.S. standards of individual rights—in a sense, a replay of the Jewish emigration issue writ large with emphasis now on the various Soviet "dissidents." Although overlapping, the two groups differed distinctly in an ideological sense. The human rights group was predominantly liberal and humanistic, the strategic superiority group largely military and considerably right of center.

What both groups had in common was the assumption that detente could be used to force changes in Soviet behavior, that it is something the United States "gives," but should "give" only for certain concessions. This was especially true of the human rights group, which reversed the idea of linkage—in effect, advocating links first, detente afterward. For both groups, detente was expendable. The strategic superiority group tended to believe that any meaningful detente with the Soviet Union was impossible, no matter what. The human rights group considered detente worthless unless the Soviet Union met its standards of conduct.

The voluminous and generally sympathetic coverage the media gave to these two positions might suggest that no important segment of U.S. society still believed in the idea of detente. This was not the case. Important elite groups supported the Nixon-Ford-Kissinger policy, if often with certain reservations. Their main spokesman was the American Committee on

East-West Accord, composed of more than 100 U.S. business leaders, former ambassadors, university presidents, nuclear scientists and other scholars, plus several publishers and labor leaders.[39]

Members of the American Committee maintained that the national interest of the United States could be served only by continuing to improve relations with the Soviet Union. It held that the detente process faltered at least as much because of U.S. policies as Soviet policies. While stressing the need for adequate defense, it disputed the claims of the strategic superiority group about the nature and extent of the Soviet military buildup, and especially argued the inutility of nuclear weapons as other than deterrents.

The pro-detente group differed with the human rights group more on tactics and methods than on moral principle. While the human rights advocates asserted that detente would mean a harder Soviet line against "dissidents," the pro-detente advocates maintained that the opposite was true, that relaxation of international tensions encourages internal liberalization and that the broadening of human rights in the Soviet Union, like Jewish emigration, is possible only under conditions of an evolving detente relationship. The pro-detente group also held that there is no way the United States can compel changes in Soviet internal policies, that efforts to do so will inevitably fail—in fact, make more difficulty for the "dissidents"—and, if pushed far enough, will make detente impossible. If the trade act affair ended with neither trade nor increased Jewish emigration, it was argued, the risk here is having neither human rights nor detente.

Detente can be compared to a bicycle. It requires forward movement. If it slowed down considerably during the Ford presidency, after the first half-year of the Carter administration it came to a virtual stop. It was not clear whether this resulted more from intention, disinterest, or maladroitness. Certainly President Carter had not formally repudiated detente. He said repeatedly that he wanted arms and other agreements with the Soviet Union. At the same time, his handling of Soviet relations was such that the atmosphere of detente, which is necessary for further agreements, suffered greatly.

The president started off by needling the Soviet leaders on human rights. He then shattered the rigid and somewhat prim official Soviet mind set by publicly announcing, in advance, new SALT proposals at variance with the Vladivostok agreement. He first rejected and then accepted Ford's appointee as ambassador to Moscow, notwithstanding that diplomat's reputed anti-Soviet orientation. This was followed by a public challenge to Soviet influence in various parts of the world and a tightening of restrictions on Soviet trade, already laboring under MFN discrimination. When signals of Soviet unhappiness with these developments reached the White House, Carter told congressional leaders that he did not intend to be "concerned everytime Brezhnev sneezes."

And yet the administration's position was ambiguous. The president appeared unmoved by the strident tones of the strategic superiority group of detente opponents, especially since its leaders took a harder line than the Joint Chiefs of Staff and were in the vanguard of opposition to certain Carter appointments, notably that of Paul Warnke as director of the Arms Control and Disarmament Agency and chief SALT negotiator.[40] His secretary of defense, Harold Brown, a cautious proponent of the SALT agreements, also did not accept many tenets of the strategic superiority group.

On the other hand, no matter how much he might want an arms agreement, it was uncertain whether Carter was willing to face up to the issues of SALT in ways likely to produce an accord. His rejection of the B-1 bomber appeared to have little to do with U.S.-Soviet relations. Indeed, his option in favor of the strategic cruise missile apparently was taken without regard for the fact that it was certain to complicate further the SALT negotiations.[41] How much the president would be willing to compromise on the number and range of cruise missiles in return for Soviet compromises on the Backfire bomber so as to preclude its use as a strategic weapon was not clear. Nor was it clear that if he should make such compromises and stick with the general outlines of the Vladivostok ceilings, which seemed to be the only basis for reaching an initial agreement, that he would be either able or willing to exercise the political leadership needed to win ratification of a treaty that included them.

President Carter explicitly repudiated the concept of linkage, particularly any connection between arms agreements and his posture on human rights. Actually, linkage never existed in the way it was often popularly pictured, a trade agreement for an arms agreement, for example. Yet a certain linkage exists in the very nature of things in the sense of an intimate connection between the state of U.S.-Soviet relations generally, that is, the atmosphere of detente, and almost any important agreement between the two countries. In an atmosphere of detente, many things can be undertaken that otherwise would be impossible. Already, after the first Carter SALT efforts indicated a repudiation of the Vladivostok accord, the Kremlin had indicated that it might no longer be willing to waive exclusion of U.S. forward based strategic systems in Europe. It was this apparent inability, or unwillingness, to understand this kind of linkage that constituted the major contradiction in the Carter administration's handling of U.S. Soviet relations.

Overall, it was probably the president's position on human rights that had the greatest impact on the atmosphere of detente. In contrast to Ford, who declined to see Solzhenitzyn, the hero of both groups of anti-detente forces, Carter received one Soviet dissident at the White House, wrote a personal letter to another, and generally associated himself with the position of calling other countries to account for violations of U.S. human rights norms. The administration's June report to the congressionally established Commission on Security and the Cooperation in Europe, for example, while not focusing exclusively on the Soviet performance, nonetheless particularly stressed the situation in the USSR and Eastern Europe.[42] The president appeared to be altogether sincere in this approach. What was lacking was some indication of its practicability.

Secretary of State Cyrus Vance tended to be a supporter of the more pragmatic view of the pro-detente advocates on human rights, and his adviser on Soviet affairs, Marshall D. Shulman, was in general, if cautious, agreement with their views.[43] But their input seemed less decisive than that of Zbigniew Brzezinski, the president's national security adviser. In earlier years, Brzezinski, who was born in Poland, often took a hard-line position on U.S.-Soviet relations. Although prior to his White House appointment he accepted detente, albeit without marked enthusiasm, he appeared to view it differently than Kissinger.[44] Opponents of detente have made much of the oft-stated Soviet point that coexistence does not apply to ideology. There were indications that Brzezinski accepted this view and perceived a necessity for the United States to take the ideological initiative. Pushing the Soviet leaders on human rights, as well as proclaiming a challenge to Soviet influence in various parts of the world, seemed to be a version of how this could be done. There was little doubt, however, that much of the impetus came from Carter himself.

Secretary of State Vance said he did not think the president's public affair with human rights would jeopardize detente.[45] Whether or not he was correct depended on how far Carter went with the issue and on how much leadership he was prepared to exercise on behalf of detente generally.

Regardless of Carter's demurrers, Moscow tended to see his human rights initiatives as one of selective morality directed primarily at the USSR and its bevy of Eastern European communist regimes.[46] The Soviet leaders in recent years have developed considerable sophistication about the United States. It does not, however, extend to accepting a Woodrow Wilson reincarnated as a born-again Southern Baptist as a natural phenomenon. Predictably, Moscow's reaction became sharply critical. Criticism of the United States, although still markedly less than during the cold war years, once again was widespread in the Soviet press.

Despite this, if Carter were to taper off his emphasis on human rights, at least as far as Moscow is concerned, and renew the lost momentum toward overall detente, U.S.-Soviet relations almost certainly could recover their earlier promise.

But Carter would have to do both, and it was not certain at the end of 1977 either that he understood this or that he could swing it if he did. With regard to the human rights issue, it was a question of whether he had painted himself into a corner. The nature of the problem was apparent at the Belgrade Conference to review compliance with the Helsinki Agreement. The August 1977 report of the U.S. Commission to monitor the Helsinki accord was far more critical of Soviet compliance than was the president's report to the Commission in June.[47] While U.S. representatives at the Belgrade Conference spoke in comparatively restrained tones, most of their efforts still consisted of needling the USSR. Nevertheless, even before the conference adjourned there was grumbling in Congress that the administration was not pushing hard enough on positions Carter himself had espoused so prominently.

Despite this, negotiations on SALT seemed, at the end of 1977, likely to produce an agreement. But the administration had backed off from the sweeping proposals advanced in the spring, and anti-detente forces were predicting they could defeat a treaty in the Senate. In any event, an agreement was certain to face stiff opposition. It would take vigorous presidential leadership to overcome these hurdles, but it could be undertaken without losing face and with good chances of success. The anti-detente constituency in the public at large is more articulate than numerous, and the American people have invariably responded to White House guidance on such matters. A serious administration effort on behalf of a SALT treaty would find strong allies and be more than a match for Senator Jackson and the American Committee on the Present Danger. Having made his point on human rights, Carter could begin to instruct the country about the international realities involved. Earnest efforts for detente could quite honestly, and accurately, be portrayed as efforts to further freedom of expression and movement. Even a White House statement about the importance of the "no use of force in changing borders" part of the Helsinki Agreement, which was its original focal point, would contribute. If the administration did not feel, for domestic political reasons, that it could actively urge Congress to repeal the Jackson-Vanik amendment, the president could at least proclaim his hope that some substitute could be found for the restrictive provisions of the trade act. (The-once-solid position of the Jewish organizations on this issue showed signs of changing, since it was clear that the Jackson-Vanik amendment was counterproductive in terms of Jewish emigration. Some Jewish leaders, in fact, seemed to be hoping for a show of administration interest to help them with their own constituencies.)

But the presidential leadership required would have to be not only vigorous but adroit. In Washington, there were few signs it was forthcoming. Wholly aside from its positions and nonpositions, the administration seemed unable to bridge the distance between Pennsylvania Avenue and Capitol Hill. Top foreign policy priority had been given to the controversial Panama Canal Treaty, whose fate, despite this emphasis, was uncertain. This meant that congressional consideration of a SALT treaty—to say nothing of possible amendments to the trade act—would likely be put off until late spring or summer 1978, when election politics would predominate and all politicians tend to avoid anything controversial.

It was not clear how Moscow viewed all these developments. In the summer of 1977, the Kremlin was hoping for a signal to which it could make a favorable response.[48] In July, Carter made a somewhat double-edged speech in Charleston, South Carolina, both promising to "redouble" efforts to explain his policies to the Soviet Union and at the same time warning the USSR that he would not be pressured.[49] Almost as if they had combed the text of this speech to find something favorable, first Georgi Arbatov, the Kremlin's chief expert on the United States, and then Brezhnev himself heralded Carter's remarks as "positive."[50] Soviet initiatives for reopening the SALT negotiations followed. But if detente were really to be given a new lease on life, something more than the rather ambiguous Charleston speech, something addressed to Americans more than to Russians, was necessary.

Although Brezhnev seemed to have put all his eggs in the detente basket, there were limits to how far he would, and could, go. Even if the "dissidents" pose no threat to the Soviet regime, it simply is not in the nature of things for the Soviet Union suddenly to embrace Western democratic-type individual freedoms. Also, linkage, like all else in international relations, can work both ways. Moscow has its own critics of detente protesting that thus far it had been mainly a one-way street in favor of the United States.[51] From their point of view, the record is at least questionable. Since the initiation of detente in 1972, the Soviet Union had lost influence in the Middle East; German relations were not what was expected, especially in regard to Berlin; the United States had raised the ante in SALT with the announcement of plans to develop two new weapons systems (the cruise missile and the neutron bomb); SALT I had expired with no treaty on even the Vladivostok accord; detente had been used to interfere with Soviet internal affairs; and the big trade breakthrough, originally seen as an integral part of the detente relationship, had not materialized.

Against these perceptions, continued lack of forward movement would risk dispelling what was left of the detente atmosphere. If this occurred, one could anticipate ultimately some shift of Soviet policy toward a less cooperative line. This would likely mean not a return to the all out hostility and confrontation of the cold war—at least not at first—but rather a "cool war," with greatly diminished communication between the two sides and a continued arms race. Even a cool war, however, would sacrifice much of what had been accomplished by detente and abandonment of hope for future positive achievements. In addition, of course, there would be no guarantee that a cool war would remain cool; it could easily turn cold and then hot.

Even if detente were to survive the 1977 crisis, one had to keep in mind that Brezhnev would not stay in office forever, and that waiting in the wings were some preferring a harder line. There was no assurance whatsoever that if a new Soviet leadership did not find detente already securely on the road it would not opt for, or feel compelled to follow, a less benign policy than Brezhnev's. Sharp shifts in foreign policy as a result of perceived inability to cooperate with the West have a long tradition in both Russian and Soviet history, going back at least to Napoleonic times. Such a feeling of frustration in more recent times produced the Nazi-Soviet pact and Stalin's cold war isolation.

In any event, the consequences of letting detente go down the drain are unpredictable. Should it happen, the West would confront a Soviet Union not only resentful and doubly suspicious but also a Soviet Union with much of the great military muscle the strategic superiority group was talking about. In such a case, the future would be foreboding.

One thing seemed sure at the end of 1977: The whole question of detente appeared to be near some kind of crux. And the situation was as Kissinger put it in his "Pacem in Terris" address: "Opportunities cannot be hoarded; once past they are usually irretrievable."[52]

NOTES

1. Henry Kissinger, "Detente with the Soviet Union: The Reality of Competition and the Imperative of Cooperation," *Department of State Bulletin*, October 14, 1974, p. 154.

2. *Ibid.*, p. 1.

3. The twin sets of misperceptions are discussed in Fred Warner Neal, *U.S. Foreign Policy and the Soviet Union* (Santa Barbara, Calif.: Center for the Study of Democratic Institutions, 1962); and "A Review of American-Soviet Relations: Detente in Perspective," *Commercial Law Journal*, September 1975, pp. 338–89.

4. For Stalin's views, see an account of the Nineteenth Congress of the Communist party of the Soviet Union in Leo Gruliow, ed., *Current Soviet Policies* (New York: Praeger, 1953).

5. For Khrushchev's pronouncements at the twentieth and twenty-first Congresses, see Leo Gruliow, ed., *Current Soviet Policies*, vol. 2, and *Current Soviet Policies*, vol. 3 (New York: Praeger, 1957 and 1959).

6. Neal, *U.S. Foreign Policy and the Soviet Union*, pp. 34–36.

7. See, for example *Pravda*, August 8, 1965; December 18, 1965; and March 15, 1966.

8. Cf. Kissinger, "Detente with the Soviet Union," p. 4.

9. Richard M. Nixon, "Asia after Vietnam," *Foreign Affairs* 46, no. 1 (October 1967): 111–25.

10. (Henry Kissinger's doctoral dissertation, published as *A World Restored* (New York: Grosset & Dunlap, 1964). The author describes how Metternich played off Napoleonic France against Tsar Alexander I's Russia.

11. This scenario was reported by those involved in it. See Fred Warner Neal, "The Moscow Declaration," *Center Magazine* 5, no. 5 (September/October 1972): 26–31.

12. *Pravda*, March 30, 1972.

13. For some reason, U.S. critics frequently assert that there is no Russian word for "*detente*." See, for example, James R. Schlesinger, "Detente and the Military Balance: The Need for a Bigger Budget," in Fred Warner Neal, ed., *Pacem in Terris, vol. 4, American-Soviet Detente, Peace and National Security*, (Santa Barbara, Calif.: The Fund for Peace and the Center for the Study of Democratic Institutions, 1976).

14. Fred Warner Neal, "A Leaf from Metternich," *The Nation* 213, no. 6. (September 6, 1971): 162–64.

15. For the text of the Declaration of Principles, see *Department of State Bulletin*, June 26, 1972, pp. 898–99. See also discussion in Neal, "The Moscow Declaration"; and "A Liberal's Case for Keeping the President," *Center Magazine* 7, no. 3 (May/June 1974): 4–11.

16. See, for example, Department of State Bulletin, June 26, 1972; Neal, "The Moscow Declaration"; and "A Liberal's Case for Keeping the President."

17. Henry Kissinger, "The Nature of the National Dialogue on Foreign Policy," in Fred Warner Neal and Mary Kersey Harvey, eds., *Pacem in Terris, vol. 3, The Nixon-Kissinger Foreign Policy: Opportunities and Contradictions* (Santa Barbara, Calif.: Center for the Study of Democratic Institutions, 1974).

18. *New York Times*, December 8, 1973.

19. Kissinger, "Detente with the Soviet Union."

20. Neal, "A Liberal's Case for Keeping the President," p. 9.

21. Richard M. Nixon, "The Real Road to Peace," *U.S. News and World Report*," March 26, 1972, pp. 32–33.

22. The quotation is from Nixon, "The Real Road to Peace." As an example of the idea that hopes were built too high, George Kennan, a supporter of detente, although disliking the word, wrote in the *Saturday Review* (March 6, 1976), pp. 12–17, that "as a result of this overselling, many people came to address to the behavior of both countries expectations that were unreal and could not be met fully." (Ibid, p. 12) It may have been overdramatized, but it was seldom, if ever, "oversold," at least by Nixon and Kissinger.

23. These are Soviet figures, but they jibe fairly well with Western estimates. Cf. *Foreign Affairs Newsletter*, February 15, 1975, pp. 2–3.

24. For the text of the Final Act, see *Department of State Bulletin*, September 1, 1975, pp. 323–50.

25. For the Vladivostok agreement, see *Department of State Bulletin*, December 23, 1974, pp. 879–81.

26. For the Soviet view, see Georgi Arbatov, the Kremlin's chief American-ologist, in *Pravda*, February 5, 1977. Other Soviet views are quoted in Fred Warner Neal, "Can the Soviet-American Detente be Salvaged?" *Center Report*, (April 1975). 9–12; and "Report from the Kremlin," *World Issues*, October/December 1976, pp. 11–13.

27. *Washington Post*, February 18, 1975, p. 1.

28. The positions expressed by General George S. Brown, chairman of the Joint Chiefs of Staff, are illustrative of this point. *New York Times*, February 1, 1977, p. 9. See also remarks of Politburo member Boris Ponomarev quoted in Neal, "Report from the Kremlin."

29. *Washington Post*, December 1, 1975.

30. On this point, see analysis of U.S. Representative Les Aspin in Neal, *Pacem in Terris*, vol. 4, p. 123; Admiral Elmo Zumwalt (U.S.N., Ret.) has a differing view. Ibid., pp. 114–24.

31. *Washington Post*, December 1, 1975.

32. Kissinger, "The Nature of the National Dialogue on Foreign Policy," p. 11.

33. *Department of State Bulletin*, February 23, 1975, p. 211.

34. Kissinger, "The Nature of the National Dialogue on Foreign Policy."

35. Kissinger, "Detente with the Soviet Union," p. 5

36. *New York Times*, January 31, 1976. Even before Angola, the administration was not pressing Congress to amend the trade act, in fact because such urging would have had no chance of success.

37. *Department of State Bulletin*, February 23, 1976, p. 210.

38. Cf. *Washington Post*, February 20, 1977, p. 18.

39. It was earlier called the American Committee on U.S.-Soviet Relations. The statements of the American Committee and the Committee on the Present Danger are compared in *New York Times*, January 11, 1977, p. 33. See also Fred Warner Neal, "The Salvagers of Detente," *World Issues*, February/March 1977, pp. 27–29.

40. *New York Times*, February 1, 1977, p. 9.

41. While the USSR regarded the B-1 as simply an improvement in existing U.S. bombing capacity, the strategic cruise missile was seen as a new weapons system. Cf. Fred Warner Neal, "Carter Image in Russia: Still Out of Focus," in "Views," *Newsday*, July 22, 1977. A thorough treatment of the cruise missile by Kosta Tsipsis in *Scientific American*, (February 1977), pp. 20–29, discusses how seriously this weapon would complicate an arms agreement.

42. "Second Semiannual Report to the Commission on Security and Cooperation in Europe, December 1, 1976–June 1, 1977," *Department of State Special Report*, no. 34, June 1977.

43. For Shulman's views, see U.S., Congress, House of Representatives, Committee on Foreign Affairs, 93 Detente, Cong., 2d sess., 1974.

44. See, for example, Brzezinski's remarks in report of Arden House meeting, *Politics and Commerce in US-USSR Relations: What Should United States Policy Be?* Graduate School of Business, Columbia University, March 31–April 3, 1976.

45. *Los Angeles Times*, March 5, 1977, p. 1.

46. Neal, "Views."

47. *New York Times*, August 6, 1977, p. 1.

48. Neal, "Views."

49. *New York Times*, July 22, 1977, p. A-3.

50. *Los Angeles Times*, August 4, 1977, Pt. 1, p. 15; and August 17, 1977, Pt. 1, p. 22.

51. Neal, "Report from the Kremlin."

52. Kissinger, "The Nature of the National Dialogue on Foreign Policy," p. 10.

3 Detente and the Sino-Soviet-U.S. Triangle

Thomas W. Robinson

INTRODUCTION

Detente—the relaxation of tensions in selected areas—has been a feature of U.S.-Soviet relations since the resolution of the Cuban missile crisis in 1962 and of U.S.-Sino relations since the Shanghai Communique of 1972. The resultant improvement of ties between the United States and the two major communist countries has been facilitated by the Sino-Soviet split and, in turn, has contributed to the worsening of the conflict between them. In fact, since the very inception of communist rule in China in 1949, the foreign policies of all three states have been intertwined to such a degree that, in retrospect, it is difficult to separate cause and effect. To be sure, such has not always been the view. Most studies have analyzed the foreign policy of only one side of the triangle. A realistic assessment of a single state's policy, to say nothing of any of the dyads, requires a more general inquiry focusing on the triangle as a whole and on the changing structure of the international political system itself.

A proper approach would be to rewrite the post-1949 international political history in terms of the triangle, and then to construct a model of triangular international politics on the basis of the reciprocal influences of four levels of determinants: domestic factors, national interests and power, the policies of the other two states, and the configuration of the international political system. That has not been done yet.[1] Meanwhile, several partial approximations provide useful substitutes. The most common is to infuse a notion of how the character of the "strategic triangle"* influences the foreign

---

*By "strategic triangle" is meant the Sino-Soviet-U.S. subsystem. It dominates international politics because of the exceeding importance of these three states, because each is a large landmass around which politics in its region revolves (there are no other such states), and because each points nuclear weapons at the others' heads. The foundation of post-World War II international politics is the combination of nuclear deterrence and the ability to transmit other aspects of national power at significant distances outside national boundaries. The United States has been the principal actor in international politics precisely because of those abilities, and the

policy of one of the three states, for example, the People's Republic of China (PRC), through analysis of the comparative relations which that state has developed with the other two—in this case, with the United States and the Soviet Union. Only rarely, however, is there any attempt to draw conclusions as to how the triangle as a whole operates or how it affects the policies of the state in question.

More to the point are bilateral studies[2] for instance, Sino-Soviet or U.S.-Sino relations. These almost always include an analysis of the influence of the policy of the third state on the dyad in question, but even in this instance there is distressingly little work on the overall triangular system.

Finally, there is a combination of these alternatives, an approach that concentrates on three sets of bilateral relations, but that also includes the policies of the third state and then generalizes from the political history and the contemporary issues that develop among the three states. That is the approach adopted here. It assumes that the triangle, although actually a unitary and integral whole, for analytic purposes can be broken down into three bilateral relations, with the remaining state acting as a parametric variable. Such an approach seems realistic, since most of the activity constituting triangular politics does take place along one or another leg of the triangle, and since the policies adopted by one state toward another are undertaken with an eye on the reaction of the third or are initiated to adjust indirectly to the policy departures of the third state. Thus, when speaking, as below, of "China as a factor in U.S.-Soviet relations," one is inspecting the U.S.-Soviet side of the triangle as it is modified by the policy of China.* Indeed, in this case, as in the two others, stress will be more or less equally divided between the dyad in question and the policy of the third state. Once this task is finished, conclusions can be drawn about the nature of the triangle as a whole.

This approach has at least two drawbacks. One is that breaking down the totality into its three constituent parts may miss important features of the triangular system that would naturally emerge from an analysis remaining at the most general level. Another drawback is that an approach stressing comparative policies and issues will have to make do with an ad hoc set of categories that in addition will vary with the dyad under discussion, instead

---

Soviet Union has shared such capability since the early 1960s. China does not yet have the ability to project its power at long distances, but makes up for it—partially by ideological braggadocio, partly by acting as if it already possessed the requisite means or soon will, and partly by attempting to convince Moscow and Washington that it heads a new alliance of Third World states that balances the alliance systems centered on the other two.

---

*In this and in all subsequent mention of China, reference is made to the People's Republic of China.

of the more complete and elegant group of variables associated with the four levels of determinants mentioned above. On the other hand, two advantages present themselves. One is that a creative tension is set up between the fact that while no one dyad is considered to be primary, it is necessary to begin somewhere and to make later analyses dependent upon prior inquiry. The other is that an emphasis on issues and policies enables some forecasting, albeit of a purely extrapolative sort.

CHINA AS A FACTOR IN U.S.-SOVIET RELATIONS

Any discussion of triangular political and security developments must immediately confront the problem of how to evaluate the "China factor" in the respective policies of the United States and the Soviet Union. Several topics immediately arise. First, what is meant by the "China factor?" Have there not been several meanings of this term? Second, what has been the history of the role of the People's Republic of China (PRC) between the United States and Soviet Russia as concerns the interests, power, and policies of the three states? Third, are there not aspects of Soviet Union, U.S., and PRC policies and interrelations that can best be understood in terms of the "rules" (if they exist) of triangular international politics? Of the changing nature of the international political system as a whole? Or of the need to respond in some common manner to challenges from the environment? Let us briefly examine each of these topics.

There are at least two meanings of the term "China factor." The first merely refers to variants of China's policy toward the United States and the Soviet Union, and separate Soviet and U.S. responses to that policy. The way in which Peking's policies influence U.S.-Soviet relations in turn is not always explicitly described or analyzed. For instance, writers in Moscow sometimes criticize China for taking an anti-Soviet stand on important issues of Marxist-Leninist doctrine or on relations with nonruling parties, but do not always draw the conclusion that such "deviations" make it more difficult for the Soviet Union to carry out its policy goals toward the United States[3] In similar manner, U.S. writers sometimes describe China's policy toward the United States as springing from its ideology, national interest, and cultural considerations, and derive U.S.-Sino relations directly therefrom, neglecting the Soviet component.[4]

One reason for attaching this disassociated meaning to the term stems from the fact that for long periods the "China factor" has been constant because China's policies toward the United States and the Soviet Union have been relatively invariant, as have U.S.-Sino or Sino-Soviet relations. Since the late 1950s, China's policy has been consistently anti-Soviet, and, from 1950 to 1972, constantly anti-U.S. Because changes in U.S.-Soviet relations in the post-1945 period seemed to depend on other issues, the conclusion was sometimes drawn that China has not been a factor in U.S.-Soviet relations at all or a residual factor at best.[5] Even after 1972, when the interdependence of Sino-Soviet relations and U.S.-Sino relations was made explicit, and the character of U.S.-Soviet relations shifted accordingly, it was often presumed that, China's policy toward the other two having established a new constancy, U.S.-Soviet relations were no longer affected and depended as before on a complex of other factors.[6] The overall Sino-Soviet-U.S. triangular context of U.S.-Sino relations is often overlooked in such an approach.

The second meaning of the "China factor," far from reducing the term to variants in China's policy toward the United States and the Soviet Union (and then sometimes ignoring them), concentrates on changes in Soviet and U.S. policies toward each other in response to their changing relations with Peking. These changes are sometimes viewed as restricted purely or mostly to variations in their respective bilateral relations with China.[7] Changes in Soviet and U.S. policies toward each other are occasionally viewed in expanded triangular terms, that is, with the realization that the policies of all three states are linked in a triangular system that dominates all of international politics.[8] In this more general view, whatever one state does vis-à-vis either of the other two—or even toward third states, regions, or issues not seemingly connected with the mutual relations among the three—affects the policies and the bilateral ties of the other two. Whether stemming from bilateral relations with China or from triangular relations among the three, this meaning of the term concentrates on China's effect on U.S.-Soviet relations rather than, as in the first meaning, on China's policy and its separate relations with that country.

These two approaches to the "China factor" inevitably affect evaluation of the history of China's role in the development of post-World War II U.S.-Soviet relations. If one restricts the "China factor" to indicate changes in U.S.-Sino and Sino-Soviet relations brought about by variations in the PRC's foreign policy, it follows that China has not been central to U.S.-Soviet relations. On the other hand, if China has been important to U.S. and Soviet foreign policies, respectively, the two superpowers have managed to insulate the "China factor" from their own common problems. This restricted meaning leads to a relatively simple analysis of the role of the "China factor" by dissociating the Sino-Soviet-U.S. triangle into its three bilateral components: U.S.-Soviet, Sino-Soviet, and U.S.-Sino. Implications follow for the way U.S.-Soviet relations are viewed by scholars and statesmen. The cold war was something that took place principally between the United States and the Soviet Union, and China was neither a catalyst nor a major factor in that conflict.[9] The Sino-Soviet split occurred for reasons internal to the international communist movement and not, for the most part, over differences over what strategy to adopt toward the United States.[10] The long period of U.S.-Sino discord was the product of differences of ideology, interest, and power between China and the United States, but not of their respective attitudes and policies toward the Soviet Union.[11]

On the other hand, if one adopts the expanded meaning of the term "China factor"—changing U.S.-Soviet interactions in response to changes in their relations with China—quite different conclusions can be drawn. While the Sino-Soviet-U.S. triangle is usefully analyzed in terms of activities along the three bilateral legs, in reality the legs have always been mutually linked, not mutually isolated. Since the signing of the Sino-Soviet alliance in 1950, what one state has done vis-à-vis either of the other two has vitally affected relations among the three. China, therefore, has always been central to U.S.-Soviet relations. For instance, the Sino-Soviet alliance so greatly changed the international balance of power that it permanently affected U.S. policy toward the Soviet Union, its own allies, and almost every substantive international issue.[12] The Sino-Soviet split arose partly because of differences over how to deal with the United States, particularly over the "missile gap" issue of the late 1950s, and over China's attempt to involve the Soviet Union militarily in the offshore islands and the Taiwan crisis of 1958.[13]

U.S.-Soviet detente resulted not only from the necessity to avoid a nuclear holocaust but also from the Soviet Union's desire to protect itself from conflict in Europe while facing a perceived threat from China in the East.[14] U.S.-Sino detente after 1972 was organically connected with China's fear of a Soviet attack, not merely domestic political developments and the impending end of the Vietnam conflict.[15] In this analysis, then, the "China factor," like the "U.S. factor" or the "Soviet factor," stands at the very center of U.S.-Soviet relations by virtue of the triangular nature of their connections. To analyze matters in terms of the restricted meaning of the "China factor" is, in this view, as inaccurate in the 1970s as it was in the 1950s.

It would be a mistake, however, to make too much of the apparent exclusiveness of the two approaches. Not only have the three states alternated, since 1950, between which variant they utilize, but the very nature of the triangle has changed over the last quarter century. At times, it was entirely appropriate to approach matters from the viewpoint of bilateral state relations, while at other times the broader, triangular viewpoint seemed more suitable. Prior to the death of Stalin in 1953, and after the Sino-Soviet border clashes of 1969, the case seems strong—in reality and in terms of the three states' actions—for assessing developments in terms of triangular state relations. Between 1953 and 1969, the more restrictive, bilateral approach seems more appropriate. Given U.S.-Sino estrangement and the Sino-Soviet split, decision makers in the three capitals could, and did, act as if their policies toward either of the other two states had little or no connection with their relations with the third.[16]

The nature of triangular relations has changed since 1950 in ways that make it increasingly appropriate to adopt the broader, interdependent approach to the question of China's role in U.S.-Soviet relations. Most importantly, the power of the PRC has grown relatively more rapidly than that of the United States or the Soviet Union.[17] It is no longer possible to treat Peking as a junior partner in a coalition, as the Soviet Union attempted to do in the early 1950s; or to ignore it, the United States attempted to do, for the most part, until the late 1960s. It is no longer possible for either nuclear superpower to overawe, for long, a combination of the other two. Of perhaps equal importance is the growth of Soviet power,[18] which has driven China and the United States closer together than at least China would wish—and this trend seems likely to continue. The growing relative equality of power among the three nations counters Soviet power to some extent and gives all three states, particularly China, a degree of policy independence that none previously possessed. Finally, the very magnitude of power available to all three, and the "power distance"* each maintains vis-à-vis fourth states, means that an alliance between any two of the three states would have exceedingly serious consequences for the third. Policy makers in all three capitals must, above all, guard against such an eventuality, however unlikely present differences make it seem.

Paradoxically, the weakest party in a triangle sometimes possesses the most freedom of maneuver, as China's role between the United States and the Soviet Union demonstrates. Despite its relative weakness in overall power, China's position between the superpowers is relatively strong. Because it opposes both powers on issues of substance, it is Peking, not Washington or Moscow, which can decide whether, and to what extent, to soften that opposition and hence improve relations. This is particularly true with regard to Sino-Soviet relations, since it is primarily China's policy that prevents solution to outstanding problems.[19] Thus its leverage on the United States is considerable, while all Moscow must do is to continue to await intra-Chinese leadership developments.[20] Moreover, in the emerging U.S.-Soviet competition for China's favor, the United States must offer more than the Soviet Union because there is a natural propensity for the post-Maoist Chinese leadership to attempt to free itself from the shackles of Mao's too anti-Soviet policy.† But Washington can offer less, since it cannot, with-

---

*By this the fact is referred to that in most every measure of national power, and surely in aggregate national power, the United States, China, and the USSR far outdistance all other states. It is true that in a few of the measures of power, China's power does not greatly exceed, or in some instances, does not even equal those of the fourth power, say Japan or West Germany. Overall, however, China seems to equal its standing in the eyes of the rest of the world as the third ranking power. Its contenders possess special limitations, such as no deployable military power in the case of Japan, or fixation upon the Soviet threat in the case of West Germany. Each of these is tied, therefore, to the United States.

†China's anti-Soviet policy is much the product of Mao himself, as is noted later on and in footnote 41.

out severe damage to its position in the Far East and elsewhere, grant Peking what it wants most from Washington: Taiwan. Moscow, on the other hand, can offer more, in the sense that there are many variant solutions to the border dispute, to say nothing of offering to improve economic ties and at least discussing ideological differences. Finally, as China's power grows, it will have the capability to intervene in situations farther from its borders, where at present the United States and the USSR (or their allies or proxies) are the only outside forces capable of inserting themselves.[21] This, too, will enhance China's range of maneuver between the United States and the Soviet Union, since at least one local disputant can usually be found who will be only too glad to appeal to Peking in an attempt to tilt the balance to its side.

China's position is not supreme, however. The United States and the Soviet Union can at any time agree, directly or tacitly, on a series of measures that could renew China's isolation or increasingly threaten its territorial integrity. The Soviet Union already poses such a direct threat, and the Soviet-Indian alliance could take on offensive dimensions. The United States still maintains forces in northeast and east Asia, and continues its support of the Nationalists on Taiwan.* On China's periphery, only Southeast Asia is not dominated by the two superpowers, but even here both remain active, with Hanoi leaning toward Moscow and Thailand again seeking closer ties with the United States. There is, of course, almost no probability of an anti-China U.S.-Soviet alliance, but the 4,500-mile Sino-Soviet border, the persistence of regional fears of China, and the presence of Soviet and U.S. power all around China's periphery place ultimate limits on Peking's maneuverability between Washington and Moscow. China's options are reduced to three: to improve relations with the Soviet Union and then pressure the United States to give way on Taiwan; to further improve U.S.-Sino relations as a means of girding for a struggle with Moscow; or to transform the nature of the triangle by attempting to rally a united Third World to its side. The probability of the first and the second are approximately equal and that of the third virtually nil.

There is no doubt that the Chinese leadership would like to arrive first at a general settlement with the United States—including resolution of the status of Taiwan and the problem of the U.S. defense treaty with the

---

*The partial reversal in July 1977 of U.S. withdrawal of ground forces from South Korea and the negative results of the Vance trip to China in August 1977 (U.S. commitment to the defense of Taiwan, with or without a treaty, was responsible for the lack of progress toward full recognition of Peking) demonstrate the extent of U.S. realization that its military policy is the most important element in northeast Asian stability. Although the defense treaty with Taiwan may lapse for political reasons, there seems little doubt that there will be some sort of support for the defense of Taiwan. And nobody, including Moscow and Peking, wishes to see Washington change its defense treaty relations with Seoul, Tokyo, or Manila.

Nationalists, formal diplomatic recognition, resolving the frozen assets issue, and extension of most-favored-nation status.* This would allow Peking to concentrate its attention and energy on the Soviet Union, which will always be the greater military threat, and which, by reason of geographic propinquity, will always require more policy attention. But U.S. policy has hardened on most issues, Washington has after all, obtained most of what it wants from China—representation at Peking, continued protection of Taiwan, and trade with both Chinas. Moreover, the longer the Taiwan issue remains unsettled, the harder it will be to resolve, for Taiwan is becoming increasingly more viable politically and successful economically.† It is undoubtedly true that the Carter administration is willing to go some farther distance in seeking a compromise with Peking, but the intractable nature of the differences between the two countries makes it unlikely that full resolution will come soon. Moreover, the post-Mao leadership must also renew its interest in foreign policy matters if there are to be successful negotiations. It is still not clear that it feels confident enough of its internal unity to jeopardize the status quo with the United States by risking failure of negotiations over Taiwan.[22]

The United States and the Soviet Union can also continue officially to ignore China in certain of their bilateral dealings, however unrealistic that policy may be. Presently, the SALT talks, the conventional force reduction discussions, trade and technological relations, and Middle Eastern and southern African security talks are all conducted without China's presence, as if the "China factor" did not count for much. But China *is* still "there." In all these substantive and geographic policy areas, China is a behind-the-scenes presence that more and more influences negotiations and outcomes.

---

*Prior to the 1977 Vance visit to Peking, this had been China's strategy. However, the barren results of that visit, and the renewed unity and confidence of the Chinese leadership after the Eleventh Party Congress, may lead Hua Kuo-teng and his associates to revise, if not totally reverse, the policy of resolving the Taiwan question first and the Sino-Soviet border question second.

†If one looks a decade into the future and presumes that the U.S. commitment to defend Taiwan is maintained (whether or not by treaty and whether or not accompanied by full diplomatic representation in Taipei), one would probably see the following: full industrialization, capability of providing for all but a nuclear missile defense, integration of the Nationalist minority with the Taiwanese majority, and revision of the Nationalist basis of rule to stress increasingly democratic modes of government and implicitly forgoing the "return to the mainland" syndrome. These are mere extrapolations of present trends. If the presumptions are altered to denunciation of the Security Treaty by the United States, *much the same* outcome is likely, with the exception that the probability of the acquisition of nuclear weapons by the Nationalists rises greatly, as does the probability that Taiwan would declare itself an independent state and seek diplomatic recognition on that basis. Whatever happens concerning the status of Taiwan, it is considered likely in this writer's opinion that independence, de facto or de jure, is the probable future for the island.

The size and disposition of China's nuclear force have been important, if unmentioned, aspects of both SALT I and SALT II negotiations. Any major reduction of forces in Europe would have to take into account the consequent ability of the Soviet Union to confront China without having to fear NATO's reaction. The Western alliance, by contrast, would remain at least partially dependent on presumed continuation of the Soviet-Chinese border confrontation.*

The United States has sought to increase trade levels with both the Soviet Union and China, but because trade with both nations is based upon the exchange of U.S. technology for primary produce, the U.S. doctrine of relatively equal treatment has meant that political criteria have become central. Indeed, the practice in technology transfer (especially in the military sphere) has been to lean to the side of China—and as a means of encouraging China to prolong its anti-Soviet policy could become an important additional factor in limiting U.S.-Soviet trade as a whole.[23] In regional conflicts in which the United States and the Soviet Union have an interest by virtue of their superpower status, China has always been a factor, if only marginal, in forcing stronger Soviet support of more radical political groups than would otherwise have been its preference.[24] To be sure, the United States and the Soviet Union have dominated the political landscape in the Middle East and southern Africa, while China has been relegated largely to supporting left-over extremist revolutionary groups that have no chance of attaining power, or to supporting established regimes through foreign aid. The latter, such as Tanzania, cannot be depended upon to support Peking's position on international issues.[25] But as China acquires the economic, transportation, and military means to increase the level of its involvement, its leadership may be able to convince regimes of consequence that China is a viable alternative to the Soviet Union or the United States.

Although the "China factor" in U.S.-Soviet relations is increasingly to be understood in the wider context of the triangular relationship, there is

---

*It is not fully appreciated in the West, although hardly ignored, how closely the military balance in Europe is tied to the Soviet-Chinese military standoff. Overall stability depends on the continuation of the military balance at both ends of the Eurasian landmass. If there is a sudden change in the balance in either Europe or Asia, it will be quickly reflected in the other sphere. More importantly, any change in Europe or Asia not accompanied by a similar change in the other geographic area would rebound to the disadvantage of the West. For instance, if a thinning out of forces along the Sino-Soviet frontier following a border agreement were not accompanied by a similar force reduction in Europe, the Soviet Union would obviously be in a position to increase its pressure on the West, as would China in Asia. Similarily, if force reductions in Europe were not followed by a similar Sino-Soviet agreement, the Soviet leaders could step up the pressure on Peking. The risk of war between the two communist giants would rise greatly, and with it the probability of some kind of U.S. military involvement or aid to China to restore the status quo ante. Either way, disjoint change is injurious to U.S. interests.

another set of causative factors associated with the changing character of the international system (and perhaps best termed "environmental" elements) that affects all three states equally. These include world food production and distribution; the sources and rates of technological change; the sources and pricing of raw materials, especially oil; the utilization and conservation of common resources such as the oceans; and pollution control. By way of illustration, let us address the first three of these. It matters greatly to the United States, China, and the Soviet Union that there is a potential world food shortage, that both China and the Soviet Union are either chronically short of food or operate on a thin food-to-population margin, and that the United States and its close allies, Canada and Australia, are normally the only surplus food producers in the globe. Given Soviet refusal to modify its system of agricultural production (which is the source of the Soviet shortfall in production) and the constantly threatening land-to-population ratio in China, the "politics of food" are likely to work to the long-term advantage of the United States.[26]

Much the same can be said for technology. Technological change continues to accelerate, and the major source of technological advance continues to be the capitalist West (including Japan). For the foreseeable future, China and the Soviet Union will continue to be net consumers of technology. They could, to be sure, attempt to solve this common problem by agreeing to put aside some of their political differences, but this would probably cause the Western nations to reduce the flow of technology to them so that there might be no long-term net gain from such cooperation. Hence, the imbalance of technology limits China's maneuverability between the United States and the Soviet Union, and undoubtedly causes Peking to think twice about jeopardizing its budding ties with Washington in favor of improved relations with Moscow.

The emergence of oil as a world political issue, and of the Organization of Petroleum Exporting Countries (OPEC) as an international political actor, impinges upon and complicates the U.S.-Chinese-Soviet triangular relationship. U.S. ties with OPEC are direct and mutually dependent in nature: OPEC exchanges oil for U.S. technological and military and industrial goods. The dilemma for the United States is how to manage that exchange so as simultaneously to avoid financial deterioration in the West as a whole, to ensure a continuous flow of oil, and to protect Israel. The Soviet Union and China are effectively excluded from this closed system; nonetheless, each has interests in OPEC-related matters, and some aspects of intratriangular relations are reproduced, some modified, by the oil factor. In contrast to the U.S. situation of mutual dependence, the Soviet Union encourages OPEC to continue to use its new power to weaken the West (although not Japan) and perhaps help to bring about radical regime changes in Western Europe favorable to itself. Current trends seem to point in this direction, so Moscow need only wait.[27] China, on the other hand, seeks to appeal directly to OPEC against the West and the Soviet Union as part of its campaign to unify the Third World against both superpowers. The trouble with this tactic is that because of its current anti-Soviet stance, Peking does not wish to see the West too weakened through economic collapse or inability to finance oil purchases. So neither China nor the Soviet Union can take significant advantage of the oil factor in world politics. Even to Japan, to which both Peking and Moscow wish to sell oil as means of keeping Tokyo away from the other, China cannot charge prices significantly below OPEC levels, lest it be accused of undercutting potential Third World allies.

What, by way of summary, can we say of the "China factor" in U.S.-Soviet relations? Six generalizations seem appropriate:

1. The "China factor" in U.S.-Soviet relations is exceedingly complex and cannot be separated from developments in U.S.-Sino or Sino-Soviet relations, whether taken separately or regarded as interacting elements in the Sino-Soviet-U.S. triangle.

2. Which definition, restrictive or expanded, of the "China factor" one should adopt depends on the time period and the issue under consideration. The restrictive meaning better explains developments from the mid-1950s to the late 1960s because of the frozen nature of U.S.-Sino relations and the deteriorating state of Sino-Soviet relations.

3. During the early 1950s and the 1970s, the expanded meaning more accurately reflects reality. China's policy changes were directly dependent upon Peking's relations with Washington and Moscow, taken together, while the PRC's power grew relatively more rapidly than that of the United States and the Soviet Union, even considering the nuclear capability of the two superpowers. But there are still important issue-areas where Washington and Moscow pretend, successfully, that China's role can be ignored, if only temporarily.

4. Because of the Sino-Soviet dispute, the U.S. range of options within the triangle was greatest from 1969 to the mid-1970s. Continuation of that dispute formed the essential presumption, and was the most important external factor, in the success of Secretary of State Kissinger's policy shifts during that time. But now China has the greatest potential for maneuver, especially in the post-Mao, post-Kissinger era. Not only does Peking hold the key to improved Sino-Soviet relations, but improvement in U.S.-Sino ties is nearing its natural limits while renewed U.S.-Soviet military competition threatens U.S.-Soviet detente. The most probable future is thus improved Sino-Soviet ties, exacerbation of U.S.-Soviet relations, with further improvements in U.S.-Sino relations only problematic.

5. The form the triangle assumes thus hinges on when, and how far, Peking intends to proceed in repairing its relations with Moscow and, to a

lesser extent, with Washington. In turn, these questions depend chiefly on developments in China's domestic political situation that, although in flux, seem increasingly likely to move away from Mao's out-and-out anti-Sovietism in foreign policy and toward revisionism (in Mao's meaning of the term) at home. There is comparatively little that the United States can do, or would be willing to do, to influence China's policy, directly through foreign policy concessions or indirectly through threats or inducements. The degree of the PRC's maneuverability between Moscow and Washington is increasingly large, and goes beyond its power position vis-à-vis either of the two nuclear superpowers. The potential for change in the triangle rests largely in Peking's hands.

6.   The Asian regional roles of the United States and the Soviet Union are predicated not only on the long-term mix of their respective ideologies, power, and interests but also on the regional and, potentially, the global role of China and of China's propensity to expand its geographic and functional involvement to areas and issues remote from Asia. Only by addressing the "China factor" in global terms can its overall part in Soviet and U.S. policies be assessed.

THE UNITED STATES AS A FACTOR IN SINO-SOVIET RELATIONS

Having approached the tripartite relationship among the United States, China, and the Soviet Union by focusing on China's role in U.S.-Soviet relations, let us turn to the second leg of the triangle and consider the United States position between the Soviet Union and China.

Perhaps the most important lesson of the history of the "U.S. factor" in the ties, such as they have been, between Moscow and Peking is that Washington has always been an element in Sino-Soviet relations, whether or not U.S. policy makers knew so or approved.[28]

Corresponding to the previous distinction between the restricted and expanded meaning of the role that Peking played between Washington and Moscow, it is useful to speak of "active" and "passive" roles for the United States. During the early 1950s and again in the early and mid-1970s, the U.S. role was "active" in the sense that the policy initiatives Washington undertook toward one of the communist nations directly and almost immediately influenced the course of Sino-Soviet relations. This is true whether Washington thought it was merely reacting defensively to what it perceived to be the predatory ambitions of a presumably united communist bloc during the 1950s or whether Washington sought to take advantage of the serious differences that separated Moscow and Peking by the late 1960s. In the intervening period, the United States was a "passive" element in the sense that from the mid-1950s to the late 1960s (that is, during the course of the decline in Sino-Soviet relations beginning with marginal ideological differences and ending with open border warfare in 1969) perhaps the most persistent of the Sino-Soviet differences was how to deal with the United States.[29]

Whatever the United States did, then, was meaningful to developments in the Soviet-Chinese imbroglio. The United States played a relatively active role in Sino-Soviet relations when the "China factor" in U.S.-Soviet relations was best described by the "expanded" definition noted previously. When the U.S. role in Sino-Soviet relations was passive, the China factor in U.S.-Soviet relations correspondingly best fitted the "restricted" definition.

Until the 1970s, however, the United States did not, or could not, take advantage of the increased maneuverability that stemmed from the Sino-Soviet conflict for a number of reasons. The cold war with Moscow, with all the attitudinal structure that it implied for the American mind, kept Peking more closely tied to Moscow than it desired, while the Korean War and its sequelae in the Taiwan Straits and Indochina prevented Washington and Peking from attempting to settle their mutual problems, much less thinking in common terms about the Soviet Union. There were, to be sure, a few moments when China and the United States could have broken out of the vicious circle that had developed—in 1955, at the outset of Chou En-lai's "peaceful coexistence" drive; in 1961, at the beginning of the Kennedy administration; and in 1965, when a pre-Cultural Revolution China began seriously to fear the consequences of Soviet military development. But in each case, domestic and international developments intervened to render stillborn efforts on either side—Dulles's intransigence at Geneva, Mao's unwillingness to accept Kennedy's offer of food assistance, and the growing role of U.S. ground forces in Vietnam.[30]

As for U.S.-Soviet developments, the United States not only had to "educate" the Soviet leaders in the safety rules of the nuclear game but it had to overcome repeated Soviet attempts to turn temporary advantages, for example in Berlin and Cuba, into permanent revisions of the East-West balance of power. These efforts, combined with the Soviet decision after the Cuban missile crisis in 1962 to invest in the strategic capability necessary eventually to equal or outdistance the United States militarily, led to the era of detente characterized by negotiations, trade, and technological transfer. The exacerbation of the Sino-Soviet dispute only reinforced the Soviet decision to seek to improve relations with the United States. For Washington, the result, just as in the case of its attitude toward Peking, was an initial reluctance to take advantage of Sino-Soviet discord to enhance its own foreign policy maneuverability.[31]

It took actual conflict along the Sino-Soviet border, globalization of Soviet military activity, the end of the Vietnam conflict, and Kissinger's perspicacity to cause U.S. policy makers finally to recognize the enormous potential that lay in becoming an active participant in Sino-Soviet problems.

This brought together, for the first time since Korea, the three legs of the triangle. After 1969, U.S. foreign policy throughout the globe was predicated on maximizing and utilizing the freedom of maneuver that the Moscow-Peking dispute provided. Its success—in the Middle East, Southeast Asia (at least in the sense of enabling the withdrawal of U.S. forces from Vietnam), China itself, and the nuclear arms treaties with the Soviet Union—was directly, although not solely, attributable to the belated decision to take advantage of ever-worsening Sino-Soviet relations.[32]

But if the United States had at last become centrally involved in Sino-Soviet relations, it was not merely because of the short-term advantages that seemed to accrue. As noted earlier, fundamental changes had occurred in the power relations among the three states since the early 1950s. The Soviet Union had risen to become the relative equivalent of the United States in deliverable military power, while China had gained enough power (relative to its pre-1949 past and to the two superpowers) that it could no longer be completely ignored in most international crises and negotiations. For this reason alone, it was impossible for the United States not to play some kind of role in Sino-Soviet relations. It follows that the pattern of relations developed among the three powers during the post-1969 years will likely be the norm for the foreseeable future. Thus, for forecasting purposes, one should pay less attention to how the "U.S. factor" affected Sino-Soviet relations during the period up to 1969 than to its impact in the early and middle 1970s.

The history of Sino-Soviet-U.S. interactions since 1949 helps to indicate the range of roles (which amount, in some instances, to policy choices) that the United States could be assigned or that it could assume as the Sino-Soviet situation changes. These are six in number. Washington could, as in the 1950s, be assigned the role of capitalist bête noire, the number one common opponent of, and threat to, the two major communist states. This would occur were Moscow and Peking to resolve their major differences and reestablish a close alliance. Or the United States could continue to be regarded as the separate opponent of each, common enemy number two. This would be the case were Moscow and Peking to prolong their dispute, but feel assured that neither would attack the other. These two roles would stem from intracommunist developments over which the United States would have little control. In each of these cases, a measure of cold war-like, East-West division would be reestablished and U.S. policy would have to react accordingly.

The third possible role assumes independent action on Washington's part, and thus amounts to a policy choice. In this instance, Washington would take a quasi-neutral position in Sino-Soviet relations, "treating them equally" in fact as well as in declaration, even were a tempting opportunity to arise. This would be a possibility were Moscow or Peking to feel increasingly threatened by the other and feel the need to seek assurances of support or neutrality from Washington. Alternately, the United States could decide, for balance of power purposes—as it has, despite an ostensive policy of neutrality—to become the proto-ally of one or the other, probably of the weaker, and hence China. This fourth possibility also amounts to an independent policy option, and carries with it the assumption that Washington would be willing to be used, occasionally, by one or the other of the communist antagonists for its own purposes. That may not be entirely consonant with overall U.S. interests. It also presumes that Washington would try to influence the course of developments by taking sides, however gently, in the various disputes separating the Soviet Union and China.*

If the situation changed so drastically that action (presumably military) of one of the communist powers threatened decisively to upset the Sino-Soviet balance, a fifth alternative role would, perforce, present itself to U.S. decision makers. Washington would have to decide whether it would wish to become the full, if temporary, ally of one power in order to prevent the outbreak of war (which, under foreseeable conditions, would be thermonuclear) or even to support the aggravated state in actual combat. Obviously, these are extreme circumstances whose probability of occurrence is unlikely. But since the future course of Sino-Soviet relations is itself unpredictable and because both the Soviet Union and China are militarily capable of initiating such a conflict, such a policy option for the United States at least ought to be raised.[33]

If a full alliance with one side is the most undesirable choice for the United States, the last possibility, a joint Sino-Soviet-U.S. condominium, is the best, if the least likely, option. Nonetheless, for some purposes—confronting environmental challenges or preventing nuclear dispersion, for instance—a limited harmony of interests is possible, and as a long-term policy goal it is highly desirable. Such an association would be the natural successor to any of the previously listed options except the first, depending on the specific character of the resolution of Sino-Soviet differences and the U.S. role in that process.

The choice among these roles is, of course, not for the United States alone to make. If history is any guide, Washington will be less likely to enjoy the luxury of choosing among options than to be forced into assuming a role by circumstances (as in the first two possibilities outlined above). The major determinant will probably be the changing nature of politics in China, that is, the character of the post-Maoist Chinese leadership and variations in PRC

---

*A "proto-alliance" is a preliminary working arrangement that has some of the language of an unwritten agreement, that could at some point in the future lead to a more explicitly cooperative arrangement, written or unwritten, and that should be regarded by third parties as leading in that direction. This definition fit the Sino-American situation after 1972 exactly.

policy toward the Soviet Union.* It is instructive to note, however, that at one time or another since 1949, the United States has already assumed four of these six roles. In the early and middle 1950s, Washington adopted a policy of all-out resistance to the perceived expansionist ambitions of a Sino-Soviet bloc. This corresponds to the first role. In the late 1950s and early 1960s, U.S. policy makers adopted a posture of quasi-neutrality toward the emergent Sino-Soviet dispute, corresponding to the third role. In the late 1960s and to some extent in the early 1970s, the United States sought to deal with the two communist states on a separate basis. This is the second role indicated previously. In the late 1970s, Washington attempted to maintain a balance between Moscow and Peking by leaning to the Chinese side, thus serving as a proto-ally of one against the other.†

These four alternatives remain active possibilities for the future, as do the options of full alliance with one power or attempting in the long run to fashion a triangular condominium—however unrealistic these may seem at present. But if the United States is to play an active part in Sino-Soviet relations, and thus have a say in determining its own policy options, it must decide how it wishes to involve itself in the several points of difference separating Moscow and Peking. Those differences often seem to pertain to every important question of life, but for our purposes they can be reduced to four factor groups: the border problem and attendant military questions; psychocultural differences between the two communist parties and the Han and Great Russian peoples; differences in stages of economic and political development, or "modernization"; and ideological differences, as symbolized by China's charges of Soviet "revisionism" and the Soviet response of "dogmatism." While each of these disputes lives a life of its own, it is nonetheless true that whatever policy the United States adopts toward the Soviet Union or the People's Republic of China, or both, affects the probability of their continuation, exacerbation, or resolution.

---

*By late 1977, the post-Maoist leadership still gave no sign that it was even contemplating any change in its opposition to the Soviet Union. But by then it had adopted a series of domestic changes that were as "revisionist" as could be imagined. If these domestic and foreign policies are linked, and if ideology remains a strong component of Chinese attitudes, amelioration in Sino-Soviet relations cannot be far off.

†Although no official U.S. spokesman would admit to that statement, the policy was nevertheless plain, whether it be out of design or the results of trends among the three states. U.S. policy toward the Soviet Union did stiffen, and Washington's attitude toward Peking did soften. There was a great deal of concern over the apparently predatory nature of the Soviet arms buildup, while the military concern with China was how to strengthen Peking against the Soviet Union. The Carter administration's human rights campaign was directed largely against the USSR, and hardly at all against China (which had a far worse record than the Soviet Union, at least after 1953). Washington and Peking, by 1973 at the latest, were pursuing parallel policies toward Moscow, and by the late 1970s the question was how far it should go and how to facilitate it, not whether and if this should be the case.

For instance, it is quite apparent that the degree to which the United States provides military or technological assistance to China buttresses Peking's ability to resist Soviet threats, and purchases time for Peking to redress the power imbalance it perceives vis-à-vis the Soviet Union. It also pulls Washington and Peking closer together as anti-Moscow quasi-allies. Most of the obvious statements and recommendations as to what policy the United States should adopt toward this aspect of Sino-Soviet relations have already been made and do not warrant repetition here.[34] Suffice it to note that some U.S. support has already been rendered,[35] and that even at the present low level it has become an important aspect of triangular relations.

Less apparent but of still great importance is the attitude of Americans, official and unofficial, toward the Russians and Chinese as people and toward their respective cultures. It has often been noted that while Americans usually evince a positive personal attitude toward individual Russians and Chinese alike, there is a pronounced bias against certain aspects of Sovietized Russian culture and an equally pronounced partiality in favor of Chinese culture.[36] To the extent that perceived psychocultural differences influence U.S., Soviet, and PRC decision makers, there is a tendency, increasingly important over time, for Chinese and Americans to enjoy their cultural dissimilarity and for Chinese and Russians and Americans and Russians to find these differences ever-greater impediments to the solution of outstanding problems. While it would be unwise to make too much of such cultural attitudes, they are present and do exert a considerable, if subtle, influence on Sino-Soviet-U.S. developments and perhaps prejudice U.S. policy choices in favor of a lean-to-China's-side role.[37]

Dissimilarities in the stages and pace of economic and political development among the three nations tend to push tripartite relations in a direction opposite to that induced by military-security and psychocultural considerations. The United States, the most advanced of the three economically and (we think) politically, tends to have more in common with the Soviet Union, at least in economic matters. Both states stress specialization of function, wage incentives, bureaucratized administration, and technological solutions to social problems. China stands at the opposite end of the spectrum with regard to each of these societal characteristics, to say nothing of the obvious differences in levels of industrialization. While one should not place too much emphasis on prospects for "convergence" between U.S. and Soviet societies, there is nevertheless a trend in that direction that may accelerate in the future. With regard to China and the Soviet Union, however, a rather different process of "convergence" may already be taking place, Maoist strictures and China's policies notwithstanding. Basically, it remains to be seen whether China's experiment in attempting through Maoist idealistic voluntarism to avoid the common end points of the modernization process ultimately will be successful. Even before Mao's death, many signs pointed to massive resistance to his mixture of induced social disorder and assumed harmony between individual motivations and societal goals. Perhaps it is too soon to tell, but current signs seem to point to Soviet-style "revisionism" as the wave of the future for China.* China will not much longer be able to avoid the "iron law of development" that is evident in every society, Eastern or Western, capitalist or socialist, in the last two centuries.[38] Thus, in sum, "modernization" seems to be pulling the Soviet Union in the direction of the United States and China toward the Soviet Union. What the net result of this trend will be is difficult to determine, but political and ideological factors will surely play a major role in determining it.

While China's "modernization" is ultimately to the benefit of the United States, as it lessens the social distance between the two cultures, in the short run it may lead to a renewed linkage between China's and the United States' principal long-term opponent, the Soviet Union. If the United States decides to assist China's modernization as part of an overall anti-Soviet policy, it must be cognizant of this possibility. On the other hand, different styles of modernization are glaringly evident in China and the Soviet Union. In the Soviet Union, the peasant and the consumer have been deliberately exploited for half a century in order to provide the investment funds for heavy industry and military equipment.[39] In China under Mao, the regime made a virtue of the necessity to develop agriculture and to provide an equitable, if very low, living standard in lieu of differential wage incentives. Although the totalitarian features of the Maoist mode of development are apparent to Chinese and foreigner alike, and have come under increasing criticism both within and outside China, the potentiality exists for its modification in a humanistic direction.[40] A high volume of trade with and technological assistance (especially in heavy industry) from the United States and other Western nations, including Japan, would provide at least the possibility that China could avoid having to follow the Soviet developmental path. Increased trade and technological assistance would also encourage the Peking leadership to ameliorate its attitude toward the United States and other Western nations.

It is too early to conclude that Sino-Soviet ideological differences will moderate after Mao's death. Certainly any successor leadership in China will pay lip service to Mao's thought, though policy content may be very different. †

---

*Pro forma obeisance to Maoist ideals (some of them) and to the man himself does not hide changes in policy: restoration of discipline, material incentives, quality in education, scientific progress, comparative liberality in culture and the arts, stress on production over revolution, and regularity of bureaucratic procedure. All spell revisionism in the Chinese context.

†What better way to ensure successful de-Maoification than to conduct it in his name? The Chinese have learned the lesson of the Soviet mistake in denouncing Stalin, thus denying

The Maoist efforts to vaccinate the Chinese leadership against the Soviet revisionist virus may have induced at least temporary immunity, but for two reasons China in the future may be unable to carry on the kind of ideological vendetta against Moscow that has been seen during the last two decades. The first reason stems from the modernization impetus described above. China, as a society and polity, may come to resemble more and more the Soviet Union as industrialization, bureaucratization, and division of labor proceed. As that becomes apparent to the Chinese leadership, they may find themselves in ever-lessening disagreement with their Soviet counterparts. The second reason is the extreme imbalance in the anti-Soviet nature of China's foreign policy. Every leadership crisis has entailed the purge by Mao of opponents subsequently accused of advocating some degree of improvement in Sino-Soviet relations. Most of the anti-Maoist opposition has been located in the military, which has been understandably reluctant to support policies that might embroil their country in a war they could not win. The accusatory literature has always charged defeated politicians with campaigning to dampen China's ideological criticism of the Soviet Union or advocating Soviet-induced revisionist practices at home.[41] With Mao dead, modifications in practice are being made that must some day be reflected in ideological changes.

If changes in the practical content of Sino-Soviet state relations come, as seems likely, will not an ideological modus vivendi follow? The United States has little direct influence on intracommunist ideological differences, but its actions and attitudes always indirectly affect when, whether, and how they are resolved or exacerbated. In terms of the six policy roles outlined above, in order to avoid again becoming the common or the separate enemy of China and/or the Soviet Union, the United States could stress common interests with both (such as nuclear nonproliferation) or adopt a policy of neutrality or "leaning to one side," depending upon the issue. The latter policy is quite difficult, particularly because there is a contradiction between joint U.S.-Sino interests in limiting the expansion of Soviet power and the extreme sociopolitical distances between the PRC and U.S. societies. In the long run, a policy of neutrality with regard to ideological issues may be safest for the United States.

Changes in these four aspects of the Sino-Soviet dispute (border disputes, psychocultural differences, levels of modernization, and ideological clashes) may come only after some time, and the policies of all three states

---

most of their own history. It is unlikely that Mao's successors will do that, especially since Mao is China's Lenin *and* Stalin. On the other hand, as post-Maoist practice diverges increasingly from Maoist theory, his influence will decline relative to that of Marx and Lenin: national and ideological heroes whose writings and lives may be exploited for whatever policy purpose national interest requires.

may remain relatively unaffected in the short term. Moreover, policy changes almost always result from confrontation over immediate disputes or of opportunities perceived as fleeting. The U.S. role in Sino-Soviet relations therefore depends also on policy aspects of U.S.-Sino and U.S.-Soviet relations. In each case, four issues stand forth. In the U.S.-Sino case, the issues of consequence are Taiwan, full diplomatic recognition, the terms and extent of trade, and the extent of U.S. technological transfer to China.

The Soviet Union has wisely never allowed itself to become involved in the Taiwan question, and there is very little probability that it will do so in the future. But that issue and the associated problem of recognition are linked to the Sino-Soviet border question in two senses. On the positive side (for the United States), prolongation of the Sino-Soviet border dispute provides security for Taiwan against attack from mainland China and allows Washington to continue avoiding the question of military responsibility for the Nationalists' defense. Negatively, the longer that settlement of the Taiwan issue is postponed, the greater is Peking's propensity to turn away in disgust from trying for a diplomatic accommodation with the United States and to move toward the Soviet Union. Were the Sino-Soviet border dispute to be settled tomorrow, the next day China would probably turn its military attention to unilateral solution of the Taiwan question.

As for recognition, there is little more that Washington can do to effectuate full diplomatic relations with Peking until the Taiwan question is resolved or postponed by mutual agreement. There are many ways to fudge that issue and, were Peking willing, there are ways to move to full recognition and retain Taiwan, too.[42] But it is probably too late to argue to Peking that recognition without possession of Taiwan is good for each state's policy of limiting expansion of Soviet power. Peking wants Taiwan too much for that; moreover, it can probably obtain a reasonable border treaty with Moscow any time it wishes.[43]

The questions of trade and technological assistance to China are closely related to the U.S. role in Sino-Soviet relations. Not only would increased trade and assistance encourage Peking to maintain policy independence from Moscow but it also would assist China in defending itself from a possible Soviet military attack. Of equal importance is that trade and aid should be given in a manner that supports those Chinese leaders who argue for improved ties with the United States. However, this does not necessarily obviate a possible Sino-Soviet detente in these same areas. Indeed, rather than become overly dependent on U.S. technology, China may continue to diversify its range of suppliers, which could well include greater amounts of trade with, and technological transfers from, the Soviet Union. Finally, trade and technological transfers strengthen China, since Peking will inevitably use much of it to build a more modern military force. Because a strong China that is also unfriendly to the United States, and possibly increasingly close to the Soviet Union, is obviously contrary to U.S. national interests, there may be severe limits to the lengths to which Washington can go to persuade Peking, through these inducements, to stay away from Moscow and to continue a moderate policy toward the United States.

Major U.S.-Soviet policy issues are also four in number: arms control, nuclear and conventional; the Soviet arms buildup, both strategic and conventional, in Europe and at sea; trade and technology; and third-area confrontations, particularly in the Middle East and Africa. Washington must always pay its greatest foreign policy attention to the Soviet Union, and the Sino-Soviet component of these issues therefore is often given less adequate scrutiny, sometimes on the presumption of constancy of Soviet-Chinese discord. That assumption was, of course, never valid and is even less so in the post-Maoist era. By contrast, the Soviet Union has regarded its negotiations with, and policy toward the United States in all four of these areas as partially dependent upon its policy toward China and upon Peking's own strategy. As noted earlier, the Chinese nuclear program has always been a behind-the-scenes element in SALT negotiations, and the Soviet strategic and conventional arms buildup can be partially explained by the perceived need to gird for combat with the Chinese foe. The rise in the volume of U.S.-Soviet trade and the quest for U.S. technology has come about, among other reasons, as a result of Moscow's desire to strengthen the country industrially and militarily in the event of war with China. The Soviet Union's regional policies have been increasingly forward, not only because of its leaders' greater confidence in its ability to apply military power at a distance but also because they fear that China will succeed in rallying the support of the extreme left of the regional political spectrum.[44] That fear has sometimes driven the Soviet leaders to take a stronger stance than they would have preferred, as is evident in the Middle East and southern Africa.[45]

In sum, the U.S. "detentist" policy (if it still can be called that) toward Moscow and Washington's policy of encouraging step-by-step a melioration of ties with Peking continue to be important constituents in Sino-Soviet relations. Whatever the United States does, directly as regards China or the Soviet Union or indirectly as regards substantive issues or geographic areas, affects relations between the two communist powers. The United States is a factor in each Sino-Soviet policy dispute, even if only as the subject of argument. Moreover, its own policy moves cause the Soviet and the Chinese leaders to react to such initiatives and to consider how they affect their own interrelations. Hence, while U.S. policy must, as always, be formulated principally by reference to its own range of interests, its relative national power, and the domestic political situation, its influence on the Sino-Soviet leg of the strategic triangle must always be taken into account. The operative questions for Washington are how to conduct its foreign policy so as to forestall major improvement in Moscow-Peking ties and how to cope with a partially reunited Soviet-Chinese bloc were such an improvement to occur.

With Mao having already "met God," and with the Soviet leaders trying their best to achieve a diplomatic breakthrough in the border talks, the likelihood of Soviet-Chinese detente, despite misreading of signals in Moscow and Peking, is now higher than at any time in the last two decades. This provides additional impetus, if any is needed, for refurbishing the U.S. military, settling disputes among the Western allies, expending even more resources to lower tensions in Third World areas, and setting the domestic house in order. The cost may be much higher in the not too distant future.

THE SOVIET UNION AS A FACTOR IN U.S.-SINO RELATIONS

At first glance, the Soviet Union would seem to be only a minor element in U.S.-Soviet relations, at least for the period prior to 1969. Most of the history of the relations between the three states, after all, has centered on bilateral Sino-Soviet and U.S.-Soviet encounters. What facts there are concerning the United States and the People's Republic of China before 1969 were either negative, that is, there were no positive ties—diplomatic, economic, or cultural—or they were very slow in developing. After the 1969–72 period of China's intense fear of Soviet attack, relations were largely dependent on internal developments in the two countries and the intractable nature of the Taiwan issue. A closer look, however, reveals that the Soviet Union has played a more important role in post-1949 U.S.-Sino relations than has generally been noted. In fact, Moscow's policy has always been the most important external variable in Peking-Washington relations, as a few examples will demonstrate.

Aside from the role played by the Soviet Union in assisting the Chinese communists in coming to power from 1946 to 1949,[46] the most important act by a Soviet policy maker in the quarter century after 1949 was Stalin's agreement, in the Sino-Soviet Treaty of Friendship, Alliance, and Mutual Assistance of 1950, to defend China from U.S. attack.[47] This alone forestalled any possibility of early U.S.-Sino accommodation. The 30-year duration of the treaty (even now, it should be noted, technically still in force), combined with the Korean War (which it helped make possible), kept Peking and Washington at swords' points for an unnecessarily long time. From 1950, the Soviet Union was an invisible presence at every negotiating table at which U.S. and PRC diplomats sat. Moreover, the cold war kept the United States and China apart by politically bifurcating the globe into hostile Soviet- and U.S.-led camps. Thus, from the middle 1950s to the early 1960s, separate initiatives to improve U.S.-Sino relations foundered principally on cold war suspicions—in 1955, on Dulles' insistence that China was merely acting as a Soviet handyman in carrying out the Soviet bloc's offensive against the United States;[48] and in 1961, on Mao's conviction that acceptance of Kennedy's offer of agricultural assistance would hinder the joint Sino-Soviet offensive that he urged against the U.S. "paper tiger."[49]

Even the results of the Cuban missile crisis gave evidence of the Soviet leaders' ability, even if unintended, to keep Peking and Washington apart: Moscow's decision after Cuba to seek detente with the United States isolated China within the triangle. Peking's isolation was deepened by its military action against India in 1962 (which brought both the Soviet Union and the United States to New Delhi's side), the subsequent U.S. ground intervention in Vietnam, and the near-simultaneous beginning of the Cultural Revolution in China (both of which further estranged Washington and Peking).[50] From the late 1960s it was the Soviet Union that provided the central impetus driving Washington and Peking closer together—first by threatening China with invasion and then, through its strategic buildup, by threatening the United States with a first strike nuclear capability.[51] In sum, no understanding of U.S.-Sino relations is complete without recognition that the Soviet Union has always possessed the means to influence, and often to determine, the character of their ties through its own actions.[52]

The reasons why Moscow has been so successful in influencing U.S.-Sino relations to its own advantage are obvious. First, its sheer power constrains leaders in Washington and Peking to pay their greatest policy attention to Kremlin activities and to Moscow's burgeoning potential.[53] Second, its geographic location between the West and China provides the Soviet Union with direct land access across long borders or their equivalent with both (in the case of the United States, not merely across the Bering Strait but, more importantly, with Europe, where Washington has major policy interests). This favorable geographic position has enabled Moscow to direct its initiatives first toward the one (in the 1950s, the United States and the West), then the other (China, in the late 1960s and early 1970s), and, when its power base proved sufficient, toward both, as in the middle 1970s and beyond. Third, with regard to issues, the Soviet leaders have demonstrated that they possess the capability to modify important aspects of their overall foreign policy if the result is maintenance of a high degree of influence over U.S.-Sino relations. To be sure, Moscow has often been constrained to change its policy for internal reasons or in response to U.S. or PRC policy initiatives. But the fact that Soviet decision makers are small in number, and usually need not take into account Soviet public opinion on foreign policy questions or subject themselves to democratic centralist discipline, has enabled them to vary policy more quickly than their U.S., and often their PRC counterparts. Ideology and perceived weakness in comparative overall national power vis-à-vis the United States have been the main constraints skewing Soviet policy initiatives toward the United States and China away from their objective ideal.[54] Obviously, these factors have been quite important and will continue to be so in the foreseeable future, but in comparison with the constraints on U.S. and PRC leaders, the Soviet disadvantages are relatively minor.

In general, then, the Soviet Union is in an increasingly favorable position to implement its policies toward the United States and China. But it is the very probability of success that is Moscow's greatest hindrance, for it tends to unite its two most important opponents and their allies. Fear of Soviet military power, the exigencies of geography, and their common opposition to Soviet policy initiatives drive an otherwise isolationist-autarchic China to cooperate with members of the global alliance system centered around the United States. Realizing this, the Soviet leadership feels constrained to modify its policy goals—directly as concerns China and the United States and indirectly as it concerns third states, other issues, and regions of the globe outside east Asia, Europe, and North America. With respect to U.S.-Sino relations themselves, those goals are two. In the general sense, the Soviet Union involves itself in U.S.-Sino affairs in order to prevent or render impotent an anti-Soviet combination of powers structured around a Peking-Washington tie, however tenuous that might be. More positively, Moscow seeks to set the stage for eventual rapprochement with Peking, for progressive global isolation of the United States, and for expansion of its own influence throughout the globe. Specifically, the Soviet Union wishes to delay as long as possible restoration of full diplomatic relations between the United States and China, and therefore quietly does what it can to perpetuate the Taiwan issue as a means of ensuring U.S.-Sino discord. It also wishes to discourage U.S. or other Western technological transfer, military assistance, economic assistance, or high levels of trade with China.[55]

It is difficult for Moscow to take effective measures in support of these specific goals. For the most part, the Soviet leadership must wait, passively and hopefully, for China's leadership to change its composition or its mind and return to the fold. It dares not involve itself directly in the Taiwan question, lest it position future relations with Peking for an indefinite period.* Its own global muscle-flexing has frightened the leaders of the United States and China into working together more closely. It can, and indeed has, offered Peking the prospect of strong economic ties and renewed technological assistance,[56] but China's leadership remembers with bitterness the abrupt cutoff of Soviet trade and assistance in 1959–70 and does not want to risk a repetition. There is obviously no possibility of Soviet military assistance to China so long as tensions and force levels along the border are so

---

*On many occasions in the United States and in the Soviet Union, I have queried Soviet scholars and diplomats about their intentions regarding Taiwan in event of U.S. disengagement from the island. Would the Soviet Union not replace the United States as the security guarantor of the island? Would not the USSR wish to establish a naval base on Taiwan? The answers were always no. As one Soviet remarked: "We have seen what an albatross Taiwan has been for you. We do not want it hung around our neck in turn." These opinions are both credible and backed up by Soviet sources: There is no hint of a Soviet wish to become involved in the Taiwan question.

high. So the Soviet Union is seemingly stymied in developing specific, workable policies to serve its policy goals toward China and the United States.[57]

Where is the balance between Moscow's success over the long run in influencing important aspects of PRC and U.S. policy and behavior patterns to conform to its own goals, on the one hand, and these short-term obstacles, on the other? Perhaps the answer is best expressed in cost-benefit terms. As noted above, the chief benefit to the Soviet Union in the post-1949 history of U.S.-Sino relations lay in the distinctly unfriendly character of those relations (until 1972) and the incomplete nature of their diplomatic, economic, and cultural ties thereafter. To have been instrumental in so thoroughly separating their principal opponents for over a decade can only be counted as an enormous diplomatic victory for the Soviet leaders. (This is not to deny, of course, the innate importance of U.S.-Sino differences, which would persist, perhaps even increase, were the Soviet factor somehow to be subtracted from the equation.) In the post-1972 period, there have been some benefits to the Soviet Union (and corresponding costs to the United States and China) associated with the closure of the political distance between the two countries and the threat of actual U.S.-Sino cooperation against the Soviet Union.[58] For instance, the very fact that China and the United States stand as a bulwark against the expansion of Soviet influence in Asia has provided Moscow with renewed incentive for "leapfrogging" over north and east Asia and concentrating its policy attention on India, the Middle East, and Africa. A similar benefit, if it can be called that, follows from the Kremlin's perceived necessity after 1972 to build up Soviet military strength (conventional and nuclear) in order to deter potential military threats from the two states and their allies. U.S.-Sino detente has therefore probably provided an additional stimulus, if any were needed, for Moscow to increase military strength at a rate faster than previously, detente with the United States notwithstanding. This has proved of immediate "benefit" to the Soviet military, but has also enabled Moscow to make its presence more strongly felt in areas farther away from its own borders and sphere of influence. The results of this redirection of policy attention and acceleration of military buildup are graphically illustrated in the effectiveness of Soviet policy in southern Africa. Moscow would not have had as much incentive to intervene in Angola, with all the subsequent benefits for its African policy, had the United States and China not agreed to put aside some of their differences in the face of the Soviet challenge in Asia.[59]

The benefits to the Soviet Union of U.S.-Sino separation, or even a measure of U.S.-PRC detente, are evident, but the costs are also high and mounting fast. China and the United States, separately or in concert, are directing an increasing share of their policy attention and foreign policy resources to deterring Soviet military support and to countering Soviet influence wherever it is found, in Asia or elsewhere. The two countries are already cooperating, directly or tacitly, in restricting further expansion of Soviet influence in Asia and the Third World.* U.S.-Sino cooperation, if continued in its present direction, may eventually ensue in close, de facto policy alignment against the Soviet Union on many issues of consequence to the three states, and hence to world politics as a whole. This would mean an informal global network of alignments directed against Soviet expansion. There could be no greater political defeat for Moscow than engendering a hostile combination of all the states of major political, economic, and military consequence. The Soviet Union has already found it necessary (as indeed it has for more than a decade) to redirect its policies toward third countries and issues in order to counter competing U.S. and PRC policies. If this trend continues, the consequence could be the mortgaging of much of the rest of Soviet policy to counteract the impact of a nascent U.S.-Sino coalition. If the Kremlin leadership is unsuccessful in reversing these trends, the Soviet Union could become isolated in world politics—continuing to rule over its East European sphere of influence, but shut out from most other areas and confronted at every turn by a very powerful combination of states.

The Soviet Union would surely prefer to maximize the probability of retaining present benefits and at the same time avoid the costs associated with these deleterious possibilities. Above all, that means doing whatever it can to forestall further U.S.-Sino cooperation. The question is whether it can succeed in doing so, and if so, how. In other words, what is Moscow likely to do (presuming that the Kremlin's own analysis of its changing role in the Sino-Soviet-U.S. triangle is roughly similar to that outlined here)? Perhaps the most likely policy alternative is to do nothing different in its conduct toward China and the United States. Basically, this alternative has two facets.

Toward the United States, the Soviet Union would continue to try to overtake Washington in military power, economic strength, and general political influence, while at the same time attempting to reach a series of interim agreements with Washington designed to beguile the United States into believing that long-term improvement of relations is still possible. More specifically, the Soviet Union would likely seek new SALT and other arms limitation agreements, but not at the expense of its goal of outdistancing the United States in overall military strength; attempt to reestablish the primacy of its influence in the Middle East by arming the more radical Arab regimes for another military strike at Israel, while at the same time verbally supporting an overall peace settlement; oppose and belittle U.S. initiatives in

---

*Examples include China's tacit encouragement of Japanese-South Korean-U.S. military steadfastness in northeast Asia; separate but parallel movement toward New Delhi in the hopes of loosening Soviet-Indian bonds; a similar approach to Egypt in the field of military aid; and support of African regimes that adopt or maintain an anti-Soviet stance.

human rights, while claiming innate superiority over the United States in that area; and continue to invest in producer goods at a rate such that Soviet economic growth will continue to surpass that of the United States (using trade with the West to purchase the advanced technology to make that possible) and produce enough consumer goods to keep the Soviet citizenry reasonably content.

Toward China, the Soviet Union will no doubt continue to offer to settle the border question, while dangling the possibility of resolving ideological differences. At the same time, Moscow will compete with Peking for influence in communist and noncommunist states with common borders, in the Third World, and on ideological and substantive state issues. As to specific issues, there seems little incentive for Moscow to initiate military conflict of any kind with China; indeed, the Soviet leaders may conclude that a timely withdrawal of some border forces would materially enhance prospects for an overall agreement. Nor is it likely, so long as China's leadership maintains strong control of the population, that Moscow will attempt to foster dissident minority movements in Sinkiang or Inner Mongolia. On the other hand, there seems little doubt that the Soviet Union will persist in competing with China for Japan's favor, principally through trade inducements, while continuing to refuse to compromise with Tokyo in fisheries and ownership of the disputed islands. With regard to North Korea and North Vietnam, Moscow also seems likely to sustain its competition with Peking for their allegiance, and the present standoff will thus likely endure. Finally, in South Asia, the Middle East, and Africa, the Soviet Union will undoubtedly persevere in trying to keep China out of these regions by varying its stands on local issues in the hope of gaining or retaining the support of ruling elites. This can be accomplished either by moving left in response to Peking's verbal assaults or by supplying economic and military assistance that China cannot match.

The net effect of these general and specific policies appears to be dual. On the one hand, the Kremlin leaders intend them to lead to a global-political situation wherein the Soviet Union will replace the United States as the world's most powerful and respected state. The overall balance of power between the United States and Soviet-led alliance systems would perceptibly and unalterably tip to the Soviet side. In this scenario, Peking would eventually come to terms with Moscow, and the world would thus march, still peaceably, toward the Soviet version of communism. Were China and the United States not to react, separately or in concert, to these policies and goals, there seems to be little reason why this Soviet-preferred world would not come to pass.

The trouble with this scenario, and with the Soviet vision as a whole, is that it presumes that neither the United States nor China will take effective countermeasures. It does not, therefore, address the root of the problem of

Soviet policy (which, not coincidentally, is the essential shortcoming of all Soviet policy since 1917): Moscow has not tried to carry out its program through cooperative attempts to resolve conflicts of interest with other nations, and it therefore has been generally unsuccessful in isolating its most troublesome opponents, capitalist or communist. Moscow is attempting to isolate its opponents through competition with both the United States and China throughout the globe, but because its power is now so great that the Western world and China are being driven together out of fear—just as the United States and Europe were in the early 1950s in response to the threatening potential of the Sino-Soviet alliance. So long as China and the United States feel themselves to be on the same side of the power equation, Moscow's policies will foster that otherwise unlikely combination of revolutionary communists and status quo capitalists that it fears and hopes to avoid.

The future, therefore, is not solely in Soviet hands. Moscow has no choice but to continue its global competition with both China and the United States—such is the iron law of international politics—and it can no longer do anything definite to hinder improvement in U.S.-Sino relations. It must, as noted previously, avoid involvement in the Taiwan issue. It can do nothing to prevent technological transfer and possible improvement in trade between its two opponents, except perhaps drive them to higher levels through its threats. The question of formal U.S. recognition of the PRC is one with which, by definition, only Washington and Peking can deal. And Soviet policy toward Japan and Korea and Vietnam and India is relatively fixed by geography and existing alliances.

The Soviet Union is thus in a dilemma when it seeks to play a role in U.S.-Sino relations that will enhance prospects for achieving its own foreign policy goals. It must do what it is doing, but its very actions tend to create their own opposition. Perhaps China and the United States will not, in the end, be able to overcome their differences sufficiently to establish a strong working relationship, a principal purpose of which would be to keep the Soviet Union in line. No doubt the Soviet Union will govern its "China policy" with exceeding caution until the post-Mao Chinese leadership clearly emerges. Peking might then feel under somewhat less pressure to compromise with Washington. Finally, it is possible that the seriousness of the threat to Moscow of North American-European-Asian cooperation would be lessened by the looseness of that coalition and by the prospect of large increases in Soviet strength. The balance of power mechanism (which, despite all that has been said, is still the basic operating principle of international politics) does not, after all, operate perfectly. But given time and the likely trends outlined above, the Soviet Union may ultimately face a global combination of powers designed to freeze the Kremlin out of the Third World and to limit the direct exercise of Soviet power to its present East European sphere of influence.

NOTES

1. A thorough analysis would have to use systems dynamics as a methodology, which by definition is the only approach general enough to encompass all relevant variables. *The Limits to Growth* (Washington, D.C., Potomac Associates, 1972 and 1974) was influencial precisely because it used this means of inquiry. What is lacking in the study of international relations is an agreed-on theory, which is to say, agreement on what variables count and how much. For a preliminary statement of how the four levels can be linked, see Thomas W. Robinson, "Political and Strategic Aspects of Chinese Foreign Policy," in Donald C. Hellmann, ed., *China and Japan: The New Balance of Power* (Lexington, Mass.: Heath, 1976), pp. 198–224.

2. On U.S.-Soviet relations, see Adam Ulam, *The Rivals: America and Russia Since World War II* (New York: Viking, 1971); on U.S.-Sino relations, Gene T. Hsiao, ed., *Sino-American Detente and Its Policy Implications Next Decade* (New York: Praeger, 1974); and on Sino-Soviet relations, see Alfred D. Low, *Sino-Soviet Dispute: An Analysis of the Polemics* (Rutherford, N.J.: Fairleigh Dickenson University Press, 1976).

3. See, for instance, O. B. Borisov and B. T. Koloskov, *Soviet-Chinese Relations, 1945–1970* (Bloomington, Ind.: Indiana University Press, 1975); and G. V. Astafyev and A. M. Dubinskii, eds., *Vneshnyaya Politika i Mezhdunarodniye Otnosheniya Kitaiskoi Narodnoi Respubliki (The Foreign Policy and International Relations of the Chinese People's Republic), 1949–1973* (Moscow: Mysl, 1974).

4. John K. Fairbank, *The United States and China* (Cambridge, Mass.: Harvard University Press, 1971).

5. The best examples are the Soviet-American Strategic Arms Limitations Treaties. See John Newhouse, *Cold Dawn: The Story of SALT* (New York: Holt, Rinehart and Winston, 1973); and Mason Willrich and John B. Rhinelander, eds., *SALT: The Moscow Agreements and Beyond* (New York: Free Press, 1974). Only in the case of the ABM agreement was China's force, such as it was, a factor, and that element disappeared once the new treaty was signed and estimates of China's missile force were severely downgraded.

6. This is particularly true of recent writers on detente who have concentrated on the threat of the Soviet military buildup and who have presumed that, Soviet-Chinese relations being continuously bad, things would remain that way, even after Mao's death. Specialists in U.S.-Sino relations, on the other hand, sometimes went to the opposite extreme of calling for a (gradual) sellout of Taiwan in order to prevent China from renewing its ties with Moscow. On detente, see, inter alia, Arthur Cox, *The Dynamics of Detente* (New York: Norton, 1976); Richard Pipes, "Why the Soviet Union Thinks It Could Fight and Win a Nuclear War," *Commentary*, July 1977, pp. 21–34; Albert Weeks, *The Troubled Detente* (New York: New York University Press, 1977); and Robert W. Tucker, "Beyond Detente," *Commentary*, March 1977, pp. 42–50.

7. Gargi Dutt, "China and the Shift in Superpower Relations," *International Studies*, October–December 1974, pp. 635–62; and Harold C. Hinton, "The United States and the Sino-Soviet Confrontation," *Orbis*, Spring 1975, pp. 25–46.

8. Vernon Aspaturian, "The USSR, the USA and China in the Seventies," *Survey*, Spring 1973, pp. 103–22; William E. Griffith, ed., *The World and the Great Power Triangles* (Cambridge, Mass.: MIT Press, 1975); Michel Tatu, *The Great Power Triangle: Washington, Moscow, Peking* (Paris: Atlantic Institute, 1970); and Ronald J. Yalem, "Tripolarity and World Politics," *Yearbook of World Affairs* (London: Stevens and Sons, 1974), pp. 23–42.

9. The best book on the origins of the cold war is John Lewis Gaddis, *The United States and the Origins of the Cold War, 1941–1947* (New York: Columbia University Press, 1972). It does not rate the China issue as a terribly important element in precipitating the cold war, although after 1950 China's policy was surely instrumental in continuing it. Perhaps the best revisionist volume on the subject, that of Thomas G. Paterson, *Soviet-American Confrontation: Postwar Reconstruction and the Origins of the Cold War* (Baltimore: Johns Hopkins University Press, 1973), hardly mentions China at all.

10. Oton Ambroz, *Realignment of World Power: The Russo-Chinese Schism Under the Impact of Mao Tse-Tung's Last Revolution* (New York: Speller, 1972).

11. See Foster Rhea Dulles, *American Policy Toward Communist China, 1949–1969* (New York: Crowell, 1972).

12. John Spanier, *American Foreign Policy Since World War II* (New York: Praeger, 1973); Howard Boorman et al, *Moscow-Peking Axis* (New York: Harper, 1957).

13. Donald S. Zagoria, *The Sino-Soviet Conflict, 1956–1961* (Princeton, N.J.: Princeton University Press, 1972); Nikita Khrushchev, *Khrushchev Remembers* and *Khrushchev Remembers: The Last Testament* (Boston: Little, Brown, 1970 and 1974).

14. Adam Ulam, *Expansion and Coexistence: The History of Soviet Foreign Policy* (New York: Praeger, 1968).

15. Thomas W. Robinson, "The Sino-Soviet Border Situation, 1969–1975," Hudson Institute, HI-2364-RR, November 1975.

16. All of the major East-West differences and all of the crises during this period shared this characteristic. All the crises of those years were bilateral in form, and when one power attempted to trilateralize an issue—as China did in the Taiwan Straits crisis of 1958—it was rebuffed by its erstwhile partner. For details, see Thomas W. Robinson, "The View from Peking: China's Policies Towards the United States, the Soviet Union, and Japan," *Pacific Affairs*, Fall 1972, pp. 333–55.

17. This is admittedly a challenging statement. The components of national power are many and, moreover, expressible only in situationally relevant terms or in terms of other states' perceptions of one's own power. The most important changes in China's power were the recovery of national unity after 1949 and the ability of a strong government to pursue its interests abroad. Moreover, most other states perceived China as moving into the same league, even though as a junior partner, as the United States and the Soviet Union. The Sino-U.S. statement in the Korean War, China's defeat of India in the late 1950s and the early 1960s, and Peking's acquisition of nuclear weapons were milestones along the paths of massive increases in China's power and Soviet and U.S. perceptions thereof. It is true that the Cultural Revolution, the Soviet border buildup after 1969, the disarray in Chinese politics in the early and mid-1970s, and China's disinvestment in military hardware all called into question that reality and those assessments of its power. Nonetheless, it is also true that China is the only state in the world that can, and has, stood up militarily to the Soviet Union and the United States, and to which both superpowers devote more diplomatic and military attention than any other third state. For a development of the concept of power in international relations and its application to the Sino-Soviet-U.S. triangle, see Thomas W. Robinson, "China in a Tripolar World: An Approach to the Theory and Practice of Three State International Relations," unpublished manuscript, 1973.

18. This is amply documented in the annual *U.S. Military Posture* statements of the Joint Chiefs of Staff; the annual *Report of the Secretary of Defense* (Washington, D.C.: Government Printing Office, 1970–   ); and in the annuals *The Military Balance* and *Strategic Survey* (London: International Institute for Strategic Studies, 1970–   ).

19. See Thomas W. Robinson, "The Sino-Soviet Border Dispute: Background, Development, and the March 1969 Clashes," *American Political Science Review* 66, no. 4 (December 1972): 1175–202; and "The Sino-Soviet Border Situation, 1969–1975.": 1175–1202.

20. This has been Moscow's stated policy since the overthrow of Khrushchev in 1964. For details, see ibid. Occasionally, the Soviet leaders lapse into a fit of frustration with China [as in the Aleksandrov editorial in *Pravda*, May 14, 1977] but the established policy will in all probability continue. Moscow has nowhere to go, and of its policy options a strategy of "watch and wait" has the highest probability of success. For a translation of the Aleksandrov editorial, "Peking: A Course Arrived at Disrupting International Detente Under Cover of Anti-Sovietism," see *Current Digest of the Soviet Press*, June 8, 1977, pp. 1–4.

21. If one inspects China's policy toward various regions, its ability to influence local

events drops precipitously with distance. The PRC has most to say in the area around its periphery, that is, in Asia. China has less to say about the Middle East and Africa simply because it cannot apply its power at such great distances. For Chinese and Soviet policies in these areas, see Alvin Z. Rubinstein, ed., *Soviet and Chinese Influence in the Third World* (New York: Praeger, 1975).

22. For an analysis of the Eleventh Congress, see David Bonavia, "Hua Spells Out the New Gospel," *Far Eastern Economic Review*, September 2, 1977, pp. 8–12. The Congress documents are in *Peking Review*, August 26 and September 2, 1977.

23. Indeed, this seems to be the direction in which the United States is moving. See "Brown Sets New Technology Policy Expected to Favor China's Needs," *New York Times*, September 11, 1977, p. 1,; and Michael P. Pillsbury, "Future Sino-American Security Ties: The View from Tokyo, Moscow, and Peking," *International Security*, Spring 1977, pp. 124–40.

24. See, for instance, Raymond Duncan, ed., *Soviet Policy in Developing Countries* (Waltham, Mass.: Ginn-Blaisdell, 1970); Roger E. Kanet, ed., *The Soviet Union and Developing Countries* (Baltimore: Johns Hopkins University Press, 1974); Olas M. Smolansky, *The Soviet Union and the Arab East Under Khrushchev* (Harrisburg, Pa.: Bucknell University Press, 1974); and Robert H. Donaldson, *Soviet Policy Toward India: Ideology and Strategy* (Cambridge, Mass.: Harvard University Press, 1974).

25. This is amply demonstrated by Tanzania's actions after China's completion of the Tanzanian railroad project. Tanzanian Premier Julius Nyerere thanked the Chinese for their efforts, sent most Chinese home, and continued his policy of neutrality. See George T. Yu, "Chinese Aid to Africa: The Tanzania-Zambia Railway," in Warren Weinstein, ed., *Chinese and Soviet Aid to Africa* (New York: Praeger, 1975), pp. 29–55.

26. Lester R. Brown, *By Bread Alone* (New York: Praeger, 1974); and Mihajlo Mesarovic and Edward Pestel, *Mankind at the Turning Point* (New York: Dutton, 1974).

27. Donald L. M. Blackmer and Sidney Tarrow, *Communism in Italy and France* (Princeton, N.J.: Princeton University Press, 1975); and Walter Z. Laquer, " 'Eurocommunism' and Its Friends," *Commentary*, August 1976, pp. 25–30.

28. See Robinson, "China in a Tripolar World," for illustrations.

29. In addition to the two sources in note 13, see William E. Griffith, *The Sino-Soviet Rift* (Cambridge, Mass.: MIT Press, 1964); William E. Griffith, *Sino-Soviet Relations, 1964–1965* (Cambridge, Mass.: MIT Press, 1967); and David Floyd, *Mao Against Khrushchev: A Short History of the Sino-Soviet Conflict* (New York: Praeger, 1963).

30. Roderick MacFarquhar, ed., *Sino-American Relations, 1949–1971* (New York: Praeger, 1972).

31. This received official sanction in both Soviet and U.S. pronouncements on detente. On the Soviet side, see Adam Ulam, *Expansion and Coexistence*, chs. 11–13 on the U.S. side, see *U.S. Foreign Policy for the 1970's: Building for Peace*, 1–4, (Washington, D.C.: Superintendent of Documents, 1971–74). These represent the personal views of Henry Kissinger, then secretary of state.

32. Thomas W. Robinson, "United States-China Relations Since the Shanghai Communique and Prospects for the Future," in *Proceedings of the Fifth Sino-American Conference on Mainland China* (Taipei: Institute of International Relations, 1976), pp. 726–57.

33. The Sino-Soviet military balance, tending steadily toward rough equality since 1973, makes conflict ever more unlikely. See *The Military Balance* and *Strategic Survey* (London: The International Institute for Strategic Studies), annual surveys for the years since 1972. However, it is the overall increase in Soviet power that pulls the United States and China together, and that trend is likely to continue.

34. See Michael P. Pillsbury, "U.S.-Chinese Military Ties?" *Foreign Policy*, no. 20 (Fall 1975): 50–64; and A. Doak Barnett, "Military-Security Relations Between China and the United States," *Foreign Affairs*, April 1977, pp. 584–97.

35. Barnett, "Military Security Relations." On August 26, 1977, the Department of De-

fense issued new regulations on the export of technology that observers perceived, correctly, as designed to facilitate supplying certain types of U.S. military technology to China. See U.S. Department of Defense, Office of Assistant Secretary of Defense (Public Affairs), "Interim DOD Policy Statement on Export Control of United States Technology."

36. For a good recent example of U.S. reactions to the Soviet Union, see Hedrick Smith, *The Russians* (New York: Ballantine, 1976). Most of the U.S. travel literature on China in the 1970s is quite positive, if rather uncritical. The best is exemplified by Ross Terrill, *800,000,000: The Real China* (Boston: Atlantic/Little, Brown, 1972); and *Flowers on an Iron Tree* (Boston: Little, Brown, 1975).

37. It is true that a reaction against a too-positive view of China as a whole is already developing in the United States, leading perhaps to a proper separation of U.S. views of China-as-Cathay from views of China-as-a-communist-ruled-state. Attitudes toward the former aspect seem likely to remain positive; toward the latter, probably increasingly neutral or negative. If this useful separation is made, a lean-to-the-Chinese-side role for the United States will have to be justified more on power politics/national interest grounds than moral and human rights reasons. See Edward Luttwak, "Seeing China Plain," *Commentary*, December 1972, pp. 27–33.

38. S. N. Eisenstadt, *Modernization: Protest and Change* (Englewood Cliffs, N.J.: Prentice-Hall, 1966); Alex Inkeles and David H. Smith, *Becoming Modern: Individual Changes in Six Developing Countries* (Cambridge, Mass.: Harvard University Press, 1974); Cyril Black *et al., The Modernization of Japan and Russia* (New York: Free Press, 1975).

39. Merle Fainsod, *How Russia Is Ruled* (Cambridge, Mass.: Harvard University Press, 1964); Roy Medvedev, *Let History Judge: The Origins and Consequences of Stalinism* (New York: Vintage Books, 1973).

40. That modification would have to come from a combination of post-Maoist changes in China's policy, as already seems evident from the post-Maoist policies outlined earlier, the unavoidable concomitants of modernization, and an interpretation of Maoist thought emphasizing tolerance and humanism. Such strains do exist throughout Mao's writings, although obviously they have taken a back seat to the more totalitarian aspects. Even in his later years when Mao's actions were more radical, his writings tended to moderate somewhat. For this, see Stuart Schram, ed., *Chairman Mao Talks to the People* (New York: Pantheon, 1974).

41. On Liu Shao-chi, see Lowell Ditmer, *Liu Shao-chi and the Cultural Revolution* (Berkeley, Calif.: University of California Press, 1974); on Lin Piao, see Thomas W. Robinson, *Lin Piao: A Chinese Military Politician* (forthcoming); on Lo Jui-ching, see Harry Harding and Melvin Gurtov, "The Purge of Lo Jui-ching: The Politics of Chinese Strategic Planning." (Santa Monica, Calif.: Rand Corporation, 1970).

42. Victor H. Li, "De-Recognizing Taiwan: The Legal Problems" (New York: Carnegie Endowment for International Peace, 1977); and the forthcoming book by Ralph Clough to be published in 1978 by the Brookings Institution, Washington.

43. Robinson, "The Sino-Soviet Border Situation."

44. Cf. Rubinstein, *Soviet and Chinese Influence in the Third World;* Roger E. Kanet and Donna Bahry, eds., *Soviet Economic and Political Relations with the Developing World* (New York: Praeger, 1975); and Kanet, *The Soviet Union and the Developing Nations.*

45. Robert O. Freedman, *Soviet Policy Toward the Middle East Since 1970* (New York: Praeger, 1975); and Robert Leguold, "Soviet and Chinese Influence in Black Africa," in Rubinstein, *Soviet and Chinese Influence in the Third World*, pp. 154–75.

46. O. B. Borisov and B. T. Koloskov, *Sino-Soviet Relations, 1945–1970* (Bloomington, Ind.: Indiana University Press, 1975).

47. Max Beloff, *Soviet Policy in the Far East, 1944–1951* (London: Oxford University Press, 1953).

48. MacFarquhar, *Sino-American Relations, 1949–1971.*

49. See Griffith, *The Sino-Soviet Rift*, for the well-known series of Chinese letters to the

Soviet Union on the subject of bloc strategy toward the West. The various Kennedy administration initiatives toward China and the negative PRC responses are described and documented in MacFarquhar, *Sino-American Relations, 1949–1971*, pp. 182–208.

50. On the consequences of the Sino-Indian border war, see Bhabani Sen Gupta, *The Fulcrum of Asia: Relations Among China, India, Pakistan, and the USSR* (New York: Pegasus, 1970). On the linkage between the Vietnam War and the Cultural Revolution, see William F. Dorrill, "Power, Policy, and Ideology in the Making of the Chinese Cultural Revolution," in Thomas W. Robinson, ed., *The Cultural Revolution in China* (Berkeley, Calif.: University of California Press, 1971), pp. 21–112.

51. On the Soviet strategic and conventional buildup, see Paul H. Nitze, "Assuring Strategic Stability in an Era of Detente," *Foreign Affairs*, January 1976, pp. 207–32; Jan M. Lodel, "Assuring Strategic Stability: An Alternate View," *Foreign Affairs*, April 1976, pp. 462–81; and Robert Lucas Fischer, "Defending the Central Front: The Balance of Forces," *Adelphi Papers*, no. 127, Autumn 1976. The question of the nature, extent, and direction of the Soviet buildup was the subject of a special Central Intelligence Agency study, which sought competing interpretations, publically known as "Team B" (the outside, academic consultant group) versus "Team A" (the internal analyst group). The ensuing debate can be followed in *New York Times* and *Aviation Week and Space Technology* during late spring 1976.

52. For an amplification of these views as applied to the Asian regional context, see Thomas W. Robinson, "Soviet Policy in Asia," in William E. Griffith, ed., *The Soviet Empire: Expansion and Detente* (Lexington, Mass.: Heath, 1976), pp. 285–336.

53. Although the Soviet Union's usable, exportable "power" is largely concentrated in the military field, and although Moscow continues to be constrained by significant weaknesses, both Washington and Peking became increasingly concerned with the military component. In the late 1960s and early 1970s, Washington and Peking engaged in a bit of wishful thinking about the supposedly changed nature of power as it pertained to their respective relations with the Soviet Union. The United States pretended that Moscow was in reality weak (because of the dissidents, bad harvests, poor technology, etcetera) and thus chose to ignore the enormity of the Soviet force buildup and military modernization. China, perhaps one should say Mao personally, pretended that the Soviet Union was weak for ideological reasons and that the Soviet military buildup along China's northern frontier was not a serious threat because of China's allegedly superior defense tactics. Both were incorrect: The basis of power in international relations is still disposable military power—the more so in an era of instant nuclear destruction and of the drastic shortening of conventional wars wrought by the revolution in conventional weaponry. On the new debate about the nature of power, see the series of articles in the October 1977 issue of *Foriegn Affairs;* Seyom Brown, *New Forces in World Politics* (Washington, D.C.: Brookings Institution, 1974); and Robert W. Tucker, "Beyond Detente," *Commentary*, March 1977, pp. 42–50. On the conventional weaponry revolution, see James F. Digby, "Precision-Guided Weapons," *Adelphi Papers*, no. 118, Summer 1975.

54. It is *perception* of relative power that counts in international politics. The Soviet leaders have always perceived themselves as relatively weak vis-à-vis the United States, and have attempted to compensate for their weakness in creativity/quality by emphasizing quantity. That, plus aspects of the Russian national character, explains much of the recent arms buildup. For an exposition on the role of perception in international politics, see Robert Jervis, *The Logic of Images in International Relations* (Princeton, N.J.: Princeton University Press, 1976). Tibor Szamuely has written a perceptive statement of Russian character, *The Russian Tradition* (New York: McGraw-Hill, 1974).

55. Vladimir P. Lukin, "Some aspects of the American approach to Asia," *Sh. Sh. A.* (USA), May 1976; and "Maoist regime at a new stage," *Kommunist*, August 1975.

56. See Robinson, "The Sino-Soviet Border Situation, 1969–1975," for details.

57. See note 13. The July 14, 1977 outburst is an example of the frustration that Soviet

leaders feel in not being able to convince China's leaders to change the policy of anti-Sovietism, even after Mao.

58. Soviet policy from 1973 can be followed on a yearly basis in *The International Yearbook of Foreign Policy Analysis* (New York: Wiley, 1975).

59. On Angola, see Anthony R. Wilkinson, "Angola and Mozambique: The Implications of Local Power," *Survival*, September/October 1974, pp. 217–27; Kenneth L. Adelman, "Report from Angola," *Foreign Affairs*, April 1975, pp. 558–74; John A. Marcum, "Lessons of Angola," *Foreign Affairs*, April 1976, pp. 407–25; and Colin Legum, "The Soviet Union, China and the West in Southern Africa," *Foreign Affairs*, July 1976, pp. 745–62.

4 Detente and U.S.-Soviet Relations in the Middle East during the Nixon Years (1969–74)

Robert O. Freedman

Any examination of the U.S.-Soviet relationship during the presidency of Richard Nixon must take into consideration the fact that the spectrum of relations between the two superpowers was a very broad one during this period. Strategic arms; U.S.-Soviet trade; the triangular relationship among the USSR, the People's Republic of China (PRC), and the United States; Soviet Jewish emigration; Vietnam; crises in the Third World; Berlin, and a host of other issues all crowded in on one another, with a problem or development in one area of the U.S.-Soviet relationship often tending to affect the relationship in another. Consequently, to abstract totally the U.S.-Soviet relationship in the Middle East from this crowded spectrum would be somewhat artificial. Therefore it will be necessary to deal in this study with the U.S.-Soviet relationship in non-Middle Eastern areas only to the extent that developments in these areas have tended either to affect U.S.-Soviet relations in the Middle East or to be affected by them.

Because the most basic definition of detente—one accepted by both the USSR and the United States—is "the relaxation of tensions between the superpowers," and the Middle East is one area in the world that has demonstrated the capability of sharply increasing U.S.-Soviet tensions, this chapter will analyze the extent to which detente, as defined, was actually present in the U.S.-Soviet relationship in the Middle East during the 1969–74 period. In particular, attention will be paid to the question of whether Soviet actions during this period could be said to have been aimed at, or had the effect of, increasing or reducing tensions between the superpowers.[1]

The analysis is divided into three sections. The first will deal with the 1969–70 period, and will highlight Soviet behavior during the two crises in 1970: the violation of the U.S.-sponsored cease-fire agreement between Egypt and Israel in August 1970 and the Syrian invasion of Jordan in September 1970. The second section will cover the period from January 1971 through October 1972, during which a number of major agreements were signed between the United States and the Soviet Union, including the "Basic Principles of Mutual Relations" in which the two nations committed themselves to preventing "the development of situations capable of causing a dangerous exacerbation of relations" and to refrain from trying "to obtain unilateral advantages at each other's expense."[2] With the signing of this, as well as other agreements at the 1972 summit, it was widely believed that a detente relationship had come into being. This period also witnessed a clear effort by the USSR to limit the arms sent to Egypt and to discourage the Egyptians (and other Arabs) from precipitating a new war against Israel. The final period of the study extends from October 1972 until the resignation of President Nixon in August 1974, and examines Soviet behavior in two more crisis situations: the Arab-Israeli War of October 1973 and the Syrian-Israeli "war of attrition" of March-May 1974. In its conclusions, the chapter seeks to demonstrate whether there were any differences in Soviet behavior in the detent period (1973–74)—as opposed to what might be termed the pre-detente period (1969–70)—and will make some general statements about the nature of the U.S.-Soviet relationship in the Middle East and its effect on the larger U.S.-Soviet relationship.[3]

THE DIPLOMATIC BACKGROUND IN THE MIDDLE EAST

By the time Richard Nixon assumed the presidency in the United States in January 1969, the Soviet Union had been active in Middle Eastern politics for a decade and a half. Beginning with the arms deal with Nasser's Egypt in 1955, which broke the Western arms monopoly in the region, the Soviet Union had developed diplomatic, economic, and military relationships with a number of states in the area, and by 1969 had established a particularly close relationship with the Arab states of Egypt, Syria, Iraq, and Algeria. These relationships, however, were not without their problems. The Arab elites frequently complained about insufficient Soviet support against Israel, and they were suspicious of the Arab communist parties operating in their countries. In addition, they were often unhappy at the position taken by the USSR in intra-Arab quarrels, such as the one between Syria and Egypt, and intraregional disputes, such as the one between Iraq and Iran.[4] Nonetheless, despite these difficulties, Soviet relations with these key Arab states were quite good, and by 1969 it appeared that the Soviet position in the Arab world was far stronger than that of the United States.

The overall Soviet goal at this time seems to have been the elimination of Western military, economic, and political influence in the Arab world to the greatest degree possible, while substituting Soviet influence in its place. The primary strategy employed by the Soviet leadership to eliminate Western influence (one first noticeable with Kosygin's visit to Cairo in May 1966) was the establishment of an "anti-imperialist" Arab front directed against Israel and its Western supporters, particularly the United States. While this strategy, when successful, had the clear benefit of rallying all the Arab states together, and thus eliminating the need for a painful Soviet choice in intra-

Arab conflicts, it also included the possibility that the Arabs might exploit this unity and, reinforced by Soviet arms, go to war against Israel at a time not desired by the USSR, and that in turn this war could escalate to a U.S.-Soviet confrontation. Indeed, perhaps overencouraged by Soviet support, Nasser formed just such an Arab coalition in May 1967, blockaded Israeli shipping in the Straits of Tiran, and brought troops to the Israeli borders, only to be soundly defeated in the June 1967 war (as were Syria and Jordan)—a defeat that, at least temporarily, was also a defeat for Soviet armies and prestige in the region.[5]

By 1969, however, the USSR had recovered, indeed, even improved, its position in the Arab world. The Egyptian army had been reconstructed under direct Soviet supervision and, resupplied with modern Soviet weaponry, was now engaging Israel in a war of attrition along the Suez Canal.[6] The Soviet Union had also resupplied and reequipped the Syrian army, and enjoyed particularly close relations with Syria's Jedid regime. Soviet relations were also good, albeit a bit more distant, with the Al-Bakr regime that had just come to power in Iraq and the Boumedienne regime in Algeria. The fact that these states had had no diplomatic relations with the United States, Britain, or West Germany since the 1967 war must have been perceived as yet another plus for the USSR in what it saw as a "zero-sum" contest for influence with the United States in the Middle East. Nonetheless, throughout the post-1967 war period, Soviet influence did not rise above the behavior reinforcement level in any Arab country, that is, where the USSR could demonstrate the ability to reinforce a decision taken by an Arab elite, such as Nasser's war of attrition against Israel. It never reached the stage of behavior modification, that is, where the Soviet Union could pressure its clients to take a pro-Soviet action, or abstain from an anti-Soviet action, if such a position were against the client elite's will.[7] Indeed, in many cases it appeared as if the Arabs were exploiting the Soviet drive for influence by taking large amounts of Soviet economic and military aid, while giving little in the way of political obedience in return.[8]

THE NEW U.S. ADMINISTRATION TAKES POWER

It was against this background of rising, but still limited, Soviet influence in the Middle East that the Nixon administration took office. Nixon had stated in his inaugural address that in dealing with the Soviet leaders, he wished to move from "a period of confrontation to an era of negotiation." He proposed U.S. cooperation in reaching a strategic arms agreement with the USSR, a primary Soviet objective, in return for a more cooperative Soviet position in reaching a settlement of the Arab-Israeli conflict. Indeed, in his press conference of January 27, 1969, soon after taking office, Nixon stated:

> What I want to do is to see to it that we have strategic arms talks in a way and at a time that will promote, if possible, progress on outstanding

political problems at the same time—for example, in the *problem of the Middle East*—and in other outstanding problems in which the U.S. and Soviet Union, acting together, can serve the cause of peace. (Italics mine)[9].*

It transpired, however, that in its dealings with the United States on Middle Eastern matters, the USSR was interested not in reaching a Middle East settlement, but in improving its own position in the region. This was to become evident as the United States undertook the first of a series of peace initiatives in the Middle East. Under the direction of U.S. Secretary of State William Rogers, the United States engaged the USSR in two-power talks aimed at reaching an agreement for a Middle East peace settlement. Despite a number of concessions to the Soviet position on such matters as the extent of Israeli withdrawal, the USSR nonetheless rejected the U.S. plan, seeking to portray it in the Arab world as a U.S. device to aid Israel. Indeed, Soviet opposition reportedly led an angered Nixon to order Rogers to make public the final U.S. peace offer in December 1969. (This was to be called the "Rogers Plan.")[10] In addition, in July 1969, in the midst of the U.S.-Soviet discussions, Nasser sharply escalated his war of attrition against Israeli troops in the Sinai peninsula—an action clearly reinforced by shipments of Soviet weaponry.[11] Thus, the USSR did not prove to be, as Nixon had hoped, a willing partner in the quest for an Arab-Israeli peace agreement.

Nasser's escalation of the war of attrition was to lead to a similar Israeli escalation in the form of fighter bomber attacks across the Suez Canal against Egyptian artillery emplacements. These attacks soon extended deep into Egypt as the Israelis sought to destroy Egypt's military infrastructure, so as to limit the amount of firepower the Egyptians could bring to bear along the canal. The war of attrition escalated, and Nasser found his forces increasingly unable to defend Egyptian airspace against the Israeli attacks. By January 1970, in a state of virtual desperation, Nasser flew to Moscow to seek Soviet support against Israel. According to Mohamed Heikal's description of this visit, Nasser initially wanted only Soviet SAM-3 missile crews to protect Egyptian airspace, but when the Soviet leaders stated that Egypt would have to accept an integrated system of Soviet missile crews *and* Soviet combat pilots, the Egyptian leader readily agreed.[12] In taking this major step, the Soviet leaders, for the first time, injected a Soviet military combat presence beyond the Soviet bloc, and it was to be a major Soviet presence of 21,000 troops by the time Sadat expelled the Russians in 1972.[13] In return for its military assistance against Israel, the USSR received virtual control over a

---

*It should be noted that Nixon held similarly optimistic hopes that the Soviet Union would help the United States get out of Vietnam.

number of Egyptian military, naval, and air bases (including Cairo West), and was able to utilize these bases not only to prevent Israel from attacking the Egyptian heartland* but also to maintain an air cover for the Soviet fleet in the eastern Mediterranean, which at the time lacked aircraft carriers. Coming at a time when U.S. power was in retreat in Southeast Asia (U.S. troops were being withdrawn from Vietnam under the Nixon Doctrine), the Soviet projection of force in the Middle East seemed to indicate a significant increase in Soviet influence in the Third World and a decrease in that of the United States.

The U.S. reaction to emplacement of Soviet combat forces in Egypt was very mild. Indeed, the fact that the U.S. government delayed for three months an Israeli request for more Phantom and Skyhawk jets while Rogers tried yet another peace initiative appeared to indicate that it had acquiesced in the increase in Soviet power in Egypt.[14] Perhaps emboldened by U.S. hesitation, the USSR moved its air defense installations from the Cairo-Helwan area toward the canal, and by late spring there were engagements between Israeli and Soviet airmen. With the United States preoccupied with its invasion of Cambodia (which precipitated major student demonstrations on campuses throughout the United States and the postponement of a scheduled U.S.-Sino meeting), it appeared to be only a matter of time until Soviet missiles were emplaced all along the canal, a development that would not only protect Egypt from Israeli air strikes but also provide covering antiaircraft fire for an Egyptian troop crossing of the canal itself. In an effort to prevent just such a development, Israeli fighter bombers made—at a high cost in destroyed or damaged aircraft—efforts to prevent the missiles from being emplaced. Inevitably, Soviet and Israeli aircraft became engaged in dogfights during this period, and on May 6 the United States announced it would reconsider Israeli requests for aircraft because Soviet personnel were now flying combat missions,[15] although no firm promises of new jets were to be forthcoming until September.

As the situation along the canal heated up still further in June, Kissinger, in a news conference on June 26, sought to tie the U.S. action in Cambodia to a show of firmness in the Middle East, and made the strongest U.S. statement to date attacking Soviet involvement in Egypt:

> It is, of course, nonsense to say that we did what we did in Cambodia in order to impress the Russians in the Middle East. It was not as simple as that. But we certainly have to keep in mind that the Russians will judge us by the general purposefulness of our performance everywhere. What they are doing in the Middle East, whatever their intentions, poses the gravest

---

*In an effort to avoid clashing with the Soviet Union, Israeli Defense Minister Moshe Dayan suspended all "deep penetration raids" in April.

threats in the long run for Western Europe, and Japan, and therefore, for us.[16]

Kissinger finished his briefing on a very strong note: "We are trying to expel the Soviet military presence, not so much the advisers, but the combat pilots, and the combat personnel before they become so firmly established."[17]

Meanwhile, high-ranking State Department personnel, sensitive (or perhaps oversensitive) to Soviet sensibilities, tried to spread the word that Kissinger's comments were "inadvertent, completely inadvertent."[18] Nonetheless, the message had gone forth that the United States was forcefully back in the influence-competition game in the Middle East. The message was not lost upon Egyptian Vice-President Anwar Sadat, who, as president, expelled Soviet troops from Egypt in 1972.

Soon after Kissinger's news conference, the United States succeeded in working out a 90-day cease-fire between Israel and Egypt and between Israel and Jordan. One of the elements of the cease-fire agreement, which was tied to a resumption of the diplomatic mission of special U.N. Representative Gunnar Jarring, was a standstill provision in which neither side was to improve its military position during the cease-fire period in the military status quo zones extending 50 kilometers (33 miles) east and west of the canal. Mindful of Israeli fears that Egypt and the USSR would use the cease-fire period to complete the missile emplacements along the canal, Nixon stated at a press conference on July 30: "Some concern has been expressed by Israeli government officials that, if they agree to a cease-fire, they run the risk of having a military build-up occurring during the cease-fire. We and others have attempted to assure them that this would not be the case."[19] Israeli concern, however, turned out to have been well founded, for no sooner had the cease-fire taken effect than it was violated as the Egyptians and their Soviet allies moved their SAM-3 missiles up to the canal, thus precipitating yet another Middle East crisis.

THE CEASE-FIRE VIOLATION AND THE U.S. "RESPONSE"

Almost as soon as the 90-day cease-fire went into effect, on August 7, 1970, Egyptian and Soviet crews began to move SAM-3 missiles into position along the canal. In some cases, destroyed missile emplacements were repaired; in other cases, new installations were set up, sometimes replacing dummy installations that had been put in place just before the cease-fire.[20] Heikal gives the following account of Nasser's thinking on the missile movement:

> The most important thing in Nasser's view was to finish building the missile wall. When completed, this would not only protect our armed

forces on the West Bank of the Suez Canal, but would give protection over a strip 15–20 kilometers wide on the East Bank and thus cover a crossing.[21]

According to Heikal, Nasser told the Soviet leaders: "We must have a breathing space so that we can finish our missile sites. We need to give our army a break and cut down our civilian casualties."[22]

While Egyptian reasoning in first accepting the cease-fire and then violating its provisions is quite clear, Soviet strategy is a bit more complicated. On the one hand, Egypt, the USSR's main Arab ally and its operational base for the Soviet air force and navy, had come out in favor of the cease-fire. It was unlikely, therefore, that the Soviet Union would try to veto such a position, particularly since the USSR shared the Egyptian goal of completing the missile system at no additional cost in Egyptian (or Soviet) casualties. In addition, Soviet-Israeli relations were heating up. With dogfights now taking place between Israeli and Soviet pilots, there was the possibility that the confrontation might escalate still further. Indeed, the Soviet leaders may have feared that the Israelis, suffering heavy losses in both aircraft and personnel during the war of attrition, might decide to launch an attack across the canal to destroy the missile bases—much as they had done in 1969—and that Israeli and Soviet troops might then engage in direct combat. Such a situation might quickly escalate and bring in the United States on Israel's side, a development the Soviet leaders clearly wished to prevent. (At the time, they were in the final stages of working out a treaty with West Germany, the primary NATO ally of the United States. A Soviet-U.S. military confrontation in the Middle East could well delay or even prevent such a treaty, which the USSR desired in order to consolidate its western frontiers. This would permit it to concentrate its attention on the PRC, with which it had engaged in two border battles in 1969, and with which negotiations to solve the border dispute had again broken down.)[23]

While the cease-fire clearly had advantages for the Soviet Union, the Soviet leadership was unhappy at the fact that the United States had reinserted itself into Middle Eastern politics so broadly. According to Heikal's account of Nasser's trip to Moscow, Brezhnev reportedly asked Nasser somewhat hotly, "Do you mean to tell me you are going to accept a proposal with a U.S. flag in it?"[24] Nonetheless, the Soviet leaders may have felt that the U.S. initiative would come to naught anyway, and that both Egypt and the USSR, with missiles emplaced and Egyptian crews more fully trained, would be in a much better military position at the end of the 90-day cease-fire. While the United States might protest the violations, there was little it could do to halt them; and given the fact that U.S. prestige was so heavily linked to the cease-fire, the Americans might even overlook the missile violations in their haste to bring about negotiations between the Arabs and Israelis under the auspices of Ambassador Jarring.

If this, indeed, was the trend of Soviet thinking, it was initially correct. Despite almost immediate protests by the Israelis about cease-fire violations, there was no U.S. confirmation that violations had occurred for almost a month. For their part, the Soviet leaders claimed that Israel's complaints were an attempt to sabotage the peace talks, and that it was Israel that had broken the cease-fire by building new fortified positions on its side of the canal. When the United States began complaining about the violations, the Soviet Foreign Ministry issued a statement on September 10 denying that any "ground-to-air missiles, manned by Soviet crews" had appeared in the Suez Canal Zone, and claiming that the Soviet Union "from the very beginning stood for the cease-fire, observing the importance of such a step, and did everything possible for the successful implementation of the Jarring mission."[25] Interestingly enough, the very next day *Izvestia* published a detailed article asserting that Egyptian activities in the cease-fire zone were confined to "maintenance work on old positions":

> Egypt has not altered the positions of rocket installations inside the 50 kilometer zone specified by the agreement. The measures carried out by Egypt in this zone are confined to maintenance work on old positions. Israel and the U.S.A. are trying to present these minimal measures, including the shifting of the location of rocket installations with others, which are necessary for the security of the rocket emplacements and of their personnel, as violations of the agreement.[26]

The United States, however, did not regard the Soviet-Egyptian cease-fire violations as "minimal measures" aimed at the security of the missile emplacements and their crews. The first U.S. reaction was to promise to Israel the long-sought Phantom and Skyhawk jets. This angered the Arabs. Radio Moscow broadcast the statement by Egyptian Foreign Minister Mahmoud Riad who said that as a result of the newly promised U.S. military aid to Israel, "the U.S. has brought its (cease-fire) initiative to an end."[27] Coming from Egypt, such a statement apparently meant that whatever concerns the Soviet Union may have had that the U.S. cease-fire initiative would strengthen the U.S. position in the Middle East (while, in the zero-sum game thinking of the Soviet leaders, weakening that of the USSR) could now be set aside. That the Soviet leaders had entertained such concerns was evident from another Radio Moscow broadcast the same day:

> The Imperialists and their agents do not cease their attempts to drive a wedge into Soviet-Arab relations and to blur the Arabs' understanding of the clear fact that the road to restoring justice in the Middle East and to attaining the legitimate national aims of the Arabs lies in strengthening firm friendship and cooperation with the U.S.S.R. and all other Socialist countries.[28]

While the end result of the missile violations may have strengthened the position of the Soviet Union in the Middle East, it clearly angered the U.S. leadership. Kissinger, after denouncing the Soviet Union for violating the missile agreement, told newspersons on September 16:

> Our relations with the Soviet Union have reached the point where some important decisions have to be made, especially in Moscow. . . . Events in the Middle East and in other parts of the world have raised questions of whether Soviet leaders as of now are prepared to pursue the principles that I outlined earlier; specifically, whether the Soviet leaders are prepared to forego tactical advantages they can derive from certain situations for the sake of the larger interests of peace.[29]

Kissinger's pique also may have been related to developments in Jordan where the Palestine guerrilla organizations, unhappy at King Hussein's acceptance of the cease-fire with Israel, were engaged in full-scale battles against Hussein's forces. Given the close relationship between the United States and the Hussein regime, both Kissinger and Nixon were clearly very concerned about these developments. When, two days later, an armored force from Syria (whose government had very close ties to the USSR) invaded Jordan, another crisis erupted in the Middle East.

THE JORDANIAN CRISIS

The Jordanian crisis of September 1970 was the outcome of a long struggle for power in Jordan between the government of King Hussein and a number of Palestinian guerrilla organizations that often fought among themselves while also challenging the Jordanian monarch.[30] After a series of unsuccessful truces earlier in the year, fighting in September was precipitated by Hussein's acceptance of the U.S.-sponsored cease-fire with Israel and a subsequent attempt to assassinate him. This was followed by a number of aircraft hijackings whose perpetrators, the Popular Front for the Liberation of Palestine (PFLP), had flown the hijacked aircraft and their passengers to a PFLP-controlled airstrip in Jordan. Determined not to allow this state-within-a-state situation to continue, Hussein decided to crack down on the guerrillas once and for all. The guerrilla organizations immediately united to fight him.

Complicating this already complicated situation was the attitude of the Jedid regime in Syria, which opposed the cease-fire and was the main Arab champion of the Palestinians. On September 18, it decided to invade Jordan with an armored brigade. Given the fact that two thirds of the population in Jordan are Palestinian, the Syrian leaders may have felt the dispatch of the armored brigade would be sufficient to force Hussein to terminate his attacks on the Palestinians, or possibly even to topple him. Whatever the ultimate goal of the Syrian leadership in sending tanks into Jordan, the Syrian action precipitated a crisis in U.S.-Soviet relations. Still smarting from apparent Soviet duplicity in the missile violation of the cease-fire, Kissinger reacted very strongly when the Soviet leaders were shown to have lied in claiming that Syria had not invaded Jordan. The fact that Soviet advisers had accompanied the Syrian tanks to the Jordanian border—later admitted by a Soviet official[31]—gave further evidence of Soviet involvement in, if not instigation of, the Syrian move.

In assessing Soviet motivations in supporting the Syrian move, several considerations must be taken into account. First, the Soviet relationship with the Jedid regime was a very close one,[32] and just as in the case of Nasser's decision to violate the cease-fire, the Soviet leadership clearly did not want to use up its political capital with Syria to oppose the Syrian initiative. Second, the possible Soviet payoff from such an intervention, if successful, could be considerable. For example, the regime of King Hussein was tightly linked to the West, and his overthrow could lead to yet another radical Arab regime with which the USSR could claim influence. Indeed, the overthrow of the moderate regime in the Sudan in May 1969 and its replacement by a leftist regime, which quickly developed close (albeit only temporary) ties to the USSR, and the overthrow of pro-Western King Idris in Libya in September 1969, which led to the ouster of U.S. and British forces from their Libyan bases, were both net gains for the Soviet Middle East position and seemed to set a pattern into which the ouster of King Hussein might well fit.

In addition, the fact that the United States had not opposed the regime changes in the Sudan or Libya, and had acquiesced in the emplacement of Soviet combat troops in Egypt and the violation of the U.S.-initiated cease-fire agreement, may also have led some of the Soviet leaders to expect only a mild reaction from Washington as yet another base of U.S. influence in the Middle East slipped away. Finally, the USSR was beginning to develop close relations with some of the Palestinian guerrilla organizations,[33] and even if Hussein were not toppled by the invasion, a Syrian military presence perhaps could have forced Hussein into terminating his attacks on the Palestinians, thus preserving a potential lever of Soviet influence in the Middle East. A major article in *Izvestia* on September 11 called for an agreement between Hussein and the Palestinians. A Moscow Radio broadcast in Arabic to the Arab world on September 18, 1976, several hours before the Syrian invasion, stated:

> It is in the interest of the Arab countries and the intensification of the Arab National Liberation struggle, including the Palestinian movement, to do everything necessary to stop the bloody clashes in Jordan. The reaching of a firm agreement between the Jordanian authorities and the Palestinian Fedayeen will be met with extreme satisfaction by all those interested in

settling the situation throughout the Middle East and in removing the consequence of the Israeli aggression as soon as possible.[34]

Thus, the minimum goal expressed by the Soviet Union in the Jordanian crisis was a settlement between King Hussein and the Palestinians that would preserve the Palestinians as a potential lever of Soviet influence in the Middle East while at the same time hopefully enabling the Arabs to reunite in an anti-imperialist alignment against the United States. A limited Syrian invasion in support of the Palestinians (who were getting badly beaten by Hussein at the time) might work in support of this dual goal; and should it also have the effect of toppling King Hussein's regime, the Soviet gain in the Arab world might be still greater. While the available evidence does not indicate that the USSR precipitated the Syrian invasion of Jordan, it is clear that it acquiesced in and gave support for the Syrian move.

If, on the basis of past behavior, the Soviet leaders had hoped that the United States would acquiesce in the Syrian invasion of Jordan, this anticipation was short-lived. On September 19, Nixon alerted a number of U.S. airborne units (including the 82nd Airborne Division at Fort Bragg, North Carolina, and airborne units in West Germany) and began moving the U.S. Sixth Fleet (already on partial alert because of the hijackings and a possible U.S. move to save the hostages) toward Lebanon, while warning the Soviet Union to restrain Syria. The Soviet leaders in turn criticized the U.S. military alerts and reports of new U.S. aid to Israel.[35] As the position of King Hussein deteriorated further on September 20, the Soviet chargé d'affaires was called to the State Department and warned that Israel and the United States might intervene. Reportedly, U.S. Assistant Secretary of State for Middle Eastern Affairs, Joseph Sisco, told the Soviet representatives: "Remember, you are to report very carefully to the Kremlin that we cannot give you any assurance whatever on the question of Israeli intervention or American intervention, directly in this situation."[36]

Simultaneously, Israeli and U.S. officials had begun close coordination, and as Syrian involvement grew still greater on September 21, an arrangement was worked out whereby Israeli forces would move against the Syrian forces with the United States providing air cover against any Egyptian or Soviet countermove. This cooperation became more evident as the Israelis moved tanks to the Jordan River and Israeli fighter bombers were loaded with bombs and rockets, a U.S. aircraft carrier moved to within 60 nautical miles of the Israeli coastline, and direct communications were established between the carrier and the Israeli government.[37]

Apparently the increasing U.S. show of force had some effect on the USSR, although it was not immediate. The initial TASS statement of September 19, 1970 tacitly supported the Syrian intervention: "Soviet official circles express the hope the peoples of the Arab countries, their leaders and governments and Arab organizations will do everything possible to achieve the speediest cessation of the fratricidal war in Jordan."[38] In addition, Moscow Radio, in an English-language broadcast, warned against Western, but not Syrian, interference in the Jordanian events: "It is up to the Arabs *themselves* to eliminate the internal conflict between Arabs. Any *outside* interference would be the grossest violation of international law and of the sovereignty of the Arab states."[39] (Italics mine.)

By the following day, however, Moscow Radio was already broadcasting Jordanian charges of the Syrian invasion, although balancing the charges with Syrian denials.[40] Increasingly, Moscow Radio carried stories of a possible Western intervention in Jordan, and by the peak of the fighting on September 22, the Soviet leaders appeared to have begun to seek a graceful exit from Jordan for their Syrian clients while still preserving the Palestinians as a political movement. They sought to achieve this by calling for an Arab summit conference before Western intervention in Jordan became a reality. In a broadcast to the Arab world, Moscow Radio stated:

> It is necessary to take an effective tangible step urgently to stop the bloodshed in Jordan and to settle existing differences between the Jordanian authorities and the Palestinian Fedayeen. Naturally, the decisive word in this rests above all with the Arabs themselves. For this reason, the holding of the emergency Arab summit meetings in Cairo is an urgent vital necessity. The personal meeting of the majority of Arab leaders is necessary to discuss the situation which has emerged in Jordan in order to establish *collective* effective measures to rectify it as soon as possible. (Italics mine)
>
> The continued tension in Jordan involves dangerous consequences which directly affect the vital interests of all Arab peoples without exception. If the imperialists exploited the bloody clashes in Jordan and intervened, a blow would then be dealt to the whole Arab National Liberation Movement including the Palestinian movement. . . .[41]

Perhaps in reaction to the United States show of force in the Middle East, which the Soviet Union had done nothing to deter, the radio broadcast went on somewhat ruefully to acknowledge that the United States still retained considerable power in the region:

> International imperialism, led by the U.S., has suffered not insubstantial losses in the Arab world. But it is still very strong and has quite a few positions in the Arab countries and indeed it enjoys a certain influence in some of them. For this reason, the imperialists try with all their power and means to preserve their positions in the Arab world and when possible, to strengthen them.[42]

By September 23, the crisis was over. Hussein, without any direct U.S.

or Israeli military assistance, had beaten the Syrian tank forces, and the remnants of the tank force had begun to retreat to Syria. It remains unclear, however, whether the Syrian decision to withdraw was due to Soviet advice, the U.S. Israeli military buildup, or the refusal by Syria's air force commander, Hafiz Assad, to commit Syrian aircraft in support of the invasion. In any case, the Syrian regime that had ordered the invasion fell one month later, and Assad emerged as the ruler of Syria. Once the Jordanian crisis was over, the Soviet leadership sought to gain the credit for deterring a Western and Israeli intervention in Jordan, although it is an open question whether this Soviet posturing found many believers in the Arab world.[43]

In assessing Soviet policy during the Jordanian crisis, one can detect a two-step progression. At first, the Soviet Union gave support for the Syrian intervention, even going so far as to lie to the United States about the nature of the Syrian move. When King Hussein successfully stood up to the Syrians and the United States and Israel gave every indication of their readiness to intervene to prevent King Hussein from being overthrown, the Soviet leaders appear to have backed off and, by the peak of the crisis on September 22, the Soviet leaders were seeking to enable their client Syria, which was being defeated militarily, to withdraw in a face-saving manner. The strong show of U.S. force, coming after a series of acquiescences in Soviet Middle Eastern moves, apparently came as somewhat of a surprise to the Soviet leaders. This shock was to have its effect in Soviet policy toward the Arab-Israeli crisis during the next two years.

THE COMING OF DETENTE:
U.S.-SOVIET RELATIONS AND THE MIDDLE EAST,
JANUARY 1971–OCTOBER 1972

The death of Nasser during the last stages of the Jordanian crisis of September 1970 and the overthrow of Salah Jedid's government in Syria little more than a month later removed from power the two Arab leaders who had been closest to the USSR. These events, together with the U.S.-Soviet crisis over Jordan and another U.S.-Soviet crisis over the construction of a Soviet missile base in Cienfuegos, Cuba,[44] may have prompted the Soviet Union to adopt a more cautious policy in the Middle East, which the United States had clearly indicated was a primary area of U.S. interest. Other factors that may have prompted the Soviet leaders to take a more cautious stance included some evidence of a U.S.-Sino rapprochement[45] and the workers' riots in Poland in December 1970, which resulted in the ouster of the Gomulka regime. (The latter may have convinced the Soviet leaders that they had to donate more time and resources to their own domestic affairs lest the same thing happen to them.)

Whatever the motive, Podgorny was clearly urging caution upon the Arabs during his visit to Egypt in mid-January 1971 for ceremonies to open the Aswan Dam. According to Heikel, "Podgorny sounded such a cautious note that he profoundly shocked his hosts."[46] To determine available Soviet support for Egypt, the new Egyptian president, Anwar Sadat, journeyed to Moscow on a secret visit in March, but received little more than some general promises on arms deliveries. At this time, the Soviet leaders were preoccupied with the opening of their long-delayed Twenty-fourth Party Congress at which economic and political policy for the next five years was to be set. (The emphasis in Brezhnev's speech at the Congress on the improvement of living standards and his announcement that the rate of consumer goods production was to exceed the rate of capital goods production for the first time may have been a reflection of Soviet concern about the events in Poland.)[47] The Party Congress was upstaged, however, by the Chinese announcement that they had invited an American ping-pong team and three veteran U.S. newsmen to visit China—yet another indication of a warming in U.S.-Sino relations.

Perhaps in reaction to its own economic needs and the specter of a U.S.-Sino rapprochement, the Soviet Union became more flexible in its SALT stance in May, and an agreement in principle was reached limiting the number of ABMs on both sides.[48] According to the Kalbs' report, Nixon had sent a message to Brezhnev following the December riots in Poland suggesting that the United States might be ready to help Brezhnev modernize the Soviet economy if Brezhnev were prepared to ease the Soviet stand on a number of political issues, for example, the SALT agreements.[49] Whether or not the Kalbs' version is correct, the SALT agreement in principle did serve to improve the seriously deteriorated U.S.-Soviet relations. Relations were to improve still more in October following the achievement of a preliminary accord on Berlin and the subsequent announcement of Nixon's forthcoming visit to Moscow in May 1972. (These latter two developments may have been precipitated by Kissinger's surprise visit to Peking in July.)

While U.S.-Soviet relations improved, Soviet-Egyptian relations worsened. In the early part of May, Sadat prevented a coup by a number of high-ranking Egyptian officials, such as Ali Sabri, who had close ties to the USSR.[50] What made matters worse for the Soviet position was that Sadat's subsequent purge of Ali Sabri came on the eve of the visit of U.S. Secretary of State William Rogers to Egypt—the first visit of a U.S. secretary of state to Egypt since 1953—and appeared to many as an Egyptian goodwill gesture toward the United States. The Soviet leaders were clearly concerned about the governmental changes in Egypt, and Soviet President Podgorny rushed to Egypt to sign a 15-year Soviet-Egyptian Treaty of Friendship and Cooperation.[51] Perhaps the greatest importance of the treaty to the Soviet leaders was as a demonstration that the United States had failed in its attempts to "drive a wedge between Egypt and the USSR." Indeed, in a speech at a dinner in Cairo following the signing of the treaty, Podgorny stated:

The treaty between the Soviet Union and the United Arab Republic signifies a new blow to the plans of international imperialism which is trying in every possible way to drive a wedge into the relations between our countries, to undermine our friendship, and to divide the progressive forces.[52]

Soviet-Egyptian relations, however, received still another setback two months later when a communist-supported coup in the Sudan failed. Despite Soviet entreaties for assistance in saving the lives of communists threatened with execution, Sadat publicly took the side of Sudanese President Jaafar Nimeri at a time when Soviet-Sudanese relations were deteriorating sharply.[53]

The Middle East was not the only area in the world where the Soviet Union was experiencing difficulty. The surprise Kissinger visit to China in July and the subsequent announcement of Nixon's forthcoming visit to Peking seemed to herald the establishment of a U.S.-Sino connection, a development long feared by the USSR. Aimed, at least in part, at minimizing the impact of such an eventuality, the Soviet leaders signed a 15-year Treaty of Friendship and Cooperation with India in August.[54] India, for its part, needed such a treaty in case its steadily worsening relations with Pakistan should erupt into war, an eventuality that seemed more and more likely as the year wore on.

The India-Pakistani conflict was to cause yet another crisis in U.S.-Soviet relations: The USSR backed India and the United States supported Pakistan. Indeed, Kissinger went so far as to threaten, once India appeared to be the certain winner in the war that broke out in December, that Nixon might postpone his promised summit visit to the Soviet Union if India, after capturing East Pakistan, went on to dismantle West Pakistan.[55]

While U.S.-Soviet tensions were beginning to heat up over the Indian-Pakistani conflict, Sadat made a visit to Moscow in October in order to remove what he termed the "dark cloud" that had formed over Egyptian-Soviet relations.[56] Sadat's trip was not a successful one, however, despite further promises of Soviet military aid. Although Sadat had already proclaimed 1971 as the "year of decision" in Egypt's conflict with Israel, the Soviet leaders kept stressing the need for a "peaceful settlement of the Near East crisis," and the official Soviet description of the talks made frequent reference to "a spirit of frankness" and "exchange of opinions"—indications that there were a number of disagreements.[57]

In the period following the Soviet-Egyptian talks, the Soviet government continued to stress the need for a peaceful settlement of the Middle East conflict in its public statements on the Middle East. Despite Sadat's increasingly bellicose speeches, the Soviet leaders indicated that they would not support an Egyptian attack on Israeli-held territory, "year of decision" or not. They simply were not willing to risk a confrontation with the United States, whose president was due to visit the USSR in May 1972—and who was in the process of planning a trip to China—for the sake of an Arab ally that had proven itself "unreliable" in the Sudanese affair.* At least in part because of lack of Soviet support, Sadat's "year of decision" passed without war with Israel, and the Egyptian leader's domestic position came under increasing attack. Still seeking Soviet support, Sadat made still another trip to Moscow in February where, according to Heikal, he complained directly to Brezhnev: "In October, you promised me equipment that hasn't arrived; more was promised by Podgorny in May and hasn't arrived; more was promised by Ponamarev in July and it hasn't arrived. Why the delay?"[58]

Sadat made yet another visit to the Soviet capital in late April (just before the scheduled start of the Nixon-Brezhnev summit talks), during which he once again expressed his desire for advanced Soviet weaponry (fighter bombers and ground-to-ground missiles) and Soviet support for renewed hostilities against Israel. The Soviet leaders, with more important global issues at stake (such as the U.S. reaction to the major North Vietnamese offensive into South Vietnam and continued difficulties in completing the SALT agreement), still remained unwilling to sacrifice their relations with the United States on behalf of Egypt. Perhaps as a sop to Sadat, the communique at the conclusion of the Egyptian leader's visit contained the statement that Egypt had the right to use "other means to regain territories occupied by Israel should a peaceful solution prove impossible."[59] Even this concession to the Egyptians was rendered meaningless when several weeks later [at the conclusion of the Nixon visit to Moscow, which resulted in the signing of the SALT treaty], the United States and Soviet Union seemed to agree on defusing the Middle East crisis. It appeared that the USSR had once again demonstrated its preference for a good working relationship with the United States over any desire to support Egypt in a war against Israel. Indeed, in the "Basic Principles of Mutual Relations Between the U.S.S.R. and the U.S.A.," the superpowers pledged to do ". . . everything in their power so that conflicts or situations will not arise which would serve to increase international tensions"; stated their commitment to "preventing the development of situations capable of causing a dangerous exacerbation of their relations"; and recognized that ". . . efforts to obtain unilateral advantage at the expense of the other, directly or indirectly, are inconsistent with these objectives." Another of the "Basic Principles" stated that "the U.S.S.R. and U.S. regard commercial and economic ties as an important and necessary element in the strengthening of their bilateral relations, and thus

---

*Another factor in Soviet considerations was undoubtedly the war brewing between India and Pakistan, which would cause further complications in U.S.-Soviet relations.

will actively promote the growth of such ties."[60] The Middle East received a scant mention in the final communique, which reaffirmed the two super powers' "support for a peaceful settlement in the Middle East in accordance with U.S. Resolution No. 242."[61]

While U.S.-Soviet relations improved markedly as a result of the Moscow summit (the USSR was soon to capitalize on the atmosphere of good feelings to sign a number of highly advantageous economic agreements, including one to buy a huge amount of U.S. grain), Soviet-Egyptian relations deteriorated even further.[62] Witnessing the detente atmosphere created by the U.S.-Soviet summit, and apparently convinced that the Soviet presence in Egypt had become a political and economic burden to Egypt as well as an increasing source of friction within the Egyptian army, Sadat decided upon a dramatic action before the twentieth anniversary celebration of the Egyptian revolution to electrify his country and end the malaise that had been deepening in Egypt because of the apparently interminable continuation of the no-war, no-peace situation. Following the failure of a final arms-seeking trip by Premier Aziz-Sidky to Moscow in mid-July, on July 18 Sadat announced the "termination of the mission of the Soviet military advisers and experts, the placing of all military bases in Egypt under Egyptian control, and the call for a Soviet-Egyptian meeting to work out a new relationship between the two countries."[63] In ridding Egypt of the Soviet advisers and combat troops—a move clearly welcomed by the United States—Sadat's reasoning seemed to be that inasmuch as the Soviet leaders had been unable to get Israel to withdraw from the occupied territories by diplomatic means, and was unwilling to expel them by force, Egypt would turn to the United States and Western Europe for assistance in achieving its goals.

The Soviet Union lost heavily in Sadat's decision to expel its military forces. Although it was now far less likely to get dragged into a war with the United States in the Middle East—and this fact must have sweetened the exodus somewhat—its strategic position in the Mediterranean was clearly weakened. Without its airfields in northern Egypt, it was unable to give close-in air cover to the Soviet Mediterranean fleet; and without its airfield in southern Egypt near Aswan, it lost control over a major strategic foothold in northeast Africa. In a political sense, the deterioration of relations between the USSR and the most populous and powerful Arab state also hurt the Soviet position in the Arab world.*

After Soviet troops had been expelled, Sadat began the process of seeking support in Europe and the United States. Unfortunately, the Palestinian terrorist killing of Israeli athletes at the Munich Olympic games tor-

---

*As relations with Egypt began to deteriorate in May 1971, the Soviet leaders had sought to improve relations with Iraq (a Friendship Treaty was signed in April 1972) and the Palestine Liberation Organization[64] as a partial recompense for their diminishing influence in Egypt.

pedoed his diplomatic initiatives. The United States, whose close alignment with Israel Sadat had hoped to sever by his expulsion of the Soviet troops, stood even more strongly behind the Israeli government following the Munich massacre. The U.S. ambassador to the United Nations, George Bush, vetoed a Security Council resolution condemning Israel for its reprisal raids against Palestinian guerilla bases in Syria and Lebanon because the resolution did not also condemn the terrorist acts that provoked the reprisal raids.[65]

Meanwhile, the Soviet leadership had seized the opportunity presented by the Israeli attacks to launch a special airlift of weapons to Damascus to reinforce the Syrian defenses. This airlift, which generated front-page headlines both in the Arab and Western press, underscored the Soviet argument that the Arabs could turn only to the USSR in their time of need. Similarly, through the airlift of medical supplies and diplomatic support in the United Nations, the Soviet leaders utilized the Israeli attacks on the Palestinian guerrilla camps to dramatize their position as supporters of the Palestinians, and thus tried to win more influence in the Palestinian resistance movement.

Confronted by these disheartening developments, Sadat once again turned to the USSR, sending Egyptian Premier Aziz Sidky to Moscow in mid-October on a fence-mending mission. To facilitate the trip, Sadat, in a speech to Egypt's People's Assembly on October 15, had stated that Egypt would never have a "two-faced" foreign policy, but would always value fully the friendship of the Soviet Union.[66] Sidky's visit apparently succeeded in restoring a partial flow of arms from the USSR. The Soviet price (or Sadat's perception of the Soviet price) for resuming the flow of arms may have been the ouster of Egyptian Defense Minister General Sadek, one of the most outspoken anti-Soviet leaders in the Egyptian government.[67]

A temporary reconciliation was thus achieved between the Soviet Union and Egypt. Military cooperation between the two states resumed and grew until October 1973 when, armed with a plethora of Soviet weaponry, Sadat was able to launch an attack against Israel.

THE ARAB-ISRAELI WAR OF 1973

The Road to War

Soviet weaponry flowed to Egypt in large amounts in late 1972 and continued at a heavy rate until the 1973 war. According to Heikal's account, "between December 1972 and June 1973, we received more arms from the U.S.S.R. than in the whole of the two preceding years. As Sadat said, 'They are drowning me in new arms.' "[68] In sending this large amount of arms to Egypt,* the Soviet leadership was clearly seeking to regain its lost influence

---

*Included were T-62 tanks, antiaircraft missiles of SAM-3, SAM-6, and SAM-7 variety, and antitank weapons.

in Egypt, particularly as Egypt began to forge an Arab coalition against Israel. (The coalition included oil-rich Saudi Arabia, which, by April 1973, was threatening to use its oil "weapon" against the now energy-vulnerable United States if there were no change in U.S. policy toward Israel.)

The nature of the U.S.-Soviet relationship was also changing. Whereas in 1972 the USSR had needed a good relationship with the United States for a number of reasons—including the need to prevent a U.S.-Sino entente, the need to secure the SALT agreement, and the need to gain access to U.S. grain and economic credits—by 1973 the situation had changed. The U.S.-Sino relationship had not improved as rapidly as the Soviet leaders had feared. Indeed, when a June 1973 visit to the United States was arranged for Brezhnev, the Soviet Union emerged as the two-to-one leader over the PRC in summit conferences with the United States, evidence that the United States might now be favoring the USSR over the PRC. Also, the war in Vietnam had ended, removing what had been a major irritant in U.S.-Soviet relations. In addition, the Nixon administration had committed itself to both the strategic arms limitation agreement and the economic agreements, and its prestige was thus committed to the detente relationship. Indeed, Soviet leaders may have begun to reason that just as U.S. prestige had been so committed to the August 1970 Arab-Israeli cease-fire agreement that U.S. leaders had been slow to react or even acknowledge the Soviet-Egyptian violations, the United States now might be slow to acknowledge any Soviet violation of the detente relationship. (Indeed, this was to occur in the early stage of the 1973 war.)

Superimposed on the entire framework of the U.S.-Soviet relationship during 1973 was the Watergate crisis, which eroded both the U.S. position in world affairs and the domestic political position of Richard Nixon. Indeed, in a news conference prior to his visit to the United States in June 1973, Brezhnev implicitly acknowledged Nixon's weakened position: "I am not going to the U.S. with any intention of bringing pressure to bear on the President because of the Watergate affair. It would be completely indecent of me to refer to it.[69] If Brezhnev were not sufficiently acquainted with the political implications of the Watergate crisis before his arrival, the fact must have been brought home to him soon after his arrival in Washington when the Senate Select Watergate Committee decided to postpone its hearings for a week so that Nixon could meet the Soviet leader without the embarrassment of his being implicated by testimony before the committee. By June 1973, the Nixon-Brezhnev relationship had changed to one where Nixon needed Brezhnev and the detente relationship more than Brezhnev needed him. This situation was a far different one from the year before when Nixon was being actively courted by both the USSR and the PRC.

Nixon and Brezhnev signed a number of agreements during the 1973 Washington summit, among them one that pledged both countries "to avoid action that could lead to a nuclear confrontation with each other or with a third nation," an agreement that appeared to solidify further the detente relationship between the two superpowers.[70] As in the 1972 summit, the leaders of the two superpowers appeared to pay little attention to the Middle East. Indeed, only 87 words out of a total 3,200 in the final communique issued on June 24 dealt with the Middle East situation. It appeared as if Nixon and Brezhnev deliberately wanted to downplay the conflict, lest it interfere with their pursuit of detente. The joint communique failed even to mention U.N. Resolution No. 242, hitherto the basis of the Soviet position for a settlement of the Arab-Israeli conflict. The text of the communique stated:

> The parties expressed their deep concern with the situation in the Middle East and exchanged opinions regarding ways of reaching a Middle East settlement. Each of the parties set forth its position on this problem.
>
> Both parties agreed to continue to exert their efforts to promote the quickest possible settlement in the Middle East. This settlement should be in accordance with the interests of all states in the area, be consistent with their independence and sovereignty, and should take into due account the legitimate interests of the Palestinian people.[71]

The Egyptian reaction to the summit communique was swift and bitter. On June 25, *Al-Ahram's* managing editor, Ali Hamadi el-Gammal, asserted: "Although we did not expect the talks between the two leaders to produce a specific position with regard to the crisis, we never thought that the problem would meet this strongly negative attitude on their part."[72] The Arab reaction to the summit's treatment of the Arab-Israeli conflict was in fact so negative that the Soviet government felt constrained to publish a special statement on Soviet policy toward the Middle East. It reiterated the main tenets of Soviet policy, including the need for total withdrawal of Israeli troops to the 1967 borders, a "peaceful solution" based on U.N. Resolution No. 242, recognition of the "legitimate interests and rights of the Palestinians," and Soviet support for the Arab states affected by "Israeli aggression" in 1967.[73] Nonetheless, the USSR continued to come under heavy attack in the Arab countries (and in the rest of the Third World as well) because its detente relationship with the United States appeared to subordinate Third-World interests to the interests of the superpowers.

In an attempt to answer such complaints, Dmitry Volsky, associate editor of *New Times*, again tried to justify the effectiveness of Soviet detente policy in an article published just prior to the September 1973 meeting of nonaligned nations:

> An unbiased examination of the international situation shows that the development of Soviet-U.S. contacts has already had a salutary effect on the

Third World. Transition from confrontation to stable peaceful coexistence makes it harder for the aggressive neo-colonial quarters to impose their diktat on the newly-emerged national states. In this respect the significance of the Agreement on the Prevention of Nuclear War signed on June 22 this year cannot be overestimated. Recall, for instance, this stipulation of the agreement: Each party will refrain from the threat or use of force against the other party, against the allies of the other party, and against other countries under circumstances which may endanger international peace and security. The parties agree that they will be guided by these considerations in the formulation of their foreign policies and in their actions in the field of international relations. . . .

Given a different world balance of strength, different international conditions, might the imperialists not have resorted to the most dangerous moves against, say, Iraq when it nationalized Iraq Petroleum, *or against the Popular Unity Government in Chile?* . . .

Such, then are the facts. They show that with the introduction of peaceful co-existence into Soviet-U.S. relations, Soviet support for the national liberation movements will increase rather than diminish, and opportunities for cooperation between the socialist nations and the developing countries will be greater. More, in a climate of detente, when the newly independent states can feel more secure and the system of neo-colonialist blocs is breaking down, these countries gain new opportunities to pursue independent home and foreign policies.[74] (Italics mine)

Volsky must have soon regretted these words, for less than a week later the Popular Unity government of Salvador Allende in Chile was overthrown, and Allende, who together with Brezhnev had been the recipient of the Lenin Peace Prize in May, was killed.*

It is still unclear to what degree the coup in Chile may have influenced the Soviet leaders to support Egypt's decision to go to war in October, but it is clear that by the end of September they had endorsed Sadat's move. The

---

*While it is not in the purview of this study to go into the background and development of the events in Chile, it is very clear that the Soviet leadership was bitterly disappointed about the overthrow of the Allende government. The Allende government was an excellent example proving that the Soviet policy of detente was working, and its overthrow appeared to indicate the opposite, particularly to a number of already suspicious leaders in the Middle East. Indeed, a *New Times* editorial following the coup in Chile, acknowledged this effect of the coup on detente:

A concentrated offensive is being waged against detente and its practical achievements. The object is at all costs to impede the progress of this process of such vital importance to the peoples. . . .

Unfortunately, it must be said that the psychological pressure applied by the enemies of international detente is not without effect. One Arab newspaper, for instance affirmed the other day that the reactionary military coup in Chile was nothing short of a consequence of detente.[75]

fact that Sadat had by this time managed to effect a reconciliation between Syria and Jordan clearly established him as the leader of an Arab alignment, which now included not only the radical states of Syria and Libya but also the conservative, pro-Western states of Jordan and Saudi Arabia. This made Egypt once again the fulcrum of Middle Eastern politics, and the Soviet leaders well may have thought that Soviet aid to Egypt during a war that would pit Israel (and most likely the United States, at least in a support capacity) against the Arab world would help create the "Arab unity on the anti-imperialist basis" they had so long desired. At the very minimum, an outbreak of war would inflame Arab feelings against the United States, much as the 1967 war had done, thus weakening the U.S. position in the Arab world still further. The Soviet leadership also may have considered the possibility that the war might bring a further nationalization of Western oil companies,[76] and possibly even an oil embargo against the United States and Western Europe, which would be a major blow to the economies of the Western world. Such developments would mean a sharp increase in influence for the USSR in its "zero-sum game" influence competition in the Middle East with the United States, and possibly even tip the "world balance of forces" toward the USSR.[77] Perhaps in an effort to reap these gains, the Soviet leaders failed to inform the United States of the coming war, despite an explicit agreement to do so reached at the 1972 Brezhnev-Nixon summit (where the two powers had pledged to warn each other if a dangerous local conflict threatened to arise, and not to seek "unilateral advantage" at the expense of the other).

In giving its support for Sadat's decision to go to war, the Soviet leadership took its biggest Middle East gamble since February 1970 when it had agreed to Nasser's request for a Soviet-manned air defense system. In taking that move in 1970, the Soviet leaders had gambled successfully that the Nixon administration, then still bogged down by Vietnam, would make no equivalent countermove. In 1973, the Soviet leaders may have reasoned that the Nixon administration was now so burdened with Watergate and the "energy crisis" that regardless of Soviet action during the war, it could not afford to jettison Nixon's detente policy with the USSR, which had proven to be one of his administration's few successes. The Soviet decision to support the Arabs could only provide ammunition for the enemies of U.S.-Soviet detente;* but the Soviet leaders, perhaps still smarting from the events in Chile, evidently decided that the benefits of aiding the Arabs outweighed

---

*Following revelations over the cost to the U.S. consumer of U.S. wheat sales to the Soviet Union, and attacks on detente by Soviet dissidents Andrei Sakharov and Aleksandr Solzhenitsyn, who warned against detente without democratization in the USSR, increasing numbers of Americans, even before the outbreak of the war, were beginning to question both the meaning and the value of detente with the Soviet Union.

the risks of angering the United States. Nonetheless, Soviet caution in the initial stages of the war indicated that the Soviet leaders were hedging their bets on their support of the Arabs until the Arab forces had secured some military successes.

Soviet Behavior During the 1973 Arab-Israeli War

In analyzing Soviet behavior during the 1973 Arab-Israeli War, one can detect a number of stages. In the first phase, soon after war broke out, the Soviet leaders were apparently trying to persuade the Egyptians to accept an in-place cease-fire to permit them to consolidate their gains and to prevent an expected Israeli counterattack from eliminating the Arab gains. An end to the war at this stage, while preserving Arab gains, would also avoid a possible confrontation with the United States.[78] When the Arabs rejected the Soviet cease-fire initiatives and proved that, at least temporarily, they had the capacity to win on the battlefield, the Soviet leaders decided to further the Arab military effort by urging other Arab nations to join the fighting and by initiating a massive airlift and sealift of weaponry to Syria (at the time bearing the brunt of the fighting) and Egypt.[79] In taking these actions, the Soviet leadership probably had two goals in mind. With the Arabs now winning, the Soviet leaders perhaps sensed the possibility of rallying the Arabs into long advocated "anti-imperialist" alignment, thus striking a blow at U.S. interests in the Middle East. By urging other Arab nations to enter the war and by beginning the airlift, the USSR demonstrated that it would supply them with the weapons necessary to fight Israel. Also, by urging Arabs to fight, the Soviet leaders may have hoped that it would not be necessary for Soviet troops to engage in fighting, thus avoiding the possibility of a U.S.-Soviet confrontation.*

Despite the massive Soviet airlift and exhortations for the other Arab states to enter the war, Secretary of State Kissinger mildly announced at a news conference on October 12: "We do not consider the (Soviet) airlift of military equipment helpful. We also do not consider that Soviet actions as of now constitute the irresponsibility that on Monday evening I pointed out would threaten detente."[80] In their analysis of this Kissinger statement, the Soviet leaders may have felt that the Nixon administration was so wedded to detente that the USSR was free to take even further action to influence the outcome of the war. If the Soviet airlift, sealift, and vocal exhortations to the Arabs were not deemed "irresponsible," then perhaps other acts would not be either. In any case, the Soviet Union stepped up its airlift and sealift

---

*The Soviet leaders may have had this goal in mind when they removed Soviet technicians and their families before the war. Without any Soviet citizens in Egypt, it would not be necessary to commit Soviet troops to save them.

operations, and there were reports that Soviet soldiers had driven tanks from Syrian ports to the battlefields. On the diplomatic front, the USSR now opposed any cease-fire unless it meant a withdrawal of Israeli forces to the borders Israel held before the June 1967 war.[81]

By October 15, the U.S. government, under heavy domestic and Israeli pressure, finally reacted to the Soviet moves by beginning an airlift of weapons to Israel. Meanwhile, the tide of battle had turned, and by October 16 the Israelis had not only crossed the old cease-fire lines with Syria and moved toward Damascus but had also crossed the Suez Canal and begun to develop a salient on the west bank that would soon threaten Cairo. Perhaps recognizing the developing crisis in the Egyptian military position, on that same day Soviet Premier Alexei Kosygin flew to Cairo for three days of talks with Sadat, who continued to deprecate the Israeli canal crossing. Although the Arab military position was now in trouble, the Soviet leaders could take comfort from the continued "anti-imperialist Arab solidarity" that was demonstrated by an Arab oil embargo against the United States because of its support of Israel. Participating in the embargo were Saudi Arabia, once the closest ally of the United States in the Arab world; Kuwait, another old ally; and a number of other Arab countries. (Moscow Radio on October 18 had urged the Arabs to use their oil weapon.)

The use of the oil weapon, however, could not stop the rapid deterioration in the position of the Egyptian army, a development that resulted in Kissinger's trip to the Soviet Union on October 20 at the Soviet leaders' "urgent request." The result of Kissinger's visit was a "cease-fire in place" agreement—a major retreat from the USSR's previous position calling for a return to the 1967 boundaries as a price for the cease-fire. The U.S.-Soviet ceasefire agreement, which was approved by the Security Council in the early hours of the morning on October 23, did not terminate the hostilities. Both sides, despite their agreement to the cease-fire, continued fighting to improve their positions. The Israelis quickly got the better of the fighting, and by October 24 Sadat was forced to appeal to both the United States and the Soviet Union to send troops to police the cease-fire.[82]

Egypt was about to suffer a major defeat, which would have meant a major defeat for Soviet prestige as well, as the USSR which had openly backed the Arabs. The Soviet leaders apparently decided to pressure Israel and the United States by alerting Soviet airborne divisions and dispatching Soviet transport planes to the airborne troops' bases. At the same time Brezhnev sent a stiff note to Nixon that reportedly stated: "I say it straight that if the United States does not find it possible to act together with us in this matter, we should be faced with the necessity urgently to consider the question of taking appropriate steps unilaterally."[83] While the Soviet leader may have been bluffing, Nixon apparently decided not to take any chances and called a nuclear alert.[84] It now appeared that not only had detente died but the two superpowers were on the verge of a nuclear confrontation. Brezhnev quickly backed off from his implied threat to intervene unilaterally. The United States, equally unwilling to see the conflict develop further, brought pressure on Israel to stop the Israeli army before it destroyed the surrounded Egyptian Third Army and marched on Cairo.* The superpowers then agreed to bring the issue back to the United Nations, and a U.N. emergency force was established to police the cease-fire.

Soviet policy makers, who had perhaps initially been hesitant about supporting the war, could point to a number of significant gains for the Soviet position in the Middle East (although many of these gains were to prove to be transient ones). Perhaps the major Soviet gain was the creation of the long-advocated "anti-imperialist" Arab front and the concomitant isolation of the United States from its erstwhile allies in the region. Not only had Syria, Iraq, Egypt, Jordan, Algeria, Kuwait, and Morocco actually employed their forces against Israel but even such staunch one-time allies of the United States as the conservative regimes of Kuwait and Saudi Arabia had, in addition to sending troops to the front, declared an oil embargo against the United States. Even the tiny Gulf sheikdom of Bahrein had ordered the United States to get out of the naval base it maintained there.[85]

On the negative side, U.S.-Soviet detente had suffered a major blow, and large numbers of Americans both inside and outside the government now openly opposed Nixon's detente policy toward the Soviet Union and the trade and strategic arms policies that accompanied it. Nor could the fact that the United States and the Soviet Union had nearly experienced a nuclear confrontation during the war have been welcome to the Soviet leaders.

On balance, the Soviet Union's prestige in the world, and particularly in the Middle East, had been greatly improved by the war. It appeared as if the Soviet Union had won a major, if not decisive, victory in the "zero-sum game" competition with the United States for influence in the Middle East. However, just as the USSR's position, which had been gravely weakened by its expulsion from Egypt in July 1972, had improved sharply only a few months later as a result of the Munich massacre, the United States, at a low point in middle Eastern prestige at the close of the war, was to improve its position radically several months later as a result of the astute "shuttle diplomacy" of Henry Kissinger and a reordering of priorities by Anwar Sadat.

In assessing Soviet behavior during this crisis, it is evident that the Soviet decision to support Egypt in starting the war was another case of behavior reinforcement, where a client's projected policy coincided with the goals of the USSR. The initial Soviet caution may have been related to doubts about the capacity of the Egyptians to wage battle successfully against

---

*As will be shown subsequently, Kissinger had additional motives for applying this pressure to Israel.

the Israelis, but once those doubts had diminshed, the Soviet Union did not hesitate to exploit the Arabs' success to enhance its own position in the region and weaken that of the United States. Kissinger's very broad definition of the limits of detente may have encouraged this rather bold Soviet action. When its Arab clients appeared to be on the verge of defeat, however, the USSR did not hesitate to threaten to intervene to salvage a major Arab (and Soviet) political, if not military, victory. Unfortunately for the Soviet leaders, subsequent events were to prove that Soviet support for Sadat did not yield any lasting political dividends.

THE SYRIAN-ISRAELI WAR OF ATTRITION, MARCH-MAY 1974

U.S.-Soviet relations clearly had suffered as a result of the war. The Arab unity created by the war, which the Soviet leaders had welcomed so warmly, began to disintegrate almost as soon as the war ended. The Ba'athist regime in Iraq, despite close ties to the USSR, rejected the Soviet-supported cease-fire agreement as being "against the will of the Arab masses." The Al-Bakr regime was so opposed to the cease-fire that it refused to attend the Algiers summit conference of Arab leaders in late November to coordinate Arab strategy. Similarly opposed to the cease-fire was Libyan leader Mu'ammar Kadafi, who characterized it as "a time bomb offered by the United States and Soviet Union."[86]

A more serious problem awaited the Soviet leaders in Egypt where Soviet influence, partially restored by massive shipments of military equipment (including Scud ground-to-ground missiles) began to erode.[87] By the end of the war, the primary alignment in the Arab world was the Egyptian-Saudi Arabian alliance, with the Egyptians supplying the military power and the Saudi Arabians the oil leverage. Kissinger clearly recognized this when he helped negotiate the cease-fire, thereby saving Sadat from probable political ruin when his armies were on the verge of being overrun by Israeli forces. Kissinger undoubtedly recalled Sadat's earlier efforts to improve relations with the West and his evident dislike for the Soviet leaders, whom he had openly opposed on a number of occasions since becoming Egypt's president in October 1970. Kissinger may have concluded that he had a unique opportunity to win over Egypt, and perhaps the rest of the Arab world as well (or at least the oil-rich states), first by prevailing upon the Israelis to accept a cease-fire, then working out an exchange of prisoners (November 7), and finally negotiating a complete disengagement agreement (January 18) that resulted in Israel's withdrawal from its salient near Cairo and from the east bank of the Suez Canal. (The latter enabled the Egyptians to control both banks of the canal for the first time since 1967.) In the process, Kissinger also negotiated the reestablishment of diplomatic relations between the United States and Egypt.* Kissinger not only managed to do this while leaving out the USSR, which had provided the weaponry to enable the Arabs to go to war in the first place, but he also secured Sadat's support in getting the oil embargo lifted, thus splitting the Arab "anti-imperialist" front that Soviet policy makers had worked so diligently to create.

After his successful "shuttle diplomacy" had secured an Egyptian-Israeli disengagement agreement, Kissinger made yet another journey to the Middle East in February. This time he shuttled back and forth between Damascus and Jerusalem to procure from the Syrian leaders the list of Israeli prisoners of war that the Israelis had demanded as a precondition to disengagement talks with Syria. It appeared that Kissinger was on the verge of achieving another diplomatic coup. This was apparently too much for the Soviet leaders. Having seen the United States so quickly replace the USSR as the leading foreign influence in Egypt (however temporarily), the Soviet leaders had no desire to see the process repeat itself in Syria. Consequently, Gromyko, who had just paid a surprise visit to Cairo, followed Kissinger to Damascus.[88] The Soviet-Syrian communique issued upon Gromyko's departure was bellicose: It demanded a fixed timetable for Israeli withdrawal from all occupied territory, and threatened a "new eruption" of war that would bring about a "threat to peace and security in the Middle East and throughout the world" if Arab demands were not met.[89] Strengthened by new shipments of Soviet arms and encouraged by Soviet support, the Syrian regime of Hafiz Assad began a war of attrition against Israeli positions in the Golan Heights with artillery, tanks, and air combat.

Apparently the Soviet and Syrian leaders hoped that by heating up the conflict in the Golan Heights they would be able to dissuade the oil-rich states from lifting the oil embargo against the United States. While Syria stepped up its level of fighting, the Soviet Union urged the Arab states in very strong terms to maintain their oil embargo. On March 12, Radio Moscow broadcast:

> If today some Arab leaders are ready to surrender in the face of American pressure and lift the ban on oil before the demands (for a total Israeli withdrawal) are fulfilled, they are challenging the whole Arab world and the progressive forces of the entire world which insist on the continued use of the oil weapon.[90]

The Soviet media also belittled Kissinger's mediation efforts. On March 17,

---

*Relations between Egypt and the United States warmed so rapidly that there soon began a steady flow of U.S. businessmen to Egypt where Sadat's economic policies provided a haven for foreign investments. This process culminated in the visit to Cairo of David Rockefeller, chairman of the Chase Manhattan Bank, who announced that Chase Manhattan was planning to open a number of "full-service banks" in Egypt.

Pravda called them "a mountain that gave birth to a mouse." Despite Syria's war of attrition and the Soviet campaign to maintain the oil embargo, Kissinger's diplomatic efforts were successful. On March 19, the oil embargo against the United States was lifted by the major oil-producing Arab states (although as a sop to the Syrians, Algeria stated that it would reexamine its embargo policy on June 1). When Libya and Syria refused to go along with the majority decision to lift the embargo, Arab unity on the "oil weapon" was broken.

The termination of the oil embargo was a significant defeat for Soviet diplomacy in the Middle East. The Soviet leadership had come out strongly for the maintenance of the oil embargo as a means of keeping the Arab world unified against the United States, and the USSR had greatly profited from the disarray caused by the embargo in both NATO and the European Economic Community. Egypt's decision to support an end to the embargo, despite all the aid the USSR had given Egypt before and during the October war, was yet another indication of the sharp diminution of Soviet influence in Egypt and the corresponding rise of U.S. influence.

Following the end of the oil embargo, the Soviet Union sought to improve its ties with Iraq, Libya, and the Palestine Liberation Organization to balance its losses in Egypt, whose leader, Anwar Sadat, now came in for direct Soviet criticism.[91] The USSR's central concern during the postembargo period was its relations with Syria. The Soviet leaders clearly were concerned that Syria might follow Egypt's example and move toward the West in return for economic and technical aid. The Syrian government's decision on March 13 to lift restrictions on the movement of private capital in and out of Syria and to permit the Syrian private sector to sign loan agreements with foreign investors must have added to the Soviet concern.[92] By supporting Syria in its war of attrition against Israel, the Soviet leaders hoped to avert a Syrian turn to the West, while at the same time isolating Sadat as the only Arab leader to reach an agreement with Israel. The Soviet leadership may also have entertained the hope that should fighting intensify sufficiently, the Arab oil-producing states might be forced by Arab public opinion to reimpose the oil embargo, and that Sadat himself might be forced to return to war. Yet in pursuing their policy of encouraging Syrian belligerence, the Soviet leaders had to toe a very narrow diplomatic line, for a new summit meeting with the United States was on the horizon and important strategic arms limitations issues between the two superpowers were under active consideration. In the East, the Soviet Union's relations with the PRC had taken another turn for the worse when the government refused to return the crew of a Soviet helicopter that had crashed on China's territory.[93] The Soviet leaders consequently adopted a policy of support for Syrian belligerency, while at the same time maintaining close contact with Kissinger in his mediation efforts. This dual policy would underscore Soviet support for the Arab cause while also enabling the Soviet leadership to claim a share of the credit should Kissinger succeed in persuading the Syrians and Israelis to accept a disengagement agreement. Moreover, a series of meetings between Kissinger and top Soviet leaders would help create a positive atmosphere for the convening of a summit conference between Nixon and Brezhnev.

The first high-level U.S.-Soviet meeting after the lifting of the oil embargo came on March 29 when Kissinger journeyed to Moscow for talks with the Soviet leadership. Strategic arms issues were the main topic of consideration (Kissinger later reported that no "conceptual breakthroughs" had been reached), but the leaders of the two superpowers also discussed the Middle East situation. The final communique, however, stated only that the "two sides would make efforts to promote the solution of the key questions of a Near East settlement."[94] Interestingly, while Western press reports of Kissinger's talks in Moscow portrayed them as being relatively unsuccessful, the Soviet media challenged this interpretation. On March 30, *Izvestia* commented: "The mood and content of the talks did not at all correspond to the pessimistic accompaniment that certain Western media provided for H. Kissinger's mission.[95]

While making these gestures toward improvement of Soviet relations with the United States, the Soviet leaders went out of their way to emphasize their support for Syrian President Hafiz Assad during his visit to Moscow in mid-April. Assad was met at the Moscow airport by all three Soviet leaders (Brezhnev, Kosygin, and Podgorny), and the Syrian president's visit received front-page coverage in both *Pravda* and *Izvestia*. In his dinner speech welcoming Assad, Brezhnev pointedly attacked Kissinger's diplomatic efforts in the Middle East:

> Against the background of reduced tensions, the aggressors and their protectors may once again attempt to evade a fundamental all-inclusive solution to the (Middle East) problem. It is by no means happenstance that recently "ersatz plans" as I would call them for a Near East settlement have been launched.[96]

Following five days of talks, described as taking place in an atmosphere of "frankness and mutual understanding," the Soviet leadership agreed to "further strengthen" Syria's defense capacity, and stated once again that Syria has a "lawful inalienable right" to use "all effective means to free its occupied lands." To underline the Soviet desire to play a role in the peace talks, the joint communique stated: "The Syrian side reemphasized the importance of the Soviet Union's participation in all stages and in all areas of a settlement aimed at establishing a just and lasting peace in the Near East."[97]

Soviet attention switched back to the United States at the end of April when Gromyko met with Kissinger in Geneva as the U.S. secretary of state was en route to the Middle East for further negotiation with Syria and Israel. While the main topic of the talks was Nixon's forthcoming visit to Moscow, *Pravda* also reported that the two leaders

> . . . exchanged opinions concerning the current situation in the talks on the Near East settlement and concerning the next stage of these talks. The two sides agreed to exert their influence in favor of a positive outcome of the talks and to maintain close contact with each other while striving to coordinate their actions in the interests of a peaceful settlement in the region.[98]

Kissinger, however, gave a far less optimistic view of the talks, stating only that "I expect we'll have Soviet understanding and I hope cooperation."[99]

Meanwhile, opposition to the proposed Nixon trip to Moscow was growing in the United States. Arguing that the United States had been cheated in its wheat deal with the Soviet Union, that the United States had been placed at a disadvantage by the SALT I agreement, and that the Soviet Union had proven itself an unworthy partner because of its aid to the Arabs during the October war and its support of the oil embargo, a growing number of prominent Americans opposed a new summit. *Pravda's* political commentator, Yuri Zhukov, acknowledged this opposition, and claimed it was organized by a "dirty coalition of reactionary forces made up of imperialist circles, the American military-industrial complex, West German revanchists, NATO generals, and Zionists and adventurers of every stripe." Zhukov hailed the forces in the world working for detente, lavishing particular praise on West German Chancellor Willy Brandt, and stating that Kissinger's meetings with Brezhnev and Gromyko "inspired confidence that the forthcoming Soviet-American summit talks will be a new step forward in making the process of detente irreversible."[100]

Gromyko again met Kissinger on May 7 to reiterate the Soviet leadership's continued desire to remain closely involved in the disengagement talks and to foster detente, while at the same time supplying the weapons for Syria's war of attrition. Kissinger acceded to the Soviet desire, evidently hoping that frequent meetings would serve to limit Soviet obstructionism of a peaceful settlement. Soviet concern about detente must have been sharply reinforced when West German Chancellor Brandt was forced to resign over a spy scandal involving East Germany on May 9. With Brandt gone from the European political scene, and with a Watergate-weakened Nixon under increasing attack by the opponents of detente in the United States, Brezhnev may have seen the whole structure of his detente policy toward the West in danger of collapse. In the Middle East, despite Soviet aid in its war of attrition, Syria appeared to be close to signing a Kissinger-mediated agreement with Israel. Indeed, despite two bloody Palestinian terrorist attacks on Israeli settlements, (the latter killing 24 Israeli schoolchildren at Maalot on

May 15), Kissinger had managed to work out the outlines of an agreement by the latter part of May. Apparently concluding at this point that it was better to acquiesce in the inevitable and thereby work to improve severely damaged U.S.-Soviet relations, Gromyko was sent to Damascus to salvage at least some prestige for the USSR in the U.S.-mediated agreement. Gromyko received an acknowledgment from the Syrian government of the USSR's right to participate in all stages of a peace settlement, an assurance much like Assad had given the Soviet leaders during his April visit to Moscow. In addition, the joint communique issued upon the conclusion of Gromyko's visit stated:

> The Soviet Union and the Syrian Arab Republic affirm the durability of the relations that have been established between them and the durability of the friendship between the peoples of the two countries, and they declare that *they will let no one disturb these relations and this friendship.*[101] (Italics mine)

The Syrian-Israeli disengagement agreement ended the period of direct military confrontation between Israel and the Arab states dating back to the October war, although Palestinian terrorist attacks continued to plague the Israelis. For the time being at least, the threat of renewed warfare had receded as both sides began to concentrate on diplomatic preparations for a renewal of the Geneva peace conference. In this atmosphere, the United States set the date of Nixon's visit to the Soviet Union—indeed, a Syrian-Israeli disengagement agreement may well have been the price exacted by Kissinger for the visit. The Soviet leadership could perhaps hope that the momentum toward "irreversible detente" interrupted by the October war was again proceeding. As a result of the disengagement agreement, U.S. prestige rose sharply in the Arab world, and it appeared to many observers that the United States was in the process of replacing the Soviet Union as the dominant foreign influence among the Arabs, an impression that was to be reinforced by Nixon's triumphant tour of the Middle East in mid-June.

In assessing Soviet policy during the Syrian war of attrition against Israel, one can see yet another example of Soviet behavior reinforcement of a client whose goals, at least initially, matched those of the USSR. While the Syrian goal in waging its war of attrition was apparently to improve its negotiating position vis-à-vis Israel, the Soviet leaders appear to have hoped to use the renewed fighting as a means, first, to prevent the lifting of the oil embargo (a goal shared by the Syrians) and, second, after the embargo was lifted, to continue the Arab-Israeli conflict to reinforce the Soviet position in Syria. Syria's decision to accept the disengagement agreement was a limited defeat of this Soviet goal. That the disengagement agreement facilitated Nixon's visit to Moscow to reinforce what had become a somewhat shaky U.S.-USSR detente relationship must have been some solace to the Soviet leadership.

CONCLUSIONS

In assessing Soviet behavior during the four Middle Eastern crises between 1970 and 1974, one can detect a number of similarities. In each case,
the USSR was reinforcing behavior already decided upon by a client state,
and the Soviet leadership evidently viewed the net result of the client state's
action as strengthening the overall position of the Soviet Union in the Middle East while weakening that of the United States. In each case, an increase
in tension was caused by the Soviet-reinforced client state's action, both on a
regional basis and between the superpowers. Similarly, once each crisis was
underway, the USSR was to take action (not always successfully) to try to
avoid its escalation into a major confrontation between the United States and
the Soviet Union—except in the case of the missile violation. In the missile
violation crisis, Soviet endorsement of Nasser's acceptance of the U.S.-spon-
sored cease-fire (which terminated the Soviet-Israeli clashes along the Suez
Canal, and thus eliminated the possibility of the canal war's escalation into a
superpower conflict) can be seen as a move to reduce tension, albeit temporarily, as moving missiles in clear violation of the cease-fire raised the level
of U.S.-Soviet tension. In the Jordanian crisis, while the USSR apparently
endorsed the Syrian move into Jordan, its call for an Arab summit to deal
with the Jordanian crisis appears to have been a face-saving gesture to enable
its client to withdraw gracefully from what had become an untenable position
(particularly with Israel and the United States on the verge of intervention)
and to end the crisis.

In the 1973 war, the USSR again exacerbated tensions by its actions.
Not only did it support the initiation of the war, but once the war was
underway its airlifts to Syria and Egypt and its endeavors to widen the war
by urging the other Arab states to participate intensified the crisis. However,
by withdrawing its civilians and technicians before the war began and by
urging the other Arab states to fight, the Soviet leaders, during the initial
stages of the war, took steps designed to avoid being drawn into the conflict.
When the battle turned against Egypt, however, the USSR threatened to
intervene unilaterally—a threat not too dissimilar to the one made by the
United States in support of Jordan in 1970, except that the Soviet action
came after it had supported its client's decision to go to war in the first place.
The Soviet leaders, therefore, tried to save their client from the consequences of its own action. Both the Jordanian crisis in 1970 and the 1973 war
prompted strong U.S. counteraction, and the end result was a sharp rise in
U.S.-Soviet tension. Finally, during the Syrian war of attrition, the USSR
deliberately sought to raise the level of tension to prevent a settlement that
might further weaken the Soviet Union's position in the Middle East. Coming at a time when the United States was trying to work out a peace settlement between Israel and Syria, this action also raised U.S.-Soviet tensions.
Nonetheless, the war of attrition did not erupt into a full-scale war or a

U.S.-Soviet confrontation, at least partially as a result of close U.S.-Soviet communication during the crisis.

If, on the basis of these four crises, it has been demonstrated that Soviet actions had the effect of increasing tensions in the Middle East and between the superpowers, can one point to any differences in Soviet behavior during the pre-detente crises of 1970 and the post-detente period crises of 1973 and 1974? In other words, did the agreements signed between Brezhnev and Nixon at the 1972 and 1973 summit conferences have any effect in limiting Soviet behavior? An analysis of the available evidence would tend to indicate that the only significant difference—if significant is the proper word—between the two periods was that during the 1973–74 crises, unlike 1970, the Soviet leadership gave a great deal of lip service to detente. In both crises, the USSR's goal was the same: to exploit the situation to strengthen its position in the Middle East in what it saw as a zero-sum game competition for influence with the United States.

What, then, can be said about the effect of these crises in the Middle East on the larger U.S.-Soviet relationship? Since 1969, both Kissinger and Nixon had urged the USSR to play a responsible role in the Middle East (although Soviet behavior in 1969 and 1970 did not meet the criteria of responsibility). After the 1972 and 1973 summits, when it appeared that the Soviet leadership had pledged itself to a responsible role in international affairs, many Americans felt that detente had been achieved. In 1973 and 1974, when the Soviet leaders appeared to renege on their promises, and again began behaving in crises as they had done in 1970, that is, before detente, a negative U.S. reaction to detente set in. While the Nixon administration's prestige was still committed to detente—and Kissinger made such fatuous statements as the one on October 12, 1973, saying that the USSR was not behaving irresponsibly in the war—the U.S. Congress, whose role in foreign affairs was growing, became highly disenchanted. This disenchantment, caused in large part by Soviet behavior in the war and in its oil embargo aftermath, was at least partially responsible for the imposition of a four-year $300 million ceiling on credits for the USSR (the Stevenson amendment to the trade bill), along with other economic restrictions on trade. In addition, numerous congresspersons began to raise serious questions about the desirability of a SALT II agreement, contending that the USSR could not be trusted to keep it. Soviet behavior in the Middle East, therefore, caused a general chill in U.S.-Soviet relations that later Soviet behavior in Angola served only to reinforce.

Ironically, while the USSR violated the rules of detente in 1973 and 1974 in an effort to improve its Middle East position (when Soviet leaders perceived that the general world situation, unlike the 1971–72 period, gave them the opportunity to take such action), it was the United States that emerged with the better Middle Eastern position at the close of the Nixon administration. By August 1974, despite all the Soviet aid to the Arab cause during the October 1973 war, the majority of Arab states, with Egypt in the lead, evidently concluded that their interests would be better served, at least temporarily, by cooperation with the United States. A Soviet policymaker, viewing this situation from the Kremlin, may well have asked himself whether Soviet assistance to its client states in each of these crisis situations had been worth the costs and risks involved.

NOTES

1. For general studies of the Soviet-U.S. relationship in the wider context of U.S. policy during this period, see the relevant sections of Henry Brandon, *The Retreat of American Power* (New York: Dell, 1973); and Marvin Kalb and Bernard Kalb, *Kissinger* (New York: Dell, 1975). For Kissinger's view of Soviet-U.S. relations and detente a month after Nixon's resignation, see *Bureau of Public Affairs Special Report: Secretary Kissinger's Statement on U.S.-Soviet Relations to the Senate Foreign Relations Committee September 19, 1974* (Department of State, Office of Media Services). See also Helmut Sonnenfeldt, "The Meaning of Detente," *Naval War College Review* 28, no. 1 (Summer 1975): 3–8. For authoritative Soviet interpretations of detente, see G. Shakhnazarov, "Peaceful Coexistence and Social Progress," *Pravda*, December 27, 1975 [translated in *Current Digest of the Soviet Press*, hereinafter referred to as *CDSP*], 27, no. 52, pp. 1–4); and G. Arbatov, "On Soviet-American Relations," *Pravda*, April 2, 1976 (translated in *CDSP* 28, no. 13, pp. 1–5). See also Brezhnev's speeches to the twenty-fourth and twenty-fifth CPSU Congresses. For very useful academic analyses of detente, see David D. Finley, "Detente and Soviet-American Trade: An Approach to a Political Balance Sheet," *Studies in Comparative Communism*, 8, nos. 1 & 2 (Spring/Summer 1975): 66–80; and Robert Conquest et al. "Detente: An Evaluation," *Survey* 20, nos. 2 and 3 (Spring/Summer 1974): 1–27.

The term "tension" will be defined throughout this paper as a state of strained relations between the superpowers resulting from an action by one or both of them.

2. The document was published in *New Times* (Moscow) no. 23 (1972): 39.

3. For studies concentrating on U.S.-Soviet relations in the Middle East during this period, see Yair Evron, *The Middle East: Nations, Superpowers and Wars* (New York: Praeger, 1973); Robert O. Freedman, *Soviet Policy Toward the Middle East Since 1970* (New York: Praeger, 1975); Robert J. Pranger, *American Policy for Peace in the Middle East 1969–1971* (Washington, D.C.: American Enterprise Institute, 1971); and Lawrence L. Whetten, *The Canal War* (Cambridge, Mass.: MIT Press, 1974). For a very useful collection of documents on the Soviet involvement in the Middle East, see Yaacov Ro'l, ed., *From Encroachment to Involvement: A Documentary Study of Soviet Policy in the Middle East 1945–1973* (New York: Wiley, 1974). See also Jon D. Glassman, *Arms for the Arabs: The USSR and War in the Middle East* (Baltimore: Johns Hopkins University Press, 1975); and Abraham Becker, "The Superpowers in the Arab-Israeli Conflict," in Abraham S. Becker et al., *The Economics and Politics of the Middle East* (New York: American Elsevier, 1975).

4. For a description of some of the Soviet difficulties, see Freedman, *Soviet Policy Toward the Middle East Since 1970*, Ch. 1.

5. For a useful analysis of the 1967 war, see Walter Lacqueur, *The Road to Jerusalem* (New York: MacMillan, 1968).

6. A detailed description of the various stages of the war of attrition along the Suez Canal is found in Whetten, *The Canal War*.

7. For a theoretical description of the concepts of behavior reinforcement and behavior modification as they influence relationships, see J. David Singer, "Inter-nation Influence: A Formal Model," in the influence theory section of James Rosenau, ed., *International Politics*

and Foreign Policy (New York: Macmillan, 1969). See also Alvin Z. Rubinstein, "Assessing Influence as a Problem in Foreign Policy Analysis," in *Soviet and Chinese Influence in the Third World*, ed. A. Z. Rubinstein (New York: Praeger, 1976).

8. For a detailed analysis of this "exploitation," see Robert O. Freedman, "The Soviet Union and the Middle East: The High Cost of Influence," *Naval War College Review* 24, no. 5 (January 1972): 15–34.

9. Cited in Kalb and Kalb, *Kissinger*, p. 125.

10. Ibid., p. 218. Two weeks after the announcement of the Rogers Plan, the State Department announced that the Soviet reply to the U.S. Middle East proposal of October 28 was not "constructively responsive" (Pranger, op. cit., p. 17). Another factor leading to the publication of the Rogers Plan may have been the "leaks" of several versions of it.

11. For an analysis that argues that the USSR was hesitant, at least initially, in supporting Nasser's war of attrition, see Alvin Z. Rubinstein, *Red Star on the Nile* (Princeton, N.J.: Princeton University Press, 1977), p. 8.

12. Mohamed Heikal, *The Road to Ramadan* (New York: Quadrangle, 1975), p. 86.

13. Ibid., p. 175.

14. For a further discussion of this point, see Glassman, *Arms for the Arabs*, p.77.

15. Whetten, *The Canal War*, p. 99.

16. Kalb and Kalb, *Kissinger*, pp. 221–22.

17. Ibid., pp. 222.

18. Ibid., p. 223. This version of the event, if true, is another indication of what might be termed an oversensitivity to Soviet feelings that the author has observed during a number of interviews with State Department officials. The leading example of this, of course, was Kissinger himself when he advised President Ford in 1975 not to meet with Aleksandr Solzhenitsyn.

19. Cited in Whetten, *The Canal War*, p. 117.

20. Heikal, p. 96.

21. Ibid., p. 93.

22. Ibid., p. 95.

23. For a Soviet view of Sino-Soviet relations during this period, see O. B. Borisov and B. T. Koloskov, *Sino-Soviet Relations* (Moscow: Progress Publishers, 1975), Chs. 8 and 9.

24. Heikal, *The Road to Ramadan*, p. 95.

25. *Pravda*, September 10, 1970.

26. *Izvestia*, September 11, 1970, translated in *Mizan*, Supplement A, no. 5 (September/October 1970): 1–2.

27. TASS International Report, September 16, 1970.

28. Radio Moscow (in Arabic), September 16, 1970.

29. Kalb and Kalb, *Kissinger*, pp. 240–41.

30. For a detailed examination of the Palestinian guerrilla movement, see William B. Quandt et al., *The Politics of Palestinian Nationalism* (Berkeley, Calif: University of California Press, 1973). See also Malcolm Kerr, *The Arab Cold War*, 3rd ed. (New York: Oxford, 1971), Ch. 7.

31. Brandon, *The Retreat of American Power*, p. 137.

32. For a detailed study of this relationship, see Avigdor Levy, "The Syrian Communists and the Ba'th Power Struggle 1966–1970," in *The USSR and the Middle East*, ed. Michael Confino and Shimon Shamir (New York: Wiley, 1973), pp. 395–417.

33. For an analysis of Soviet policy toward the Palestinians during this period, see Robert O. Freedman, "Soviet Policy Toward International Terrorism: A Case Study of the USSR and the PLO," in *International Terrorism*, ed. Yonah Alexander (New York: Praeger, 1976), pp. 115–47.

34. Moscow Radio, September 18, 1970.

35. Kalb and Kalb, *Kissinger*, p. 231. The Soviet representative during these meetings was Yuli M. Vorontosov, Soviet chargé d'affaires, who took Soviet Ambassador Anatoly Dobrynin's place while the latter was on vacation.

36. Ibid., p. 232.

37. Ibid., pp. 237–38.

38. Moscow Radio, September 19, 1970.

39. Ibid.

40. TASS International Service, September 20, 1970.

41. Moscow Radio, September 22, 1970.

42. Ibid.

43. TASS International Service, September 23, 1970; *Pravda*, September 24, 1970.

44. For a description of this crisis see Kalb and Kalb, *Kissinger*, pp. 241–47; and Brandon, *The Retreat of American Power* pp. 280–83.

45. Nixon had, for the first time, called "communist China" by its official name, The People's Republic of China, in a toast to visiting Rumanian Party Leader Ceasescu on October 26, 1970, and Dobrynin called Kissinger to ask for an explanation (Kalb and Kalb, *Kissinger*, p. 267).

46. Heikal, *The Road to Ramadan*, p. 117.

47. Leonid Brezhnev, "Report of the Central Committee of the Communist Party of the Soviet Union to the twenty-fourth Congress of the CPSU," in (Documents of) *The Twenty-fourth Congress of the Communist Party of the Soviet Union March 30-April 9, 1971* (Moscow: Moscow Press Agency Publishing House, 1971), p. 50.

48. Kalb and Kalb, *Kissinger*, p. 247. For a detailed view of the SALT negotiations, see John Newhouse, *Cold Dawn: The Story of SALT* (New York: Holt, Rinehart and Winston, 1973).

49. Kalb and Kalb, *Kissinger*, p. 245. (According to Kalb and Kalb, the note was sent on January 9, 1971. Podgorny's visit to Egypt did not take place until mid-January. It is therefore possible that some of the caution shown by the Soviet leader during his visit may have been due to a desire not to upset the possibility of a new relationship with the United States that might bring economic benefits to the USSR.)

50. For a detailed examination of these events, see Freedman, *Soviet Policy Toward the Middle East Since 1970*, pp. 49–52.

51. Ibid., p. 51.

52. Ibid.

53. Ibid., pp. 52–55.

54. For a useful analysis of this treaty, see William J. Brands, "Soviet Influence in India," in Rubinstein,, *Soviet and Chinese Influence in the Third World*, pp. 42–45.

55. Kalb and Kalb, *Kissinger*, pp. 298–99.

56. Cited in *New York Times*, October 12, 1971.

57. Freedman, *Soviet Policy Toward the Middle East Since 1970*, p. 64.

58. Heikal, *The Road to Ramadan*, p. 158.

59. *Pravda*, April 30, 1972.

60. *New Times* (Moscow), no. 23 (1972): 39.

61. Ibid., pp. 36–38.

62. For an excellent analysis of the grain deal and other Soviet-U.S. economic agreements, see Marshall Goldman, *Detente and Dollars* (New York: Basic Books, 1975), especially Ch. 7.

63. Text of statement in *New York Times*, July 19, 1972. For a more detailed treatment of Sadat's expulsion decision, see Freedman, *Soviet Policy Toward the Middle East Since 1970*, pp. 74–78.

64. For a discussion of Soviet-Iraqi relations during this period, see Freedman, *Soviet Policy Toward the Middle East Since 1970*, pp. 68–74.

65. Ibid., p. 94.

66. Cited in the report of Henry Tanner, *New York Times*, October 16, 1972.

67. Abdul Kuddous, writing in *Akhbar al-Yom*, claimed that Sadek had been fired be-

cause he failed to implement some of Sadat's directives. See the report by William Dullforce in the *Washington Post*, October 30, 1972. *Pravda*, on November 1, 1972, gave the same version.

68. Heikal, *The Road to Ramadan*, p. 181.

69. Cited in Kalb and Kalb, *Kissinger*, p. 498.

70. Ibid., p. 499.

71. The text of the communique is in *New Times* (Moscow), no. 26 (1973): 23.

72. Cited in New York Times, June 26, 1973.

73. TASS, June 27, 1973; reprinted in *Middle East Monitor* 3, no. 14 (July 15, 1973):1.

74. Dmitry Volsky, "Soviet-American Relations and the Third World," *New Times* (Moscow), no. 36 (1973): 4–6.

75. *New Times* (Moscow), no. 39 (1973): 1.

76. For a study of Soviet policy and the oil politics issue, see Robert O. Freedman, "The Soviet Union and the Politics of Middle Eastern Oil," in *Arab Oil: Impact on the Arab Countries and Global Implications*, ed. Naiem A. Sherbiny and Mark A. Tessler (New York: Praeger, 1976), pp. 305–27.

77. On this point, see Foy D. Kohler, Leon Goure, and Mose I. Harvey, *The Soviet Union and the October 1973 Arab-Israeli War* (Miami, Fla.: Center for Advanced International Studies, University of Miami, 1974).

78. For a description of early Soviet maneuvering about the cease-fire, see Heikal, *The Road to Ramadan*, pp. 209–13. For an analysis of the Soviet behavior, see Rubinstein, *Red Star on the Nile*, p. 264.

79. For detailed studies of Soviet policy during the war, see Glassman, *Arms for the Arabs*, Ch. 5; Chaim Herzog, *The War of Atonement, October 1973* (Boston: Little, Brown, 1975); Heikal, *The Road to Ramadan*; Freedman, *Soviet Policy Toward the Middle East Since 1970*; Whetten, *The Canal War*; Walter Laqueur, *Confrontation: The Middle East and World Politics* (New York: Bantam Books, 1974); William B. Quandt, *Soviet Policy in the October 1973 War* (Santa Monica, Calif.: Rand, 1976), R-1864-ISA; and Rubinstein, *Red Star on the Nile*.

80. The text of the news conference was published as a State Department Bureau of Public Affairs, News Release, October 12, 1973.

81. Not all the Nixon administration shared Kissinger's commitment to detente, however; Melvin Laird, a former defense secretary and then a presidential adviser, began openly to attack the USSR on October 16. cf. report by Bernard Gwertzman, *New York Times*, October 17, 1973. For a highly critical evaluation of Kissinger's policy during the war, see Gil Carl Alroy, *The Kissinger Experience: American Policy in the Middle East* (New York: Horizon Press, 1975).

82. Heikal, in his version of these events, claims that all Sadat wanted were Soviet and U.S. observers (Heikal, *The Road to Ramadan*, p. 251).

83. Kalb and Kalb, Kissinger, p. 553.

84. The U.S. alert and the exact nature of the Soviet moves are not yet clear. For Kissinger's statement about the alert at a press conference, and a description of the alert, see the *New York Times*, October 26, 1973.

85. For a detailed description of the actions taken by the Arab states during the war, see the *Middle East Monitor* 3, nos. 19 and 20 (1973).

86. Cited in *Brief* (Tel-Aviv), no. 69 (November 1–15, 1973): 3.

87. For a desciption of the employment of the SCUD missiles by Egypt during the war, see Glassman, *Arms for the Arabs*, pp. 137–38. The exact arrival date of the SCUDs in Egypt is not yet clear. See Quandt, *Soviet Policy During the October 1973 War*, p. 9.

88. *Pravda*, March 6, 1974, referred to the talks as having taken place in a "businesslike atmosphere," a sign of minimal achievement and cordiality.

89. *Pravda*, March 8, 1974.

90. Moscow Radio, March 12, 1974.

91. *Pravda*, March 25, 1974.

92. See the report in *Middle East Monitor* 4, no. 7 (April 1974): 1.

93. *Pravda*, March 29, 1974.

94. Ibid.

95. *Izvestia*, March 30, 1974 (translated in *CDSP* 26, no. 13, p. 11).

96. *Pravda*, April 12, 1974 (translated in *CDSP* 26, no. 16, p. 2).

97. *Pravda*, April 17, 1974 (translated *CDSP* 26 no. 16, p. 6).

98. *Pravda*, April 30, 1974 (translated in *CDSP* 26, no. 17, p. 14).

99. *New York Times*, April 30, 1974.

100. *Pravda*, May 3, 1974 (translated in *CDSP* 26, no. 18, p. 9).

101. *Pravda*, May 30, 1974 (translated in *CDSP* 26, no. 22, p. 5).

5 Oil Politics and U.S.-Soviet Relations in the Middle East

Arthur Jay Klinghoffer

The possibility that a direct U.S.-Soviet confrontation may take place within the context of an Arab-Israeli war has always been duly recognized by political analysts, but a potential superpower conflict evolving out of the turbulent maelstrom of Middle East oil politics has been given scant consideration. It should be remembered, however, that the Soviet Union is the world's largest producer of crude oil and that its oil interests in the Middle East are substantial. The Soviet Union has focused much of its attention on the oil-rich Persian Gulf, especially following its rift with Egypt in 1972, and it has developed a major oil stake in Iraq, from which it purchases crude oil. The Soviet Union strongly endorsed the Arab oil embargo of 1973–74, and Soviet naval forces, abetted by the reopening of the Suez Canal in 1975, have become a potent strategic factor in the oil lanes of the Red Sea, the Indian Ocean, and the Persian Gulf.

Simultaneously, the United States has grown increasingly dependent on oil imports from the Middle East, and the huge U.S. arms sales to Iran and Saudi Arabia are clearly related to the problem of oil supplies. Another oil embargo or interference with tankers in a narrow waterway such as the Strait of Hormuz could have a disastrous effect on the U.S. economy, and leading government spokesmen have already indicated that, faced with such an emergency, the United States would not rule out seizure of Arab oil fields. Possible Soviet behavior during an oil crisis must be seriously considered and analyzed. It is therefore imperative to examine Soviet oil policies in the Middle East and their implications for U.S.-Soviet relations in the area. Detente was partially submerged during the Arab-Israeli War of 1973; one must ask whether it could conceivably drown in the oily waters along the Arab littoral in the future.

This chapter has been published as Monograph No. 6 in the Slavic and Soviet Series by the Russian And East European Research Center, Tel Aviv University, Tel Aviv, Israel.

THE SOVIET OIL TRADE

Soviet foreign trade is harmonized with domestic economic develop-ment and national security requirements through state ownership of the means of production and distribution and a national system for controlling imports and exports. Trade can also be used as a political weapon, particu-larly as a nonviolent operative technique consistent with peaceful coexist-ence or detente, but it usually rests on solid economic foundations even when politicized. Although a specific transaction may be based on political expediency, its economic ramifications and contractual provisions are care-fully calculated. Since the Soviet Union is self-sufficient in most basic com-modities, and has a tradition of autarky to which it can return if necessary, economics is not the most important determinant of foreign policy, but is instead a major instrument used to further foreign policy goals. Trade may therefore be viewed as a means for extending political power.

The Soviet oil trade frequently has served as a political weapon. Oil has been offered to such states as Egypt, Cuba, India, and Sri Lanka at the time of optimum political impact, and the flow of oil has been used as a political lever against the People's Republic of China, Yugoslavia, Finland, and Ghana. Viewed from another angle, Soviet encouragement of embargoes against Western states and nationalization of Western oil properties is in-tended to undermine Western political influence in the producing states and to cause schisms within the oil-hungry Western alliance. The Soviet leaders see a close correlation between oil and power, and generally do not draw distinctions between the roles of privately owned oil companies and Western governments.

Although clearly politicized, Soviet oil policies are also based on rational and practical considerations. Imports* and exports must be coordinated to provide sufficient oil for domestic consumption. Products received in return for oil must be consistent with the needs of the five-year plans. The oil trade must be attuned to the natural gas trade, and domestic fuel development and consumption patterns certainly must be taken into account when formulating international oil transactions.

The Soviet Union is now the world's largest producer of crude oil (491 million metric tons in 1975 and 520 million in 1976), and it has been a major exporter since the mid-1950s.[1] In recent years, it has usually ranked among the top five exporters; its total sales of crude oil and oil products totaled 130 million metric tons in 1975. Oil sales enable the Soviet Union to import technology, and the acquisition of pipe for oil transportation is

---

*The Soviet Union is a substantial net exporter of oil but, for both economic and geopoliti-cal reasons, it imports some oil from the Middle East and North Africa. For a discussion of this issue, see the continuing discussion in this section and the section on "Soviet Oil Imports."

also fundamental to the oil trade for the USSR has had a chronic pipe shortage.

Almost half of the USSR's oil exports go to other communist-ruled states, most of which are members of the Soviet Union's trading bloc, the Council for Mutual Economic Assistance (CMEA, or Comecon). All CMEA members except Rumania are dependent on Soviet oil deliveries, and this affords the Soviet leaders an important instrument of political and economic control. A similar volume of Soviet oil exports is delivered to Western Europe in exchange for hard currency such as U.S. dollars, West German marks, or Swiss francs. A small quantity of Soviet oil is sold to Third World states, usually in barter transactions. These deals are not especially lucrative for the USSR, but they serve to promote political goodwill and to reduce the reliance of these states on Western suppliers.

Soviet oil imports are negligible when compared with exports, but are crucial to an understanding of the Soviet role in the Middle East oil trade. A small amount of oil products is supplied to the USSR by East European states, but all Soviet crude purchases are made in the Middle East and North Africa. Total imports of crude and products were 14,700,000 metric tons in 1973 and 5,400,000 in 1974.[2] It appears from preliminary estimates that purchases from Arab states increased during the period of 1975–76.

The Soviet balance of trade deficit of 1973 was reversed by the huge windfall profits of the last quarter during which world oil prices quadrupled. As a major exporter, the Soviet Union greatly benefited from the price increases, and oil sales helped provide a positive trade balance in 1974. By 1975, however, Soviet purchases of technology, grain, pipe, and petroleum equipment had become so extensive that even a jump in the value of total oil sales from $5.76 billion in 1974 to $7.8 billion in 1975 (based on only an 11.9 percent increase in volume) could not balance the increased import expenditures. This led the USSR to increase oil sales in the hard currency markets of Western Europe, but the trade deficit nevertheless persists.[3]

SOVIET OIL POLICIES IN THE MIDDLE EAST

The primary aim of Soviet oil policies in the Middle East is to limit Western oil activities and supplies. The Soviet leaders view oil as the bulwark of Western imperialism, claiming that more than half of capitalist profits derived from the Third World come from oil.[4] They point to low wages paid to Arab oil workers and control of refining and marketing operations as the keys to Western economic aggrandizement, and they maintain that oil companies operate from a position of strength within the foreign policy decision-making apparati of Western governments. The relationship between oil companies and governments traditionally has been perceived as symbiotic, with the companies providing fuel for Western armies, which, in turn, protect the overseas interests of the oil companies.[5] Oil companies are accused of supporting status quo or "reactionary" Arab governments and funding Israel with their oil profits.[6] The Suez intervention of 1956 and the U.S. and British interventions in Lebanon and Jordan in 1958 are depicted as attempts to buttress sagging Western oil fortunes. The 1967 Arab-Israeli War has been described by some Soviet analysts as oil-company-inspired Israeli aggression against Egypt and Syria. The war was allegedly encouraged by the oil companies in retaliation against the "progressive" Arab states for their oil policies.[7]

In order to undermine Western oil influence (and for ideological considerations), the USSR advocates nationalization, embargoes, and regional control over vital waterways and pipelines. It encourages direct oil agreements between the producing and consuming states, thereby bypassing the Western oil companies, and seeks to increase the socialized oil sector within Arab economies to eliminate or drastically reduce the Western presence. To weaken the effects of any Western blacklisting of oil produced by nationalized fields, the USSR offers to purchase crude from the most prolific locations (such as Sarir in Libya and Kirkuk in Iraq), and it encourages Arab oil policy independence by providing assistance with exploration drilling, provision of equipment, training of oil technicians, and marketing. It also, through the provision of credits, promotes the building of storage facilities, tankers, pipelines, and refineries, in the Arab countries. Its intent is to transform oil from the West's alleged wellhead of influence to its Achilles heel, striving to aggravate the Western energy crisis by coupling limited access to supplies with growing insecurity of transport routes. It also lauds the rising price of oil as necessary to overcome previous Western exploitation of the producing states—but it obviously derives its own political and financial benefits as well.[8]

Foreign trade may be viewed in terms of "supply" and "influence" effects.[9] The former concerns the ability to import sufficient strategic materials, the security of trade routes, and the reliability of trading partners. The latter is based on the use of exports as an instrument of political pressure that can be exploited by a country exporting a product over which it has a monopoly or directing its trade toward states that cannot easily adjust their commercial patterns to decreases in supply. Viewed from this perspective, the Soviet Union does have some interest in Iraq in regard to the "supply effect," while its ability to exert any "influence effect" in the Middle East is minimal because of the area's oil surplus. The basic aim of the Soviet Union's policy is not to advance its own oil power, however, but to undermine the "supply effect" of the Western states. One efficient means of doing so is the embargo. The Soviet Union lent verbal support to the Arab oil embargoes of 1956, 1967, and 1973–74, and managed to benefit both economically and politically while taking almost no direct risk. Further, the Soviet Union took advantage of the embargoes by increasing its own oil exports to Western states, particularly in 1973–74.[10]

The 1956 embargo was directed against Britain and France in response to their participation in the Suez War. Nevertheless, the Soviet Union augmented shipments to France in accordance with an accelerated delivery schedule negotiated prior to the war.[11] It also took advantage of the situation by increasing the flow of crude to Egypt (partially replacing British marketers in the process), and by supplying oil products to Syria, which had cut off its chief source of crude by damaging the British-owned Iraq Petroleum Company (IPC) pipeline from Iraq.[12] Most significantly, the Suez War caused the temporary closing of the Suez Canal. West European states, worried about the security of future deliveries from the Middle East, became much more receptive to Soviet offers of oil. Soviet oil sales to Western Europe increased every year during the period 1956–61, and the Italian oil company, Ente Nazionali Idrocarburi (ENI), which began to purchase Soviet crude oil in 1957, contracted with the USSR in 1960 for huge yearly deliveries.[13]

The 1967 embargo was aimed at states that diplomatically supported Israel during the Six-Day War, such as Britain and the United States, and the Soviet leaders backed the embargo to such an extent that they called for its continuation even after it was apparent that the Arabs were determined to end it.[14] Additionally, as in 1956, the USSR increased its sales to Western Europe, particularly Spain. It claimed that it had initiated no new long-term contracts, but did admit that it had extended its sales drive immediately after the war had ended.[15]

The Soviet media, accurately perceiving a growing energy crisis in the West, started calling for a new Arab embargo as early as February 1973, but the members of the Organization of Arab Petroleum Exporting Countries (OAPEC)* did not announce an embargo until October 17.[16] The triggering event was certainly the Arab-Israeli War, and the Arabs clearly did not need any encouragement from the USSR. When the Arabs were about to lift the embargo in March 1974, however, Soviet spokesmen urged its continuation and called upon the Arabs to withstand U.S. pressure to end it. They also argued that the embargo should not be terminated until Israeli troops were withdrawn from the Golan Heights.[17] By advocating an extended embargo, the USSR sought both to display support for the more radical Arab states (such as Syria) and to complicate the Israeli-Syrian and Israeli-Egyptian disengagement talks that were being conducted under U.S. auspices. Moreover, the high oil prices accompanying the embargo filled Soviet coffers

---

*The Organization of Petroleum Exporting Countries (OPEC) was founded in Baghdad on September 14, 1960 by Iran, Iraq, Kuwait, Saudi Arabia, and Venezuela. Joining later were Abu Dhabi, Algeria, Ecuador, Indonesia, Libya, Nigeria, and Qatar (Gabon is an associate member). OAPEC was created in January 1968 by Libya, Kuwait, and Saudi Arabia. Algeria, Bahrain, Egypt, Iraq, Qatar, and Syria, and the United Arab Emirates joined later.

with huge windfall profits and the oil shortage facilitated Soviet oil sales in West European markets.

First Deputy Minister of Foreign Trade Ivan Semichastonov sought to assure the Arabs that the soviet Union would not undermine the embargo by increasing its sales, but he also emphasized that all contractual obligations for oil deliveries would be met.[18] The USSR had little extra oil available for export at that time and therefore was not in a position to embark on an extensive new sales drive, but it did reroute deliveries from West Germany and other states in order to take advantage of higher prices in particular markets, such as the Netherlands.[19] It also resold oil in Western Europe that had been purchased from Arab states. This oil had been purchased at low prices in accordance with long-term sales agreements and was resold at the prevailing inflated world prices.[20] The USSR further maximized profits by stepping up oil deliveries to the two major targets of the Arab embargo, the Netherlands and the United States.[21] This action was obviously at odds with the spirit, if not the letter, of Semichastnov's statement.

The oil embargo caused dissension within the Western alliance, temporarily weakened U.S. military capability, disrupted Western economies, and brought about some diplomatic shifts favorable to the Arab cause and against Israel. The Soviet leaders realized that Western states *could* band together to form an anti-Arab bloc of consuming states and they therefore spoke out strongly against any tendencies in that direction. They hinted that Third World states could form producers' cartels for numerous products in addition to oil, and they vociferously attacked the U.S.-sponsored Washington energy conference of February 1974. Pointing to the failure to invite Arab states, they likened the conference to a "wedding without a bride."[22]

While the embargo was generally beneficial to the Soviet Union, it also produced some negative consequences. Arab states that had sold oil to the Soviet Union on a barter basis began to demand payment in hard currency at prevailing world prices. Also, the enhanced economic status of oil enabled these states to enter into barter agreements for Western technology, which was generally more sophisticated than that provided by the USSR. The embargo also encouraged energy cooperation among Western states in the form of the International Energy Agency. The price rise linked to the embargo also created an anomalous situation concerning Soviet oil sales to East European states. Although the world price of oil had quadrupled, long-term contracts with CMEA members kept prices much lower than the world average until increases were negotiated in 1975 and 1976.

For many years, the Soviet Union had been seeking credits and technological assistance from the United States and Japan for the development of the Tiumen oil fields in western Siberia, and negotiations with the United States and Japan were close to a final agreement. The Arab embargo made such an agreement much less likely,* for the United States did not want to become dependent on oil deliveries from the Soviet Union. The Arab embargo had pointed up clearly the consequences of such overseas dependence and had provided the impetus for "Project Independence," a rather halfhearted attempt to decrease U.S. reliance on foreign suppliers. As far as Japan was concerned, the embargo had underlined the need to diversify sources of supply immediately—and deliveries from Tiumen were not scheduled to begin until at least 1980. Japan therefore turned to larger crude oil deliveries from the People's Republic of China (PRC). Hopes for a Tiumen agreement faltered as U.S. participation became increasingly uncertain and Soviet estimates of the quantity of oil to be sold to Japan decreased. Since their profits from oil sales were multiplying and they could now more easily afford to buy oil equipment in Western markets, even the Soviet leaders lost much of their interest in the Tiumen negotiations. They could now develop Tiumen on their own rather than rely on U.S. and Japanese credits. Moreover, because of their improved economic position, they were unwilling to make any additional concessions on emigration in return for U.S. credits and most-favored-nation (MFN) trading status and therefore rejected the compromise on the Jackson amendment that allegedly had been worked out with the United States.

In sum, the impact of Arab embargoes generally has been consistent with and complementary to Soviet international political aims. Any future embargoes would undoubtedly elicit a supportive Soviet response, particularly since the USSR has become closely aligned with the more radical Arab states, such as Libya, Iraq, Algeria, and Syria. Future Arab embargoes are also likely to be effective, the International Energy Agency notwithstanding. Arab states now have more tankers at their disposal; they can therefore exert greater control over oil transport and limit the ability of major oil companies to divert shipments to embargoed states.[23]

Factors militating against Arab use of the embargo weapon must be also taken into account. Arab states may be reluctant to antagonize the United States too greatly for fear of becoming increasingly dependent on the Soviet Union. They must also weigh the risks of precipitating U.S. military intervention to seize Arab oil fields or a cutoff of U.S. aid and weapons.

SOVIET OIL IMPORTS: AN ADDED DIMENSION

By the late 1960s, the growth rate of Soviet oil production was decreasing, the consumption rate was increasing, and the huge production increases in western Siberia were not expected to be realized until many years in the

---

*The Jackson amendment, linking U.S. economic assistance to the USSR with Soviet emigration concessions, constituted an additional hurdle.

future. The Soviet Union therefore decided to purchase crude oil from Arab states, and the first deal was made with Algeria in 1967. Agreements with Iraq, Egypt, Libya, and Syria quickly followed. Such oil purchases were economically beneficial to the Soviet Union, for it was cheaper to import Arab oil than to transport Soviet oil from the western Siberian and Volga-Ural production areas to the population centers of the western USSR.[24] Soviet oil supplies were also conserved, and some of the Arab oil was resold at a profit to the Soviet Union's traditional customers in Western Europe. The USSR also saved money on export transportation costs as supplying European states such as Spain with Arab oil was less expensive than transporting Soviet oil to the Black Sea and then shipping it to Spain. With the Suez Canal closed, the Soviet Union also benefited from supplying its Asian customers with oil produced in Iraq and Egypt. This greatly shortened the delivery route, which otherwise would have called for circumnavigating the African continent.

Oil also served as a convenient means of repayment for arms and industrial equipment purchased by Arab states that had few commodities with which to pay their large debts to the Soviet Union. The Soviet leaders also realized that their oil purchases could help encourage Arab nationalization of Western-owned oil fields as they were augmenting the market for the output of such fields. Soviet purchases of Arab oil therefore proved to be mutually advantageous.

As a large net exporter of oil, the Soviet Union did not need to import Arab oil. It could just as easily have cut its own exports when faced with the reduced availability of oil. This, however, would have deprived the Soviet Union of some of the power associated with being an oil exporter, and particularly in exerting control over the East European oil tap. Nor did the Soviet leaders want to reduce hard currency oil sales in Western Europe when they could, at least temporarily, secure oil on attractive barter terms from Arab states.

Although purchases from Arab states and top export priority allocation had enabled the USSR to maintain a steady flow of oil to Eastern Europe (with some of the oil transported directly from Iraq to Poland and East Germany by the USSR), the burgeoning needs of Eastern Europe were soon too great for the USSR to meet. In 1969, it called upon East European states to develop their own oil ties with the Arabs and Iranians, and a substantial direct oil trade soon began.[25] (It should be noted, however, that smaller transactions had taken place as early as 1966, especially with Iran.)

The bulk of Soviet crude oil imports has come from Iraq. As a radical and generally anti-Western state, Iraq has developed close political ties with the USSR, and since July 1975 it has had a special trading status with CMEA. Iraq is also linked to the USSR through a 1972 Treaty of Friendship and Cooperation. Iraq has been willing to sell crude to the USSR partially to pay for imports of Soviet machinery and equipment, while other large Persian Gulf producers, such as Saudi Arabia, Kuwait, and Iran, have been reluctant to do so because of their basically pro-Western orientations. (Iran, however, does sell significant quantities of natural gas to the USSR.)

Major oil cooperation between the Soviet Union and Iraq began in December 1967 when the Soviet leaders agreed to assist with exploration, drilling, transport, and marketing of Iraqi oil.[26] This agreement was finalized in June and July 1969, when specific arrangements were worked out. The key provision, as stipulated in an agreement of July 4, 1969, was that Soviet assistance would be paid for with crude oil. Numerous oil deals followed as the Soviet Union additionally became involved with refinery and pipeline construction. The export of crude, carried in tankers from the Persian Gulf port of Fao, began in April 1972, the same month that the Soviet-Iraqi Treaty of Friendship and Cooperation was signed. Bolstered by both the treaty and the Soviet purchases of crude, on June 1 Iraq announced the nationalization of the Iraq Petroleum Company, whose major assets were the Kirkuk oilfields and the IPC pipeline from Kirkuk to Mediterranean terminals at Banias in Syria and Tripoli in Lebanon. At the same time, Syria nationalized that part of the IPC pipeline passing through its territory. By mid-1972, the Soviet Union was buying Iraqi crude at the Banias terminal, thereby facilitating Iraq's successful resistance to a Western boycott of Kirkuk crude. Loading tankers at both Banias and Fao, the Soviet Union received 4,084,000 metric tons of Iraqi crude in 1972, 11,010,000 in 1973, 3,888,000 in 1974, and 5,304,000 in 1975.[27]

Complications in the Soviet-Iraqi relationship led to a marked reduction in crude oil sales in 1974. As oil prices began to rise in 1973 (even before the Arab embargo), Iraq became dissatisfied with the terms of its agreement with the USSR, contending that its barter transactions were undervalued. It agreed to honor all previous oil deals with the Soviet Union, but indicated that any new agreements would stipulate payment in hard currency.[28] This Iraqi action led to a decline in oil sales to the USSR in 1974. The Soviet leaders were reluctant to part with hard currency and, following the 1973 Arab-Israeli War, Iraq was also trying to extricate itself from overreliance on trade with the USSR, so it greatly increased commercial ties with the United States and other Western powers. Further exacerbating the Soviet-Iraqi relationship was the fact that the Soviet Union was reselling some Iraqi crude at a profit, and was even undercutting the Iraqis in their own markets. For example, in January 1975, the Iraqis protested vigorously when Soviet representatives offered to sell Kirkuk crude to Spain for less than Iraq charged Spain. The Soviet Union withdrew its offer.[29]

The Soviet Union purchased Algerian crude during 1967–72, much of which was resold to Cuba and Spain, and it has been buying Egyptian crude since 1969.[30] This oil is picked up in the Gulf of Suez and is used to supply

Soviet customers in Asia. While the Suez Canal was closed, this arrangement was most convenient for the Soviet Union; in fact, it forced the plan on Egypt as a means of repaying the Egyptian debt. The per barrel book value of the oil received from Egypt was less than that of any other oil purchased by the Soviet Union.*

Formerly, Syria had relied upon the import of Soviet oil products, but Soviet oil assistance in development of production facilities helped turn Syria into a net exporter, and sales of crude to the Soviet Union have been taking place since 1972. Libya nationalized the British-Petroleum-owned Sarir oil fields in December 1971 and the Soviet Union negotiated an oil agreement with Libya in March 1972. The USSR agreed to assist with exploration, extraction, refining, and training of oil specialists in return for crude oil. Deliveries took place during 1972 and 1973, but they never reached their expected volume because of the rising price demands that Libya initiated in 1973. The USSR has been buying small quantites of oil products from South Yemen since 1969 and occasionally some diesel fuel from Kuwait. (The South Yemeni oil products are refined from Egyptian crude at Aden.)

In geopolitical terms, oil purchases from Iraq (via Fao) and Egypt were instrumental in fulfilling Soviet export commitments to Asian states while the Suez Canal was inoperative, but there were other problems associated with the Middle East oil trade. The 1973 Arab-Israeli War led to a decline in Egyptian production in the Gulf of Suez and sales to the USSR were reduced. At the same time, Israeli damage to the Syrian port of Banias prevented the loading of Iraqi crude for several weeks, and shipment of Syrian crude bound for the USSR was also disrupted by war damage at the port of Tartus.[31] In addition, a Soviet tanker was damaged during an Israeli raid. Then, in April 1976, an Iraqi-Syrian dispute led to the closing of the IPC pipeline. Thereafter, all Iraqi crude bought by the USSR had to be shipped via the Persian Gulf, but the completion of the Iraqi-Turkish pipeline in 1977 provide a new outlet to the Mediterranean.

Future Soviet purchases of Middle East oil should not rise significantly because of the Arabs' price and currency demands and the diminution of the USSR's geopolitical rationale for such transactions as a result of the reopening of the Suez Canal. The Soviet decision to forgo U.S. and Japanese assistance with the Tiumen project also plays a role in projecting the Soviet role in the Middle East. These two states were to have recieved large quantities of crude oil from the USSR in return for their credits and technological assistance. The USSR would then have been more concerned about balancing these oil exports with imports from the Middle East. From the Arab perspective, it makes more sense to sell directly to East European states

---

*Computed on the basis of statistics supplied in Soviet foreign trade yearbooks concerning the volume and total ruble value of Soviet crude oil imports from each state.

rather than to permit the USSR to play the role of oil middleman, and the Western energy shortage also provides ample opportunities for marketing Arab oil.

OIL AND GEOPOLITICS

Prior to the 1967 Arab-Israeli War, Soviet policy in the Middle East was basically a defensive one, but the USSR has since become much more active in promoting its own strategic interests. Whereas previously it had stressed undermining Western power in the area, it has since increased its own power and influence by building up its naval forces and acquiring rights to numerous port and aircraft landing facilites in the area. It has also supplied thousands of military advisers to such states as Egypt and Syria. A similar development has taken place regarding oil as the USSR began to import it from Arab states. This has created a need to protect its new supply routes. The Soviet naval presence in the Mediterranean Sea and Indian Ocean, although obviously a deterrent to Western action as well as a potential threat to Western oil security, also must be viewed as a show of strength within waters now considered strategic in the protection of its own energy source. (Although not directly relevant to this study, it should be pointed out that the Soviet naval buildup in the Indian Ocean is partially aimed at the containment of the PRC. In fact, the Soviet leaders have been advocating, although unsuccessfully, an Asian collective security arrangement that would include states extending from Iran all the way to Japan.)

The Soviet Mediterranean fleet was greatly expanded after the 1967 war and it was augmented even further in June and July 1976 in conjunction with the Lebanese crisis. The Soviet Union's first aircraft carrier, the *Kiev*, also paid its initial visit to the Mediterranean in 1976, but the Soviet deployment of its naval force thus far has been extremely cautious. The fleet has yet to take action, despite the opportunities provided by the 1973 war, the Cyprus events of 1974, and the Lebanese civil war in 1975–76. To support its naval presence, the USSR secured the use of port facilities at Latakia in Syria; Algiers; Bone and Mers el-Kebir in Algeria; and Alexandria, Port Said, and Mersa Matruh in Egypt. (Soviet rights in Egyptian ports have been curtailed since the expulsion of its military advisers in 1972 and Egypt's abrogation of the Soviet-Egyptian Treaty of Friendship and Cooperation in 1976).

The Mediterranean serves as a Soviet access route to the strategic oil lanes south and east of Suez, and its significance has been enhanced further since the reopening of the Suez Canal in June 1975.[32] Previously, Soviet naval vessels visiting the Indian Ocean had traveled all the way from Vladivostok, home base of its Pacific fleet; they can now save 3,000 sea miles by traveling from the Mediterranean fleet's headquarters at Sevastopol on the Black Sea. All Soviet ships, including the *Kiev*, are capable of passing through the Suez Canal, as they were appropriately designed to pass through other strategic channels, such as the Bosphorus and Dardanelles, in order to secure egress from the Black Sea. In contrast, many vessels in the U.S. Mediterranean fleet are unable to pass through the canal at its present width and depth.

With easier access to the Indian Ocean, the USSR is well positioned to protect its oil import route from Iraq and to interdict tankers bound for Western states or Israel. It has developed close ties with Somalia and South Yemen, states adjacent to the critical Bab el-Mandeb Strait, which joins the Red Sea with the Indian Ocean, and now has port facilities at Berbera and Kismayu, Somalia, and Aden, South Yemen. It also uses an anchorage off the south Yemeni island of Socotra. Farther afield, it has acquired port rights at Bombay and Vishakhapatnam in India and at Umm Oasr in Iraq, and its ships have the right to call at Bandar Abbas, Iran.

In January 1968, Britain announced its intent to withdraw its naval forces from the Indian Ocean and Persian Gulf by 1971; ships from the Soviet Pacific fleet made their first visit to Indian Ocean waters three months later. The growing Soviet role in the area is certainly related to the perceived power vacuum created by the British withdrawal, and the Soviet leaders have taken steps to bolster their position through friendship treaties with India, Iraq, and Somalia. The USSR appears to be devoting increased attention to the affairs of the Indian Ocean and Persian Gulf, not only because of the oil factor but also owing to decreased Soviet influence over and involvement with Egypt. The watershed year was 1972, marked by the signing of a Soviet-Iraqi friendship treaty and the expulsion of Soviet military advisers from Egypt.

Although certainly interested in extending its influence, the Soviet Union does not seek an expanded naval rivalry with the West in the Middle East. Aside from the question of cost, the USSR lacks adequate regional logistical facilities to maintain a permanent naval presence. The Soviet leaders would prefer to keep Soviet and Western naval strengths at their current moderate level, but this is unlikely because the Western states are so critically dependent on Middle East oil. The Western states are building up their naval might, not primarily as a consequence of suspected Soviet intentions in the area but from a need to protect their oil routes and access to supply from any potential Arab obstruction.[33] Despite their withdrawal of permanent naval forces, in November 1974 the British conducted joint exercises with the South Africans off Simonstown and participated, along with the United States, in the Arabian Sea exercises of the Central Treaty Organization CENTO—the most extensive CENTO naval exercises ever held. The United States has been constructing naval and air bases on the Indian Ocean island of Diego Garcia, and it has secured landing rights at the British-controlled airfield on the Omani island of Masirah. The first U.S. nuclear-powered task force to enter the Indian Ocean in 12 years was deployed in

January 1977. In addition, the French are building a naval base at Mayotte in the Comoro Islands.

The strategic importance of the Indian Ocean and Persian Gulf should increase at least temporarily as the result of a trend toward increased use of tankers and away from pipelines. While the former have become more economical, the latter suffer from political instability as well as financial malaise. The closing of the Suez Canal from 1967 to 1975 led to the use of supertankers, which could transport huge quantities of oil from the Persian Gulf to Western Europe, and these so-called superships displayed great unit cost efficiency.[34] Also contributing to the greater use of tankers was the tanker surplus of 1975–76. As oil producers held back production to drive up prices, and as consumers took conservation measures, the quantity of oil being shipped declined. Tanker rates fell, but this made tankers even more economically preferable to pipelines, and many producing states bought surplus tankers and began to form their own tanker fleets.

The Suez Canal's importance as an oil artery is declining. Tankers were only 15 percent of its traffic in 1976, as compared with 73 percent during the first half of 1967 (prior to its closure by the Arab-Israeli war).[35] Western Europe, to which the canal had been critical, shifted to circum-Africa supertankers and larger imports from Libya, and new offshore deposits were exploited by Norway and Britain. The canal had never been quite as essential for the United States, but it, too, turned to supertankers. Although the United States has no supertanker ports, oil can be unloaded in Nova Scotia and the Bahamas and then transported in smaller tankers.

From the Soviet perspective, however, the canal remains a vital waterway. Soviet oil exports to Asian states must pass through the canal because oil export facilities have not been developed on the Soviet Pacific coast, and the USSR lacks supertankers that could transport oil around Africa. The same holds true for Soviet oil imports from Iraq, particularly since the closure of the IPC pipeline in 1976. While the canal was closed, the Soviet Union resorted to some "switch deals" in order to facilitate deliveries to such states as Japan and India, but this cannot be a permanent solution to the USSR's geographic logistics problem.[36] [During that period, the top Asian priority for Soviet tankers was the oil export program to North Vietnam.]

The Soviet Union consistently advocated the reopening of the Suez Canal, claiming that its closure was beneficial to the United States and Israel. Companies from the United States, it was alleged, were increasing their profits due to their ownership of supertankers, while Israel reaped dividends from the Eilat-Ashkelon pipeline.[37] Realizing that West European states had the greatest interest in reopening the canal, the Soviet leaders encouraged them to pressure Israel into making concessions that would lead to a settlement with Egypt.[38] After the 1973 war, the Soviet Union was most cooperative when an Israeli-Egyptian agreement was reached on reopening the canal, but it proved obstructive on other issues not related to this strategic waterway, such as the Syrian-Israeli disengagement talks. Nor did it publicize its own oil and naval interests in the canal or point out the canal's importance as a link with the Soviet Far East in the event of war with the PRC. Such a war could disrupt traffic on the Trans-Siberian Railroad, and, in any case, the USSR traditionally has supplied its eastern regions with oil shipped all the way from the Black Sea.[39]

The Persian Gulf is the hub of Middle East oil traffic, and a major Soviet aim in the area is to prevent the creation of any significant Western military presence in the gulf. Once the British had indicated their intention to withdraw from the region, the Soviet leaders feared that the United States would fill the vacuum in order to protect its oil interests.[40] Moreover, the Gulf was strategically situated in regard to Soviet territory since U.S. IRBMs launched from there would be capable of hitting Soviet missile and space installations in Central Asia.[41] The Soviet leaders therefore adopted a cautious policy that would give the United States little incentive or pretext for building up its forces. (Inasmuch as the Suez Canal was closed at the time, the Soviet fleet could not have displayed much strength in the Gulf even had it so desired.)

The United States, whose military presence consisted of a tiny naval force stationed in Bahrein, also tried to play down any U.S.-Soviet rivalry in the area. In this instance, the positions of the two superpowers were rather similar: Both wanted to avoid unnecessary military expenditures and neither wanted to be drawn into any regional political squabbles. They also had a mutual interest in maintaining the free movement of oil tankers. Consequently, the Soviet Union and the United States each maintained a low profile in the area and permitted Iran to become the policeman of the Gulf. This policy is certainly understandable from the U.S. point of view, as Iran is primarily armed with U.S. weapons and is a member of the anticommunist CENTO. The Soviet quest for regional stability also led to its acceptance of the Iranian role. In effect, the often iterated Soviet formula that Persian Gulf states should handle their own affairs is really an indication of its support for the dominant Iranian position.[42]

On November 30, 1971, Iran seized Abu Musa and the Tumbs, islands claimed by the Arab emirates of Sharjah and Ras al-Khaima. Arab leaders erupted in a chorus of protest, but the Soviet leadership failed to join them. The Soviet Union has no ideological sympathy for the Iranian monarchy, but it realistically concluded that an Iranian-patrolled Gulf was preferable to directly applied U.S. force. [It should be noted, however, that Soviet acquiescence in the matter did not extend to the Iranian show of strength in support of the Omani sultanate against the South-Yemeni-backed Dhofar guerrillas. The Soviet leaders believe that the Qabbus regime is a pawn in the renewed British game of establishing influence over the movement of oil traffic in the strategic Strait of Hormuz.][43]

The United States wants to preserve the generally pro-Western status quo in the Gulf, and the keystone of its designs is extensive assistance to the Iranian and Saudi monarchies.[44] Huge arms sales for buttressing these governments are considered essential not only for the maintenance of U.S. influence but also for the maximization of the flow of oil from two of the largest suppliers of the United States.[45] Although the United States generally has operated through Iranian proxy, its arms deliveries have caused consternation in the Soviet Union, as have the presence of U.S. training officers in Saudi Arabia, U.S. military use of Diego Garcia and Masirah, the "familiarization" visit of the aircraft carrier *Constellation* to the Persian Gulf, and the threat to occupy Arab oil fields in the event of another embargo.[46] The Soviet Union, anxious to preserve a friendly image and fearful of engendering Western intervention, does not want to be drawn into Gulf disputes, such as those between Iran and Iraq or Iraq and its Kurds, so its status has been simplified by the Iran-Iraq rapprochement and the Iraqi defeat of the Kurds. The Shah of Iran and Iraqi strongman Saddam Hussein reached an accord while attending the OPEC conference at Algiers in March 1975 and a formal border treaty was signed on June 13. In the Kurdish case, the Soviet Union supported the Iraqi autonomy plan of 1974, but it was rejected by the Kurds, in part because oil-rich Kirkuk was excluded from their territory and they were not satisfied with the oil revenue distributions formula.[47] The Soviet Union preferred Iraqi control of Kirkuk in order to be assured of receiving its oil imports, so they armed Iraq for its war against the Kurds and may even have supplied pilots for the MIG 23s flown in combat.[48]

Ideologically, the Soviet Union favors the radical antimonarchical stance of the Iraqi regime, and it would view the undermining of traditional rule in Iran, Saudi Arabia, Kuwait, the United Arab Emirates, Bahrein, and Qatar as "progressive" steps. On the other hand, it is deeply involved with the Arab-Israeli and Lebanese conflicts and would prefer, at least temporarily, to downplay the radicalization of the Gulf. It fears a logistical disadvantage as a result of the combined Western forces in the area, and it also wants to secure its own oil route from the Iraqi port of Fao. Perhaps the construction of the Kirkuk-Dortyol pipeline and some progress toward settlement of the Arab-Israeli and Lebanese problems will promote greater Soviet militancy in the Gulf.

THE UNITED STATES AND MIDDLE EAST OIL

Middle East states possess the majority of the world's proven oil reserves and they are responsible for 70 percent of total world oil exports. Western Europe is dependent upon the Middle East for approximately 50 percent of the oil it consumes (plus one third from North Africa). The United States, which imports a smaller percentage of its oil, is nevertheless the world's largest oil importer, and its dependence on foreign producers is increasing. It is also true that the United States has assumed much of the Western burden for securing access to Middle East oil supplies, particularly since Britain withdrew its military presence in 1971.

U.S. crude oil production has been declining in recent years; a study by Exxon predicts that the 1970 production level will not be equaled until 1982.[49] The United States is the second largest producer of oil, but it is by far the greatest consumer, thereby necessitating increased reliance on imports. At least 40 percent of the oil consumed is now imported, and the figure will probably rise to 50 percent by 1980.[50]

Statistics dealing with U.S. oil dependency on Arab states are often highly misleading because of three factors. First, the statistics sometimes refer to the Middle East and therefore include non-Arab Iran, the third largest exporter of oil to the United States. Second, statistics may refer only to crude oil and disregard oil products. Last, and most important, however, is the fact that a large quantity of Arab oil enters the United States indirectly. Crude oil is transferred from supertankers to smaller tankers and may then appear statistically as Caribbean or Canadian crude. Furthermore, Arab oil is often refined in Caribbean states and then shipped to the United States as oil products of supposed Caribbean origin. For example, as of June 1975, the Netherlands Antilles supplied 8.4 percent of U.S. crude oil imports and 4.5 percent of oil products imports, yet the Netherlands Antilles is not a producer of crude oil. Similar patterns can be found with regard to the Bahamas and the Virgin Islands.[51]

Although statistics vary, it appears that the United States was dependent on Arab oil for approximately 9 percent of its consumption at the time the embargo was imposed in November 1973. Since then, dependence on imports has almost doubled and reliance on Arab oil as a percentage of total imported oil has more than doubled. This means that about 45 percent of the oil now imported by the United States is of direct or indirect Arab origin. This makes the United States approximately 18 percent dependent on Arab oil.[52] Dependence on the Middle East and North Africa is even greater once Iran is included in the statistics, and Iranian shipments to the United States are rapidly increasing.

The rise in U.S. oil imports during the first half of 1976 (as compared with the same time period in 1975) can be wholly attributed to increased imports of Arab oil (Saudi Arabia has overtaken Venezuela as the biggest U.S. supplier.[53]) Deliveries from certain non-Arab states, such as Nigeria, Indonesia, and Iran, are also going up and this should help compensate for deficiencies elsewhere. Venezuelan sales to the United States are not expected to increase, and Canada is in the process of phasing out all deliveries to the United States by 1981. Even the availability of Alaskan oil will not offset the burgeoning need of the United States for imported oil.

U.S. oil dependence on Arab states contains the risk of both another embargo and a potential interdiction of tankers. Of course, shipments from Iran could also fall prey to the latter. It has been estimated that the tonnage needed to import oil will rise from the 31 million deadweight tons registered in 1974 to 78 million deadweight tons in 1980, mainly because of large shipments from the distant Middle East.[54] As the trend toward supertankers continues, military interdiction of tankers becomes easier because they are large and unmaneuverable. In conjunction with another Arab-Israeli war and embargo, attempted blockades at the Strait of Hormuz and the Bab el Mandeb Strait are possible, especially if the United States attempts to deliver oil to Israel (as stipulated in its agreement with that state at the time of the 1975 disengagement accord between Israel and Egypt). Palestinian commandoes could also attack U.S. tankers passing near the shore, just as they damaged an Israeli-bound tanker in the Bab el-Mandeb Strait in June 1971. In view of the declining importance of pipelines, sabotage against them would have almost no effect on U.S. oil imports. Other conceivable causes of disruption would be internal hostilities in Iran or Saudi Arabia or a Persian Gulf clash involving Iran and Iraq or Kuwait and Iraq.[55] All these examples illustrate the exposed and vulnerable position in which the United States now finds itself.

The United States consumes 30 percent of the world's energy even though it has less than 6 percent of its population. Conservation of energy is therefore a rather obvious solution to the problem of oil imports, but it would mean a lower standard of living and reduced economic growth. Greater emphasis on domestic oil production or a shift toward increased use of coal and atomic energy are also alternatives, but they raise both environmental and cost difficulties. Since five of the world's seven largest oil companies are U.S.-owned, tighter government regulation of private oil companies is also a possibility, but such action would run counter to the prevailing capitalist ethic.

The consequences of energy dependence and proposed solutions to the American energy dilemma have been discussed by Mason Willrich, an astute observer of international oil politics, in a stimulating and most provocative article in which he maintains that energy dependence weakens U.S. links with its allies. He points out that energy deficiency compels the United States to compete with its allies for access to oil supplies, and also makes allies less willing to rely on the United States for their security. He asserts that consumer and environmental interests have gained predominance over national security interests, and that U.S. support for Israel will lose its credibility unless some U.S. oil independence is achieved. Dependence both weakens U.S. military might and encourages closer ties with Arab states. Furthermore, greater energy independence would lead to a reduction in U.S. pressure on Israel to make concessions to the Arabs.[56] Willrich concludes that:

A growing vulnerability to interruptions in its oil supply is dangerously incompatible with America's specific responsibility as guarantor of the security of the NATO countries, Japan and Israel. Energy independence for America should thus not be identified with any retreat into a Fortress America. Quite the opposite.[57]

Faced with an Arab embargo in November 1973, as well as with other concerns about oil dependence, President Richard Nixon announced "Project Independence." Supposedly, the United States would strive for oil self-sufficiency by 1980, but the report prepared by the Federal Energy Administration made it obvious that this was not to be the case. It discusses methods of stockpiling, controlling consumption, and importing from secure sources, and it further states that zero imports are "not warranted economically or politically."[58] It defined oil independence as importing "up to a point of 'acceptable' political and economic vulnerability," and it advises: "Rather than reducing imports per se, our objective should be to reduce our vulnerability to disruptions of imports for this reason, 'independence' is better than 'self-sufficiency' as a description of our objective."[59] This report made readily apparent the fact that U.S. oil imports were not going to be scaled down, and increasing U.S. oil dependency clearly bears witness to the element of political sloganeering in the "Project Independence" scheme.

Some distinctions must be made between the roles of the U.S. government and those of private U.S. oil companies, particularly as their policies have diverged increasingly in recent years. It is certainly correct to assert that the major oil companies have influenced U.S. foreign policy with an eye toward protecting or furthering their investments in the Middle East, and that many former employees of oil companies occupy senior foreign policy-making positions. It is also true that five of the "Seven Sisters," the largest international oil companies, are U.S.-owned (namely, Exxon, Texaco, Mobil, Gulf, and Standard Oil of California [Chevron]). This, however, does not mean that oil companies have operated as arms of U.S. foreign policy. For example, Texaco sold oil to Germany in 1939–40 at a time when this was not consistent with U.S. policy interests.[60] The influence of the oil companies on U.S. foreign policy has declined, and Shoshana Klebanoff's citation of 1955* as the turning point serves as a useful guideline.[61]

As oil companies have become less successful in exerting pressure on the government, they have worked out largely autonomous foreign policies. Although such policies are increasingly typical of transnational actors (for

---

*Klebanoff claims that U.S. policy became less supportive of oil company interests because the United States developed a strategic interest in the Middle East, that of counteracting a growing Soviet involvement. She also maintains that the United States had to compete with the USSR for the friendship of Arab states, and that this prevented strong backing for the oil companies when they were engaged in disputes with these states.

example, multinational corporations), they are often at odds with official government policy. For example, when Aramco, a consortium of U.S. oil companies operating in Saudi Arabia, failed in its campaign to prevent the United States from siding with Israel during the 1973 war, it then followed the dictate of King Feisal in not supplying oil to U.S. armed forces while the war was in progress. In the early stages of the Angolan civil war, Gulf paid royalties to the People's Movement for the Liberation of Angola (MPLA) while the United States was covertly aiding its opponents, the National Front for the Liberation of Angola (FNLA) and the Union for the Total Independence of Angola (UNITA). Oil companies also operated at cross-purposes with official policy when they sought to maximize their profits during the 1973–74 Arab embargo. They held back oil supplies by stockpiling oil in storage tanks and on tankers at sea, and they even sold domestically produced oil at the new inflated price of imported oil. Should the United States intervene in an Arab state in the future, it will not be acting on behalf of the oil companies, as the latter can profit despite—or because of—an oil shortage or embargo just by raising prices. Intervention, however, could be precipitated by a national energy shortage or, in a less likely scenario, by steep OPEC price increases.

In striking contrast to the United States, the Soviet Union does not have a bifurcated oil policy. The state oil trading corporation is clearly subordinate to the Council of Ministers whenever there are political considerations affecting the initiation, termination, or volume of oil trade.

SCENARIOS OF CONFRONTATION

Oil policies of the United States and the USSR tend to accentuate the antagonistic, rather than cooperative, aspects of superpower relations in the Middle East. Involvement of these two states in armed conflicts evolving out of clashing oil interests should not be expected, but such a possibility cannot be excluded from both U.S. and Soviet strategic calculations. In fact, the likelihood of an armed Soviet-U.S. confrontation over Middle East oil has been enhanced by several recent developments. The United States has become increasingly dependent on oil imports, it has built up its naval and air forces in the Indian Ocean, and it has threatened to seize Arab oil fields. The U.S. commitment to supply oil to Israel in case of an emergency furthers the risk of blockade or sea attack, while the closure of both the Tapline and IPC pipeline limits the options for oil transport and makes sealanes even more vital. The instability in Eritrea, caused by secessionist movements against Ethiopia, and the possibility of disorder in the Territory of Afars and Issas (Djibouti), engendered by France's granting of independence, must therefore be viewed with great concern.

Soviet advocacy of high prices and embargoes increases the severity of the U.S. oil bind, and the movement of Soviet naval vessels through the

Suez Canal into the Indian Ocean poses a challenge to U.S. strategic planning regarding oil imports. The closure of the IPC pipeline also affects Soviet oil imports from Iraq, and thereby makes the Soviet Union, too, more dependent on tanker transport. Growing Soviet military ties with Libya could also be a crucial factor if that state is ever the target of U.S. intervention. Last, now that a Tiumen oil agreement with the United States seems to be unlikely, the Soviet leaders will have fewer fears of the consequences of a more daring oil policy in the Middle East.

On the other hand, the United States has come to accept passively the policy of oil field nationalization, and any intervention in support of nationalized U.S. oil companies can probably be ruled out. U.S.-Arab relations have also improved as a result of larger arms and technology transfers. Moreover, Arab states do not want to antagonize the United States too much with increased use of oil as a political weapon for fear of abetting Soviet designs of increased influence. The more moderate Arab states also find U.S. services valuable in applying pressure on Israel to moderate its negotiating stance in the Arab-Israeli dispute.

The Iran-Iraq rapprochement and the quieting down of the Iraq-Kuwait controversy reduce the risk of drawing the superpowers into regional conflicts that are to some extent based on oil. The military advantage gained by Oman (with Iranian assistance) over the Dhofar guerrillas has furthered the prospects for stability near the Strait of Hormuz. As has been seen, both the Soviet Union and United States have tried to avoid a direct confrontation in the Persian Gulf by accepting Iran as the area's enforcer. Any aggressive Soviet policy in the Gulf would probably prove detrimental to Soviet attempts to neutralize and weaken the CENTO alliance.

Soviet verbal encouragement of nationalization or embargo actions should have little effect on U.S.-Soviet relations, and direct Soviet intervention to seize oil fields is extremely unlikely unless in a condition of total war. A Soviet invasion of western Iran in an attempt to link up with Iraq could then be expected. U.S. attempts to interfere with Soviet oil imports or exports in the Middle East would be rather quixotic, but there are five broad problem areas that could eventually produce a U.S.-Soviet military confrontation over oil rights: internal disruption within a Middle East state, intraregional conflict, a struggle for influence over key waterways, interdiction of U.S. tankers, and U.S. intervention to seize oil fields.

In the first scenario, a revolt takes place in Iran or Saudi Arabia, and the two superpowers become involved as a result of their support of opposing forces. The United States strives to maintain the oil and political status quo while the Soviet Union assists revolutionaries who seek to undermine the dominant U.S. influence. In the second scenario, the Soviet Union aids Iraq in a conflict with either Kuwait or Iran while the United States assists the latter. The United States might encourage Saudi intervention in support of

Kuwait and this could precipitate Soviet involvement. Soviet participation in an Iraq-Iran war could come about as a result of U.S. military assistance to Iran or Iranian interference with Iraqi tankers in the Persian Gulf. Of course, any USSR or U.S. military role could escalate from sending advisers and supplying equipment (indirect) to actual battlefield combat (direct).

In the third instance, there could be direct support for conflicting sides in the Territory of Afars and Issas (Djibouti), Eritrea, or Oman. In the fourth hypothetical situation, the United States might use armed force to challenge the Arab interdiction of tankers and the Soviets could give naval assistance to the Arabs.

All of these scenarios are possible, but not very probable. The most menacing precipitator of U.S.-Soviet confrontation is the threat or actuality of U.S. intervention. Although clearly exaggerated for maximum impact, the comments of U.S. officials on such an eventuality cannot be dismissed out of hand as pure bluffing or bravado. The combination of the disastrous economic consequences of the 1973–74 embargo and subsequent inability to adapt energy policies has produced a combustible and potent political mixture.

Voices in the United States reached a crescendo during the first half of 1975, led by a statement of U.S. options by Secretary of State Henry Kissinger in January. Discussing oil intervention, he stated:

> I am not saying that there's no circumstance where we would not use force. But it is one thing to use it in the case of a dispute over price, it's another where there's some actual strangulation of the industrialized world. . . . I want to make clear, however, that the use of force would be considered only in the gravest emergency.[62]

Secretary of Defense James Schlesinger then echoed Kissinger's remarks, mentioning "the gravest emergency" and "the strangulation of the industrial economies of the West," and stating that the latter was to be considered in the category of grave emergencies.[63] Even Tom Wicker, a generally liberal columnist for the *New York Times*, supported intervention if the Arabs were to go as far as "strangulation."[64] In March, both Kissinger and Ambassador Akins assured Saudi Arabia that the United States had no intention of seizing its oil fields.[65] Such assurances seemed logical, as the United States was about to train Saudis in oil-field protection and Saudi Arabia was trying to counteract the tendency in OPEC toward rapid oil price increases. However, implied general threats to the Arab world continued. In an interview in May, Schlesinger indicated that the United States would be "less tolerant" of a new Arab embargo and that it would probably "not remain entirely passive." He declared: "I am not going to indicate any prospective reaction other than to point out that there are economic, political or conceivably military measures in response."[66]

From the academic community, the issue of intervention was raised by Robert W. Tucker of Johns Hopkins University, who discussed the feasibility of seizing oil fields in the area stretching from Kuwait to Saudi Arabia to Qatar.[67] The aim would be to secure enough oil to break the effectiveness of the OPEC cartel, and this area would be the best target since it is responsible for 40 percent of OPEC production. Tucker's proposal showed concern not only for U.S. suffering as the consequence of an embargo but also for the economic effects of high prices. Destroying OPEC's solidarity, in addition to being an anti-Arab measure, would affect Iran, Venezuela, Nigeria, and other non-Arab OPEC members as well.

Drew Middleton, military affairs editor of the *New York Times*, criticized Tucker's choice of a target, maintaining that a U.S. attack in the Gulf would provide too much warning time. He believed that such a military action would have to originate with naval and air forces stationed in the Mediterranean, and that their moves would provide ample time for Arab sabotage of oil installations. He considered that the seizure of Libyan oil fields could be carried out with a greater element of surprise.[68] Tucker agreed that intervention in Libya could be more effective, but did not consider Libya's oil production, if seized by the United States, sufficient to undermine OPEC.[69]

Another significant contribution to the intervention debate was a pseudonymous article by "Miles Ignotus," a reputed adviser to the U.S. defense establishment, who maintained that the basic aim was to render OPEC impotent rather than to acquire needed oil. "Ignotus" recommended intervention in Saudi Arabia and ruled out Libya for the same reason as had Tucker.[70]

Any U.S. oil intervention would take place most probably during an Arab-Israeli war and an accompanying embargo, and, as Robert Freedman has observed, such an intervention would have a high likelihood of success because several Arab armies would be engaged in the struggle with Israel.[71] Intervention in an Arab state in the Gulf could bring Iran into the fray, but as "Ignotus" pointed out, Iran would possibly have to seek Soviet support in order to fight the United States and it would be reluctant to do so. "Ignotus" even suggested that the United States should offer Kuwait to Iran as a bonus for not resisting U.S. intervention in Saudi Arabia![72]

U.S. intervention in the Persian Gulf might require aircraft landing and refueling rights. Arab states and Iran could not be expected to grant them, but perhaps Israel would.[73] Another contingent is oil-field sabotage, which could probably stall oil production for several weeks. The negative world image created by U.S. intervention would also play a role—the United States would surely be portrayed as the successor of British and French neocolonialism à la Suez in 1956. Furthermore, as Japan turns more toward the PRC for oil and as Britain starts to develop the North Sea on its way to oil self-sufficiency in the next decade, the support of these allies for such a U.S. action would be questionable.

Direct Soviet counterintervention is not very probable, but a U.S. attack on oil fields where Soviet personnel are stationed (such as Sarir in Libya) could complicate matters. The United States could be expected to seize oil fields along the Persian Gulf, and the USSR would be in a poor logistical position to force a confrontation there; its naval resources in the area are limited and its fighter aircraft do not have the range to counterattack effectively unless permission to use Iraqi airfields is granted.[74] The USSR itself could possibly intervene in a defensive capacity and thereby forestall a U.S. attack. Arab states, particularly Iraq, could call upon the Soviet Union to protect their oil fields, but one of the most likely targets, Saudi Arabia, would surely be reluctant to do so because of its anticommunist attitude.[75] Alternatively, the Soviet leaders might analyze their position in the Persian Gulf and decide to apply pressure to the United States in another area where they have the advantage.[76]

The Soviet reaction to U.S. intervention cannot be predicted with any certainty, but poor logistics, past experience, a psychological disadvantage, and the absence of any critical Soviet security concern should lead to a policy of moderation rather than militancy. Despite close political and economic ties, the Soviet Union failed to intervene in North Vietnam when the United States carried out extensive bombing missions in North Vietnam and mined Haiphong Harbor. This was partially due to North Vietnam's reluctance to secure direct Soviet military involvement, but it was also true that again considerations of poor logistics, the lack of immediate security concern to the USSR, and a desire to avoid conflict with the United States were involved. In the Persian Gulf, the Soviet stake is less than that of the United States, as a result of the latter's oil dependency. Moreover, as Tucker pointed out, the "psychological onus" would be placed on the Soviet leaders, as a decision to confront the United States in defense of a secondary ally would be theirs alone.[77] "Ignotus" similarly maintains that the United States must take a calculated risk in attempting to seize oil fields, but that the Soviet Union must take a greater risk in counterattacking against U.S. troops.[78]

The most likely course of action for the Soviet Union in the event of U.S. intervention would be to operate through a combination of proxy and limited intervention, thereby minimizing the chances of a direct confrontation. The Soviet Union has shown a reluctance to commit its troops to battles outside of Eastern Europe, but it could easily send military equipment to Arab states and encourage them to engage U.S. troops. The USSR could also organize guerrilla operations against U.S.-occupied oil fields in an attempt to sabotage oil operations. Going a step further, it could provide a small number of "volunteer" pilots. Or it could choose the riskiest course of action short of direct conflict, the introduction of Soviet air cover for Arab armies.

A U.S.-Soviet oil confrontation could take place despite the post-1972 detente relationship. Both states are particularly concerned about the other's relationship with the PRC trade, reduction in defense expenditures, and European security, but this has not prevented deep involvement in the 1973 Arab-Israeli War and the Angolan civil war.[79] Although U.S.-Soviet agreements of 1972 and 1973 called for advance notice on crises that could disrupt the peace, the Soviet leaders did not warn the United States of an impending Arab attack on Israel in 1973. Indeed, once the war was in progress, they airlifted large quantities of armaments, mobilized their own forces for possible intervention, and cheered on the Arab oil embargo.[80] U.S. responses were hardly in the spirit of detente. Nor were later U.S. threats to seize Arab oil fields.

Basically, both sides interpret detente so loosely that the concept or definition of a supposed relationship is of little consequence in influencing behavior once some strategic interest is at stake. Rather than serving as a deterrent to conflict, detente has shown its greatest effectiveness as an instrument for resolving crises once they have erupted. Detente has made it possible for communication to remain open throughout periods of pique, controversy, and turbulence.

The major Arab combatants in wars with Israel are not among the largest producers of oil. This has served partially to separate the Arab-Israeli conflict from the oil issue, but the linkage between the two has been drawn tighter in recent years. The Arab oil embargo of 1973–74 was an obvious outgrowth of the Arab-Israeli War, and the fate of the Suez Canal is fundamental to both an Egyptian-Israeli settlement and the future course of oil transport in the world. Saudi Arabia's financial support for frontline states also tends to merge the two issues, as does that state's explicit linkage of its oil ties to the United States with the call for reduction of U.S. support for Israel.[81] Furthermore, any U.S. military intervention to seize oil fields would probably be precipitated by an Arab-Israeli war, and such an intervention would also undermine U.S. credibility as a mediator for terminating such a war.

Oil is explosive, both literally and figuratively, and its entry into the already combustible Arab-Israeli cauldron could produce a major conflagration.

NOTES

1. *Pravda*, March 2, 1976, p. 4; and *Pravda*, January 23, 1977, p. 1.

2. Computed on the basis of statistics provided in *Vneshniaia torgovlia SSSR za 1974 god: statisticheskii obzor* [Foreign trade of the S.U. for 1974: statistical abstract] (Moscow: Izdatelstvo "Mezhdunarodnye otnosheniia," 1975).

3. "Soviet Oil Exports Hit Highs in Volume, Revenue," *Oil and Gas Journal* 74, no. 22 (May 31, 1976): 34.

4. Ruben Andreasyan, "New Developments on the Oil Front," *New Times* (Moscow), no. 25 (June 1973): 23.

5. *Izvestiia*, April 19, 1966, p. 2.

6. Evgenii Primakov, "Economic Aspect of the Middle East Crisis," *International Affairs*, no. 6 (June 1972): 38; and Radio Moscow, December 15, 1971, in *USSR and Third World* 2, no. 1 (December 6, 1971–January 16, 1972): 28–29.

7. D. Volsky, "Iraq's Battle for Her Oil," *New Times* (Moscow), no. 35 (August 1972): 9; G. Starko, "How to Solve the Oil Problem," *New Times* (Moscow), no. 35 (August 1958): 15; Boris Rachkov, "Neftianye monopolii i agressii izrailia" ("Oil Monopolies and Israeli Aggression"), *Kommunist*, no. 12 (August 1967): 109–17; Iu. Golovin, I. Matiukhin, and B. Smirnov, "Imperializm i arabskaia neft'" (Imperialism and Arab Oil), *Mirovaia Ekonomika i Mezhdunarodnye Otnosheniia (The World Economy and International Relations)*, no. 9 (1967): 66–78; Boris Rachkov, "The Middle East Crisis and U.S. Oil Monopolies," *International Affairs*, no. 4 (April 1969): 32; and S. Astakhov, "More About the Secret Springs of the Israeli Aggression," *International Affairs*, no. 10 (October 1967): 38. Also see Aryeh Yodfat, *Arab Politics in the Soviet Mirror* (New York: Halsted Press, 1973), p. 264; and David Morison, "Soviet Interest in Middle East Oil," *Mizan* 10, no. 3 (May–June 1968): 80.

8. Ruben Andreasyan, "Oil Confrontation: New Stage," *New Times* (Moscow), no. 3 (January 1977): 18–21.

9. See Albert Hirschman, *National Power and the Structure of Foreign Trade* (Berkeley, Calif.: University of California Press, 1969), pp. 14–15, 34.

10. For a complete analysis of the Soviet role in Arab oil embargoes, see Arthur Jay Klinghoffer, "The Soviet Union and the Arab Oil Embargo of 1973–74," *International Relations* 5, no. 3 (May 1976): 1011–23.

11. William Jorden, "Oil Exports Seen as Soviet Weapon," *New York Times*, November 29, 1956, p. 4; "Soviet Oil Offer Clarified," *New York Times*, December 1, 1956, p. 4; and "Soviet Denies Offering Oil," *New York Times*, December 2, 1956, p. 35. Statistics on Soviet oil deliveries to France may be found in *Vneshniaia torgovlia SSSR za 1956 god: statisticheskii obzor (Foreign Trade of the USSR for 1956: Statistical Abstract)* (Moscow: Vneshtorgizdat, 1958), p. 93.

12. Dana Adams Schmidt, "Soviet Reported Offering French and Arabs Its Oil," *New York Times*, November 28, 1956, pp. 1, 5; and Halford Hoskins, "Problems Raised by the Soviet Oil Offensive," U.S., Congress, Senate, Committee on the Judiciary (Washington, D.C.: U.S. Government Printing Office, 1962), p. 2.

13. Walter Laqueur, *The Struggle for the Middle East: The Soviet Union in the Mediterranean, 1958–1968* (New York: Macmillan, 1969), p. 121; and J. E. Hartshorn, *Politics and World Oil Economics*, rev. ed. (New York: Praeger, 1967), p. 236.

14. For an analysis of the Soviet position, see Abraham Becker, "Oil and the Persian Gulf in Soviet Policy in the 1970's," in *The USSR and the Middle East*, ed. Michael Confino and Shimon Shamir (New York: Wiley, 1973), pp. 191, 212.

15. *Ekonomicheskaia gazeta (Economic Newspaper)*, no. 39 (September 1967): 44.

16. For early Soviet comments, see "Radio Peace and Progress, February 24, 1973," in *USSR and Third World* 3, no. 3 (February 19–April 8, 1973): 159–60; and Radio Moscow in Arabic, August 30, 1973 trans. in Foreign Broadcast Information Service, *Soviet Union* 3, no. 172 (September 5, 1973): F6.

17. "Soviet Radio Beamed to Arabs Backs Those Favoring Oil Ban," *New York Times*, March 13, 1974, p. 24; Tomas Kolesnichenko, "Meshdunarodaia nedelia" ("International Week"), *Pravda*, March 17, 1974, p. 4; and Vladimir Bol'shakov, "Meshdunarodnaia nedelia" ("International Week"), *Pravda*, March 24, 1974, p. 4.

18. Ivan Semichastnov, "The Soviet Union's Foreign Economic Ties Today," *New Times* (Moscow), no. 2 (January 1974): 8.

19. *Platt's Oilgram News Service* 52, no. 14 (January 21, 1974): 4; editorial *Washington*

Post, March 29, 1974, p. A30; Hedrick Smith, "Soviet Diplomacy: Waiting Game as Pendulum Swings Away from Moscow," *New York Times,* November 26, 1973, p. 5; and *The Petroleum Economist* 41 (January 1974): 33.

20. Frank Gardner, "Not a Bad Profit for the Soviets—300%," *Oil and Gas Journal* 72, no. 14 (April 8, 1974): 51.

21. For a detailed analysis of Soviet oil sales to the Netherlands and the United States, see Klinghoffer, "The Soviet Union and the Arab Oil Company of 1973–74," pp. 1018–20.

22. Aleksandr Zholkver, Radio Moscow in Turkish to Cyprus, February 26, 1974, trans. in Foreign Broadcast Information Service, *Soviet Union* 3, no. 40 (February 27, 1974): CC 1–2. Also see Ruben Andreasyan, Radio Moscow in Arabic, February 10, 1974, trans. in Foreign Broadcast Information Service, *Soviet Union* 3, no. 29 (February 11, 1974): CC2; and Radio Moscow in Arabic, January 14, 1974, trans. in Foreign Broadcast Information Service, *Soviet Union* 3, no. 10 (January 15, 1974): A 2–3.

23. See V. H. Oppenheim, "Arab Tankers Move Downstream," *Foreign Policy* no. 23 (Summer 1976): 117.

24. For comments on the cost advantage of importing Arab oil, see "Soviet Bloc Turns to Middle East for Oil," *World Petroleum* 39, no. 10 (September 1968): 46; Robert North, "Soviet Northern Development: The Case of NW Siberia," *Soviet Studies* 24, no. 2 (October 1972): 195–96; Jean-Jacques Berreby, "Oil in the Orient," *New Middle East,* no. 15 (December 1969): 44; and Frank Gardner, "Russians Will Endure the 'Injustices of Nature,' " *Oil and Gas Journal* 67, no. 43 (October 27, 1969): 51.

25. See "Moscow Asks Its Allies to Buy Oil in Mideast and North Africa," *New York Times,* November 24, 1969, p. 6; and *Facts on File* 29, no. 1520 (December 11–17, 1969): 814.

26. George Stocking, *Middle East Oil* (Kingsport, Tenn.: Vanderbilt University Press, 1970), p. 314; Aryeh Yodfat, "Russia's Other Middle East Pasture— Iraq," *New Middle East,* no. 38 (November 1971): 26; Aryeh Yodfat, "Unpredictable Iraq Poses a Russian Problem," *New Middle East,* no. 13 (October 1969): 17; *Mizan* 10, no. 1 (January–February 1968): 45; and Alawi Kayal, "The Control of Oil: East-West Rivalry in the Persian Gulf" (Ph.D. diss., University of Colorado, 1972), p. 238.

27. *Vneshniaia torgovlia SSSR za 1972 god: statisticheskii obzor (Foreign Trade of the USSR for 1972: Statistical Abstract)* (Moscow: Izdatel'stvo "Mezhdunarodnye otnosheniia," 1973), p. 237; *Vneshniaia torgovlia SSSR za 1974 god: statisticheskii obzor (Foreign Trade of the USSR for 1974: Statistical Abstract)* (Moscow: Izdatel'stvo "Mezhdunarodnye otnosheniia," 1973), p. 238; and *Vneshniaia torgovlia SSSR v 1975 godu: statisticheskii sbornik (Foreign Trade of the USSR in 1975: Statistical Compendium)* (Moscow: Statistika, 1976), p. 233.

28. *Middle-East Intelligence Survey* 1, no. 2 (April 15, 1973): 16.

29. *Platt's Oilgram News Service* 53, no. 20 (January 29, 1975): 1.

30. *Petroleum Intelligence Weekly* 10, no. 19 (May 10, 1971): 5; and "Spain Buying Crude Oil from Russians," *Oil and Gas Journal* 69, no. 44 (November 1, 1971): 38.

31. *Platt's Oilgram News Service* 51, no. 215 (November 6, 1973): 3; and Benjamin Shwadran, *The Middle East, Oil and the Great Powers,* 3rd ed. (New York: Wiley, 1973), p. 466.

32. For an analysis of the effects of the reopening of the Suez Canal on Soviet oil interests, see Arthur Jay Klinghoffer, "Soviet Oil Politics and the Suez Canal," *The World Today* 31, no. 10 (October 1975): 397–405.

33. Howard Bucknell III maintains that U.S. naval forces in the Indian Ocean are more vital to national security than those in the Mediterranean because of oil. See *Energy Policy and Naval Strategy* (Beverly Hills, Calif.: Sage Publications, 1975), p. 60.

34. As of the end of 1975, only 3.6 percent of world deadweight tanker tonnage was attributed to ships with U.S. registration, but many ships owned by U.S. companies were sailing under flags of convenience. Liberia accounted for 30.7 percent of the tonnage registered and Panama for 3 percent, and these two types of registration certainly helped conceal a huge U.S.-owned fleet of tankers. On the other hand, only 1.6 percent of the world's tonnage was

registered in the Soviet Union and it is unlikely that Soviet ships were masquerading under foreign flags. The fleets of East European states were also small, but it should be pointed out that the majority of Soviet oil exports is by pipeline to East European states. The Soviet Union has been self-sufficient in tankers since 1965 and, despite the modest size of its fleet, there has actually been a tanker surplus during the period 1975–77. With the Suez Canal reopened, the ship-days needed to maintain an export program from the Black Sea to Asian states has been reduced and the number of tankers necessary for this trade therefore has decreased. It must also be remembered that all Soviet tankers are capable of passing through the Suez Canal. The Soviet Union has not followed the world trend toward supertankers because such ships would not fit through the Bosphorus and Dardanelles, and all Soviet tankers are therefore smaller than the Suez Canal's maximum capacity of 60,000 deadweight. Most supertankers built in recent years are in the 250,000 to 400,000 deadweight class.

Many oil pipelines cross the middle East, but their volume is presently minimal. Tapline, which runs from the Saudi Arabian oil fields near the Persian Gulf to the Lebanese port of Sidon, has always served as a major export route for Saudi oil but it is now almost completely closed. Some oil is piped to Jordan and Lebanon for domestic consumption but no oil has been exported from Sidon since February 9, 1975. Economic considerations are responsible for closing the tap, as it is cheaper to transport oil by supertanker from the Persian Gulf. An additional factor preventing renewed utilization of the pipeline is the political turmoil in Lebanon. Saudi Arabia may construct a new pipeline linking the Persian Gulf with the Red Sea, thus freeing itself from complete dependence on the Gulf, but it is at least temporarily more dependent on transport through the Gulf and Indian Ocean than ever before.

The IPC pipeline runs from the Kirkuk oil fields in northern Iraq to Mediterranean terminals at Banias in Syria and Tripoli in Lebanon and it is capable of transporting 1.4 million barrels of oil per day. It is now linked to Fao on the Persian Gulf as well, as a spur line has been built from the North Rumailah oil fields in southern Iraq to Haditha on the IPC line. A pipeline already connected North Rumailah and Fao. The first oil passed through the new North Rumailah-Haditha link on December 27, 1975 and was exported from Fao on January 6, 1976. Because of its new pipeline complex, Iraq acquired great flexibility, as it was capable of exporting any of its oil by either the Mediterranean or Persian Gulf route. Previously, Kirkuk crude could only be piped to the Mediterranean and North Rumailah crude to the Persian Gulf. However, such did not turn out to be the case, and all Iraqi oil is now exported on tankers plying the Persian Gulf.

The Baathist regimes of Iraq and Syria have constantly been at loggerheads politically, but an economic squabble led to the closing of the IPC pipeline on April 12, 1976. Iraq and Syria disagreed over the transit fees to be paid to Syria and over the price of Iraqi crude sold to Syrian refineries. In effect, the North Rumailah-Haditha section of pipeline therefore has become an effective means of avoiding oil transport through Syria, and it was constructed with this possibility in mind. In any case, the cost advantage of Gulf supertankers over pipeline transport through Syria had already become apparent before the pipeline was closed, and the IPC carried less than its maximum volume throughout 1975 and early 1976.

While the Suez Canal was closed, Israel constructed a pipeline bypass from Eilat on the Gulf of Aqaba to Ashkelon on the Mediterranean that has lost trade since the Canal has reopened. Egypt, realizing that the Suez Canal can handle only smaller tankers, has also been building a pipeline, called the Sumed. It opened in mid-1977 and extends from Ain Soukna on the Gulf of Suez to a terminal just west of Alexandria on the Mediterranean. It will transfer oil from supertankers in the Gulf of Suez to other supertankers waiting in the Mediterranean, so it will not lead to a reduction in tanker traffic. The Sumed should attract some oil away from Eilat, as some states, such as Rumania, want to dissociate themselves from any political stigma attached to use of the Israeli pipeline. Another pipeline, running from Kirkuk, Iraq, to Dortyol, Turkey, should also be mentioned. Construction began in April 1975 following the Iraqi defeat of the Kurds, and the line became operative in March 1977. It will be able to transport an initial

25 million tons of Iraqi oil per year to the Mediterranean and it will thus counteract the tendency toward greater reliance on tankers. It will permit Iraq to bypass both Syria and the Gulf and it may serve as a route for Iraqi oil exports to the Soviet Union. See "Tankers: Bigger Surplus Than Ever," *The Petroleum Economist* 43, no. 4 (April 1976): 135; *Platt's Oilgram News Service* 51, no. 222 (November 15, 1973): 4; *Middle-East Intelligence Survey* 2, no. 1 (April 1, 1974): 8; *Middle East Economic Survey* 18, no. 32 (May 30, 1975): 8; *Middle East Economic Survey* 19, no. 9 (December 19, 1975): 2; *Middle East Economic Survey* 19, no. 11 (January 2, 1976); 1–2; *Middle East Economic Survey* 19, no. 13 (January 16, 1976): 2; *Middle East Economic Survey* 19, no. 24 (April 5, 1976): 1; and *Middle East Economic Survey* 19, no. 27 (April 26, 1976): 7.

35. Tankers: Bigger Surplus Than Ever," p. 135; S. Karpov, "Tankers and Arab Oil," *International Affairs*, no. 9 (September 1967): 116; and D. C. Watt, "Why There Is no Commercial Future for the Suez Canal," *New Middle East*, no. 4 (January 1969): 20.

36. In switch deals, the Soviets would deliver their own oil to European customers of major oil companies and, in turn, these companies would ship oil from Persian Gulf producing states to Soviet customers in Asia. See Robert Ebel, *Communist Trade in Oil and Gas* (New York: Praeger, 1970), p. 102; *Petroleum Intelligence Weekly*, May 13, 1968, p. 2; Edward Hughes, "The Russians Drill Deep in the Middle East," *Fortune*, July 1968, p. 104; Marshall Goldman, "The East Reaches for Markets," *Foreign Affairs* 47, no. 4 (July 1969): 732; Lincoln Landis, "Petroleum in Soviet Middle East Strategy" (Ph.D. diss., Georgetown University, 1969) p. 168; "Oil Agreement with U.S.S.R.," *Middle East Economic Digest* 14, no. 43 (October 23, 1970): 1242; *Petroleum Intelligence Weekly*, October 26, 1970, p. 5; and Kayal, "The Control of Oil," p. 239.

37. Evgenii Primakov, "Economic Aspect of the Middle East Crisis," *International Affairs*, no. 6 (June 1972): 40.

38. Evgenii Primakov, "Why the Canal Must be Re-Opened: A Soviet View," *New Middle East*, no. 46 (July 1972): 7.

39. See Bernhard Abrahamsson and Joseph Steckler, *Strategic Aspects of Seaborne Oil* (Beverly Hills, Calif.: Sage Publications, 1975), p. 45.

40. "The USSR and the Persian Gulf," *Mizan* 10, no. 2 (March-April 1968): 51–59.

41. *The Gulf: Implications of British Withdrawal* (Washington, D.C.: Center for Strategic and International Studies, Georgetown University, 1969), p. 17.

42. Robert Hunter, "The Soviet Dilemma in the Middle East. P. 2. Oil and the Persian Gulf," *Adelphi Papers*, no. 60 (October 1969): 14; L. Tolkunov, *Izvestiia*, February 27, 1971, in *USSR and Third World* 1, no. 3 (February 15–March 21, 1971): 121; and the communiques of diplomatic visits by Soviet and Iranian officials in *USSR and Third World* 2, no. 10 (October 23–December 3, 1972): 586; *USSR and Third World* 3, no. 3 (February 19–April 8, 1973): 170; and *USSR and Third World* 3, no. 6 (July 16–September 2, 1973): 413.

43. Radio Moscow, January 19, 1971; in USSR and Third World 1, 2 (January 11–February 14, 1971): 67; Radio Peace and Progress, January 19, 1972, in *USSR and Third World* 2, no. 2 (January 17–February 13, 1972): 112; Radio Moscow, January 9, 1973, in *USSR and Third World* 3, no. 1 (December 4, 1972–January 14, 1973): 35; and *Middle-East Intelligence Survey* 1, no. 23 (March 1, 1974): 184.

44. See address by Alfred Atherton, Jr., assistant secretary of state for Near Eastern and South Asian affairs, Louisville, Ky., U.S. Department of State, Office of Media Services (News Release, November 1975); and U.S. Department of State, Office of Media Services, *Current Policy*, no. 2 (June 1975).

45. Although it is generally pro-Western and anticommunist, Saudi Arabia has made several overtures to the USSR since the assassination of King Feisal. See *Middle East Economic Survey* 18, no. 38 (July 11, 1975): 1–2.

46. Radio Peace and Progress in Arabic, March 11, 1975, in *USSR and Third World* 5, no. 3 (February 24–March 31, 1975): 104; and Iurii Mikhailov, "Neft'i oruzhie" ("Oil and Arma-

ments"), *Pravda*, August 8, 1976, p. 5.

47. Pavel Demchenko, "Avtonomiia Irakskikh Kurdov" (Autonomy for the Iraqi Kurds"), *Pravda*, March 14, 1974, p. 5.

48. Michael Getler, "Russian Pilots, in MiG-23s, Said to Attack Kurds for Iraq," *International Herald Tribune*, October 7, 1974, p. 2.

49. "Oil Still the Key Fuel," *Oil and Gas Journal* 73, no. 45 (November 10, 1975): 161.

50. Ibid., p. 161; and editorial, *New York Times*, August 23, 1976, p. 22.

51. See *Oil and Gas Journal* 73, no. 3 (July 28, 1975): 73.

52. *Platt's Oilgram News Service* 54, no. 60 (March 29, 1976): 4; *Middle East Information Series* 26–27 (Spring/Summer 1974): 103; "U.S. Seen Relying Heavily on Arab Oil," *Oil and Gas Journal* 74, no. 1 (January 5, 1976): 54; and William Smith, "Sale of Arab Oil to US Is Doubled," *New York Times*, August 17, 1976, p. 43.

53. William Smith, "Sale of Arab Oil Is Doubled," p. 43.

54. "Tankers: US Requirements in 1980," *The Petroleum Economist* 43, no. 4 (April 1976): 147.

55. Joseph Yager and Eleanor Steinberg, eds., *Energy and US Foreign Policy* (Cambridge, Mass.: Ballinger, 1974), pp. 311–12.

56. Mason Willrich, "Energy Independence for America," *International Affairs* (London) 52, no. 1 (January 1976): 57–59.

57. *Ibid.*, p. 66.

58. Federal Energy Administration, *Project Independence: A Summary* (Washington, D.C.: U.S. Government Printing Office, November, 1974), p. 44.

59. Ibid., p. 19.

60. Anthony Sampson, *The Seven Sisters* (New York: Viking Press, 1975), p. 82.

61. Shoshana Klebanoff, *Middle East Oil and U.S. Foreign Policy* (New York: Praeger, 1974), p. 238.

62. "Kissinger on Oil, Food, and Trade," *Business Week*, January 13, 1975, p. 69.

63. Schlesinger press conference on January 14, 1975. See *Middle East Economic Survey* 18, no. 13 (January 17, 1975): i.

64. Tom Wicker, "Stating the Obvious," *New York Times*, January 12, 1975, sec., 4, p. 17. Wicker's column appeared after the Kissinger interview, as *Business Week* was distributed in advance of its January 13 cover date.

65. *Middle East Economic Survey* 18, no. 21 (March 14, 1975): 3; and *Middle East Economic Survey* 18, no. 22 (March 21, 1975): i.

66. "Now—A Tougher U.S.," *U.S. News and World Report*, May 26, 1975, pp. 26–27.

67. Robert W. Tucker, "Oil: The Issue of American Intervention," *Commentary* 59, no. 1 (January 1975); and "Further Reflections on Oil and Force," *Commentary* 59, no. 3 (March 1975).

68. Drew Middleton, "Military Men Challenge Mideast 'Force' Strategy," *New York Times*, January 10, 1975, p. 3.

69. Tucker, "Further Reflections on Oil and Force," p. 53.

70. Miles Ignotus, "Seizing Arab Oil," *Harpers*, March 1975, p. 50.

71. Robert Freedman, "The Soviet Union and the Politics of Middle East Oil," unpublished manuscript, 1975, p. 53.

72. Ignotus, "Seizing Arab Oil," p. 60.

73. See ibid., p. 51. For a different perspective, see Earl Ravenal, "The Oil-Grab Scenario," *The New Republic*, January 18, 1975, p. 16.

74. See Yager and Steinberg, *Energy and US Foreign Policy*, pp. 321–22.

75. See Ignotus, "Seizing Arab Oil, p. 58.

76. Ravenal, "The Oil-Arab Scenario," p. 16.

77. Tucker, "Further Reflections on Oil and Force," p. 54.

78. Ignotus, "Seizing Arab Oil," p. 58.

79. See Alvin Rubinstein, "The Elusive Parameters of Détente," *Orbis* 19, no. 4 (Winter 1976): 1350–51; and G. Sheffer, "Independence in Dependence of Regional Powers: The Uncomfortable Alliances in the Middle East Before and After the October 1973 War," *Orbis* 19, no. 4 (Winter 1976)*: 1526.

80. Joseph Szyliowicz, "The Embargo and U.S. Foreign Policy," in *The Energy Crisis and U.S. Foreign Policy*, ed. Joseph Szyliowicz and Bard O'Neill (New York: Praeger, 1975), p. 197; and Malcolm Mackintosh, "The Impact of the Middle East Crisis on Superpower Relations," in "The Middle East and the International System: The Impact of the 1973 War," *Adelphi Paper*, no. 114 (1975): 4.

81. John Campbell, "The Energy Crisis and U.S. Policy in the Middle East," in Szyliowicz and O'Neill, *The Energy Crisis and U.S. Foreign Policy*, p. 120.

6 East-West Commercial Contacts and Changes in Soviet Management

Alice C. Gorlin

INTRODUCTION

Soviet attitudes toward management as an area deserving of separate concern and study have shifted as often as the political winds of the Soviet Union. In 1917, the victorious Bolsheviks regarded it as a trivial problem. Lenin saw no fundamental difference between management of large, complex firms and small simple ones:

> . . . Capitalism, as it develops, itself creates *prerequisites* for "every one" *to be able* really to take part in the administration of the state. . . . it is perfectly possible, immediately, within twenty-four hours after the overthrow of the capitalists and bureaucrats, to replace them, in the control of production and distribution, in the business of *control* of labour and products, by the whole people in arms.[1]

Subsequent experience proved the naivete of Lenin's view, and the late 1920s and early 1930s saw a revival of interest in and study of management. The educational system was geared up to produce managers.

During much of the Stalin period, the social sciences, including the science of management, were mordant. The economic achievements of this period are well known, and can be attributed at least partially to the highly centralized planning and administrative apparatus, which enabled the regime to concentrate the available resources on a small number of objectives. As the economy became more highly developed, however, it also became more complex to plan and administer. Planners and administrators were overworked because they had too many decisions to make with few, if any, precedents to guide them. Furthermore, the central apparatus could not collect and process the volume of information needed for timely and rational decisions. As a result, the wrong decisions were often made and there were many costly delays. Furthermore, because prices were not based on relative scarcities, what little discretion enterprise managers exercised was often used in ways that were incompatible with planners' preferences.

The much-heralded economic reform announced in September 1965 was an attempt to deal with the above-mentioned problems by limited delegation of decision making to enterprise managers and changes in economic calculation to aid rational decision making at lower levels. More specifically, the reform provisions were as follows: abolition of the Regional Economic Councils *(Sovnarknozy)* and their replacement by ministries organized along industrial lines; reduction of the number of obligatory indicators in the enterprise plan from 35 to 40 to 8; replacement of output and costs by sales, profits, and profitability as the chief indicators of enterprise success and determinants of managerial bonuses; introduction of a charge on capital to be paid by each enterprise; and price reform to make prices more accurately reflect costs.

Associated with the economic reforms of the 1960s was a resurgence of interest in the "science" of management as practiced in the West.[2] It was believed that Soviet managers could fashion domestic adaptations of Western management science to enable them to best utilize their newly gained independence. This interest is demonstrated by the numerous works by Western authors translated or abstracted into Russian, as well as by studies of Western management by the Institute for the study of the USA and Canada and other research bodies.[3] In addition, the Soviet Union frequently sends its professionals to the United States for varying lengths of time (sometimes via exchange programs) to study management.

Another kind of exchange program that has been developed recently is working conferences of American and Soviet economists. The Soviet side has requested that the next such conference be devoted to the study of training, deployment, compensation, and productivity of labor.

Soviet interest in and respect for Western know-how is confirmed by the experience of some U.S. businessmen. Donald Kendall, chairman of Pepsico, Inc., who has had extensive contacts with Soviet officials, believes the Soviet personnel have great respect for U.S. managerial know-how.[4] The development of trade, especially contracts involving much direct U.S. involvement in the construction and/or equipping of Soviet factories, is a potentially rich source of data on attitudes such as those perceived by Kendall. The equipment at the Kama River Truck Complex alone includes approximately $0.5 billion worth of U.S. machinery and technology, to be purchased from about 100 companies.[5]

Detente between the Soviet Union and the United States is obviously significant for a number of reasons. A major concern of this study is the fact that detente has been associated with an expansion of commercial and other economic ties between the two countries. Of particular importance is the 1972 Moscow Agreement, which called for the conclusion of a trade agreement to expand trade between the countries and the extension of credits to the Soviet Union. Detente and the increased contacts that followed have, in a sense, forced the Soviet Union to become a more open society, and the commercial negotiations between the two nations are a potentially valuable source of information on the internal workings of Soviet society. The purpose of the research described in this chapter is to draw upon the negotiating experiences of U.S. companies over the past ten years to derive information about Soviet attitudes toward changes in their system of economic management.

The research described below is based on the hypothesis that the commercial relationship is not only a source of data on Soviet attitudes but may itself affect these attitudes. It is often argued that because Soviet economic reforms have failed to achieve the objective of more rapid technical progress, purchases of advanced technology from the West are being substituted for meaningful change in economic policies. However, trade involves contact between Soviet officials and Western businessmen, and such contacts themselves produce changes in Soviet attitudes toward rationality and toward their own command system. Specifically, Soviet negotiators may become increasingly disillusioned with the command system's ability to stimulate efficiency and technical progress. Direct exposure to Western ways of doing business may suggest alternative paths for the Soviet system to follow. The possibilities for both attitudinal and structural changes are explored in this paper.

AREAS OF INTEREST IN WESTERN MANAGEMENT AND QUESTION OF APPLICABILITY

During the academic year 1975–76, Soviet economist Anatoly Porokhovsky was a scholar-in-residence at the University of Michigan Business School. His project was to study selected areas of management in large U.S. corporations and to determine their applicability to Soviet management.* The specific areas Porokhovsky studied were technical aspects of labor organization, including degree of mechanization, labor location, and job description; organizational structure; internal company planning; internal management control system, including the use of transfer prices; compensation policy; and evaluation of employee performance. Porokhovsky's interest in internal practices of large firms is perhaps related to the current merger program in the Soviet Union, which, by increasing average firm size, has engendered renewed interest in problems of management within organi-

---

*Porokhovsky has a candidate degree (roughly the equivalent of a U.S. doctorate), and is currently affiliated with the Department of Economics at Moscow State University. He is not a person of especially high stature; however, it is doubtful that the Soviet Union sends young scholars to the United States without careful scrutiny of the relevance of their research topics. Thus it is likely that Porokhovsky's areas of interest are also official areas of interest, although official areas of interest are not necessarily limited to those Porokhovsky studied.

zations.[6] Porokhovsky admits that many associations (the name given to merged firms in the Soviet Union) have encountered managerial problems.

To what extent are Western-style management practices applicable to Soviet-type centrally planned economies? A number of Soviet writers argue that they are highly applicable. Critical examination of the organizational structures of large capitalist firms is said to be useful in determining the organizational structures of Soviet enterprises, forming associations, and deciding the optimal mix of centralization and decentralization within enterprises and associations.[7] This point is also made by Georgi Arbatov, head of the Institute for the Study of the USA and Canada. He says that Soviet organizational structures are insufficiently varied to adapt to particular conditions.[8] And, according to Porokhovsky, Soviet planners studied the organizational structures of U.S. firms in determining the size and structure of the Kama River Truck Complex.

Porokhovsky believes that U.S. practice in the area of internal company planning can be applied to planning for an entire Soviet industry, as some U.S. corporations are larger than Soviet industrial ministries. He argues, however, that the plan of a U.S. firm is much narrower in scope than the plan of a Soviet industry. Soviet industrial plans must be coordinated with each other, while U.S. firms essentially plan in isolation from each other. (Research on oligopoly behavior would suggest that this is a naïve view; however, from the vantage of Soviet planners, perhaps the study of collusive behavior is not desirable.)

Porokhovsky also believes Soviet planners can learn a great deal from U.S. practice in evaluating managerial performance, especially in adopting a more flexible orientation that allows success criteria to vary with the goals of the organization. He implies that Soviet practice in this area is too rigid. He points out that in U.S. firms, although the overall goal is normally profit, different success criteria, such as cost and quality, are frequently used for evaluation of units within the firm. Also, profit itself is not a primary goal for a firm trying to develop new markets. Porokhovsky believes that Soviet associations can benefit from study of U.S. practice in this area, enabling them to better evaluate performance of their member plants.

FACTORS AFFECTING INTERNATIONAL TRANSFERABILITY OF MANAGERIAL TECHNIQUES

The Soviet economy is characterized by state ownership of the means of production; centralized determination of the size and composition of output and the allocation of resources to produce it, including investment funds; and freedom of choice in the labor and consumer goods markets, with prices and wages being centrally determined and inflexible for long periods. Thus, although some markets exist as institutions through which workers find jobs and consumers buy commodities, they play only a very minor role in the allocation of resources. The mixed capitalist economy of the United States, on the other hand, is characterized by private ownership; the decentralized allocation of resources by individual firms in response to market signals; and a significant role for nonmarket institutions, such as unions and government. Markets are the most important institutions for allocation of resources, although interference by government and unions is frequent. It should also be emphasized that most markets are not perfectly competitive and therefore do not achieve the socially optimal allocation of resources.

To what extent do these differences in the economic systems of the United States and Soviet Union limit or complicate the international transfer of managerial techniques? How important is the market setting in which Western firms operate? Porokhovsky points out that because of differences in economic systems, certain practices simply are not transferable, for example, U.S. practice in the labor relations area.

Lack of autonomy of Soviet enterprises may be an obstacle to the application of Western managerial techniques in the Soviet Union. For example, by studying the organizational structures of Western firms, Soviet managers may learn how to adapt the organizational structures of their enterprises to technology, the nature of product demand, and other relevant factors. However, such study will be to no avail unless managers have the right to determine the internal organizational structures of their enterprises. Porokhovsky emphasizes that the revival of interest in Western practices coincided with the economic reform of the 1960s precisely because Soviet managers gained increased independence at that time. It is now clear, however, that the reform has contributed only marginally, if at all, to increased independence of enterprises. Although there is some evidence that the multiplant associations will operate with more independence than ordinary enterprises, it is still an open question as to whether restrictions on enterprises will be an obstacle to adoption of Western techniques.

Economic system differences are not the only obstacle to international transfer of Western managerial techniques. Barry Richman and Melvyn Copen emphasize cultural differences and different attitudes toward success.[9] David Granick takes a similar approach in attributing national differences in the methodology for setting transfer prices to different routes toward managerial success.[10]

Leon Smolinski also shed light on the applicability question in a recent paper on the influence of East European economic thought and reform in the Soviet Union.[11] He forcefully illustrates how Soviet discussions of reforms in East Europe become quite ideological and hostile if the Soviet leaders perceive that there are "deviations" toward capitalism in these countries. In contrast, they take a more practical and nonideological view of practices in capitalist countries, as there is no question of adopting capitalism internally, just one of applying some of its intrafirm techniques. This is one possible, although partial, explanation for Smolinski's conclusion that the influence of East European economic theory and reforms in the Soviet Union is limited. Smolinski refers to an article by a Soviet economist who criticizes his colleagues for their excessive interest in the management of large U.S. corporations and corresponding lack of interest in socialist economies. Smolinski suggests that this phenomenon may be a vindication of Galbraith's view that "the logic of the new industrial state is stronger than ideological or systemic differences among countries."[12]

A final factor affecting the transferability of Western managerial techniques is the state of Soviet managerial education. It is clear from Richman's research that Soviet managerial education has tended to be narrowly technical, and until recently management was not even considered a separate field of study.[13] A recent assessment of the training of economists applies equally to managerial personnel in general, and shows that little has changed since Richman's research was published in 1967.

> There is . . . a long-standing conception that economists should be qualified only in one narrow branch, that it was enough for them to have only skills in day-to-day production planning or a narrow functional-economic training. The work experience of large production associations has shown that neither kind of specialist was prepared to handle the comprehensive planning and analysis of the activity of modern enterprise, that such work was beyond their ability. Only economists who have wide-ranging knowledge can cope with it.[14]

The economic reform of the 1960s gave some impetus to educational change when it became clear that many managerial personnel were competent in such narrow areas that they could not take advantage of their increased independence. There is some evidence of adaptation of the educational system to current needs. For example, as an experiment, a number of higher schools are now training economists in a broad range of subjects, as opposed to a narrow range of specialities.[15] Arguments are made in favor of education that stresses the solution of various managerial problems in concrete situations, which sounds very much like the case method used in U.S. business schools. Increasing acceptance of the idea that many managerial skills are general and do not depend on the branch of industry has led to calls for more centralization in education.[16]

Teaching new skills to older employees is also an area of concern. One weakness of this approach is that most retraining programs do not last more than two months, certainly not enough time to instill new approaches to problem solving. A number of ministries have drawn up five-year plans for raising the qualifications of employees, although such long-term planning is proceeding slowly. An additional problem is that enterprise managers do not encourage their employees to get additional education because their absence from work for one to two months hampers plan fulfillment.[17]

Retraining is occurring at all levels of the industrial hierarchy. Retraining of top ministerial personnel is centered at the Institute for Management of the National Economy, which was established in 1971.[18] Retraining is also taking place at the initiative of foreign firms: Fiat has established a training center at the Volga Automobile Works in Togliattigrad. The Fiat officials who started the school were concerned that they would be unable to complete their contract if the usual Soviet managerial practices were adhered to.[19] Another potential arena for managerial education is the network of corporations that the Soviet Union has established in the West as a mechanism for furthering East-West trade, for example, London's Moscow Narodny Bank and Morflot American Shipping.[20]

The Soviet leaders are acutely aware of the fact that in the United States the majority of executives were not trained as engineers but as management specialists, in contrast to their own situation. Current changes in Soviet managerial education are being accompanied by a departure from the traditional view of the enterprise director as a technician. "The director of a growing enterprise does not have time to deal personally with technical and technological problems; he has to delegate authority and devote himself to management as such."[21] Although change is clearly in the air, Soviet commentators acknowledge that they have by no means mastered the science of management. As one Soviet commentator put it, "One might say that we are still only approaching an understanding of the essence of managerial education, its role in the modern world, its advantages and the need for it."[22]

TRANSFER PRICING

Before turning to the insights and opinions of U.S. businessmen on the issues discussed, the question of international transferability of managerial techniques should be dealt with in more detail. The focus of the discussion is on transfer prices as a decision tool and their applicability in the Soviet setting. It is suggested that the Soviet leaders are overoptimistic about the extent to which Western managerial techniques can be applied in the Soviet economy. In the case of transfer pricing, and probably other areas of management as well, system differences may be a solid barrier to transferability.

Transfer pricing has been chosen as an illustration of potential difficulties because, with the growing size of firms in both the United States and Soviet Union, it has acquired increasing importance. Transfer pricing was particularly stressed by Porokhovsky as an area in which Soviet managers could learn much from U.S. practices. He believes that in calculating transfer prices, Soviet managers can adjust state-set prices in ways similar to the adjustment of market prices in the United States.

According to Western theory, transfer pricing has two major objectives, the first of which relates to performance evaluation. If the divisions of a firm operate with relative autonomy, they may be treated as profit centers. The "profits" of a division should represent that division's contribution to the overall profits of the firm. If transfers of goods and services take place among independent divisions of a firm, transfer prices are needed to evaluate these internal "sales." In other words, the transfer prices are a prerequisite to calculation of divisional profit figures. The second objective of transfer pricing is to motivate divisions to allocate resources so that total profits are maximized.

Western literature stresses that in order for transfer pricing to aid the evaluation of divisions' contributions to overall profits, divisions must have real market alternatives, as reflected in the transfer prices. Otherwise, the revenues of a selling division depend only on output, and in order to maximize profits it must minimize costs.

Determination of the correct transfer price to use in any situation is a very complex problem[23] and actual practice in Western firms does not always conform to ideal practice. For example, transfer prices are sometimes calculated according to a cost-plus-profit formula, and such prices are useless both as a guide to decisions and as a tool of performance evaluation. Many Western businessmen, however, seem to be aware of these problems, and in many situations where tranfer pricing is inappropriate it is simply not used.

Soviet theory and practice in this area, on the other hand, do not reflect an appreciation of the complexity of the transfer price problem. Furthermore, Soviet interest in this area of management does not make sense because of the nature of the environment facing the Soviet enterprise and its internal divisions.* The requisite independence of enterprises and divisions is lacking. Not only do divisions have very little choice as to customers and suppliers, that is, transactions in the external market, but enterprises and associations have very little choice in these areas either. Important input, such as raw materials and semifabricates, continue to be centrally allocated, and suppliers and customers are paired with each other in the annual plan. Thus the producing units in the case of scarce inputs cannot normally shop around for suppliers, nor can they choose among competing customers. Even if enterprises and their divisions had the choice of buying or selling on the external market, they would rarely be able to exercise this right because of the pervading seller's market. A division of a Soviet enterprise thus might prefer to buy an input on the external market (if the transfer price exceeded the wholesale price), but it would have difficulty obtaining sufficient quantities. Conversely, a division would normally have no trouble locating customers if it chose to sell externally rather than to another division of the enterprise. If the item in question were in short supply, however, the man-

---

*In the Soviet context, an enterprise may be a single-plant independent producer or a multiplant association. A division may be a shop of a very large plant or a member plant of an association.

agement of the enterprise would try to discourage such behavior, possibly by setting a high transfer price for the item.

The previous description of the Soviet environment raises the question of what does decentralization mean within an enterprise in a planned economy. Plan fulfillment is obligatory for all enterprises and associations; management, in order to ensure fulfillment, must divide the planned tasks among divisions. The role of transfer prices as a decision tool would therefore seem to be nil.

In practice, Soviet transfer prices are usually equal to the planned divisional *sebestoimost'* (variable costs), plus the division's share of total enterprise profits. Such transfer prices are predetermined to provide a certain acceptable profit level for each division; therefore, all divisions earn some profits, unless they greatly overspend. For example, a division that produces certain parts for assembly elsewhere in the enterprise may be less efficient than an outside producer. The enterprise could increase its total profits by purchasing these parts from an outside supplier. The transfer price as calculated does not reflect this alternative. Indeed, internal subcontracting is regarded as an end in itself, and some Soviet economists suggest that the profitability of semifabricates should be predetermined at an artificially high level in order to encourage their internal production. Other similar examples in the Soviet literature reflect a Soviet view of transfer prices as a method of inducing enterprises to behave in certain ways rather than as an aid to decision making.

As previously mentioned, Granick has tried to explain international differences in the methods for setting transfer prices by different criteria of managerial success. Such an explanation seems particularly appropriate to the Soviet case (not treated in Granick's paper). In the Soviet Union, plan fulfillment is essential to success as a manager. Managers set internal transfer prices so that divisions, as well as the enterprise as a whole, will fulfill their plans. The determinants of managerial success in the U.S. economy (profits and growth of the company) are very different, and thus the applicability of U.S. theory and practice in this area to Soviet industry is probably limited.

Since Soviet enterprise divisions have very little independence of action, at present they logically should be treated as cost centers rather than profit centers. But will the need for internal decentralization become greater with the creation of associations? Until the late 1960s, the vast majority of Soviet enterprises consisted of a single plant, so there was no pressing need for internal decentralization. Porokhovsky claims that this has changed with the increasing importance of associations. The majority of the associations created so far are relatively small, however, consisting of three to five plants in a small area. In such associations, internal decentralization would certainly not be mandatory. In the large so-called "industrial" associations, there is greater potential for transfer pricing. The members of these associations operate with significant autonomy in a legal sense, and these associations are spread over a wide geographic area. Whether or not internal decentralization will accompany this industrial reorganization remains to be seen. At present, however, Soviet interest in this particular Western management tool appears to be misplaced.[24]

INSIGHTS OF U.S. BUSINESSMEN

The potential of commerical contacts as a source of information on Soviet attitudes and practices in the area of management has already been mentioned. In order to obtain respondents' insights and impressions on the question of international transferability of managerial techniques and on whether increased U.S.-USSR trade, which has been facilitated by detente, has contributed to change in the Soviet managerial system, a questionnaire was drawn up and sent to the presidents of approximately 450 U.S. companies that have had commerical negotiations with the Soviet Union in the past ten years.* A total of 128 completed questionnaires were received. From analysis of the responses, it is hypothesized that new directions in Soviet management that seem Western influenced may be partially a result of the commerical relationship.

Respondents were asked to indicate their degree of agreement or disagreement with 33 statements based on their companies' negotiating experiences. It was emphasized that the questionnaire sought perceptions and impressions and did not expect factual certainty to be the basis of responses. Table 1 summarizes the responses to questionnaire statements 27–33, which are the statements relevant to the topic of this chapter.

Analysis of the responses to the seven statements (27–33) suggests several hypotheses about Soviet attitudes toward Western managerial practices. First, and not surprisingly, it is clear that Soviet awareness of and interest in Western management is far greater than actual adoption. More than two thirds of the respondents agreed with statements 27 and 28 (agreement with 28 was more intense), while less than one third agreed with statement 29. A significant minority (almost 30 percent) disagreed with statement 29, while 39 percent were undecided or felt they had insufficient information to respond.

Statements 30–32 are relevant to the impact of the commercial relationship on Soviet attitudes (awareness, interest, and adoption) toward Western management. The response to statement 30 indicates a general consensus that contact with Western firms has increased Soviet awareness of Western managerial practices; more than three fourths of the respondents agreed

*Part of the questionnaire sought information on numerous aspects of U.S. companies' negotiating experiences with the Soviet Union; these results are not included in this article.

TABLE 1: Perceptions of Soviet Attitudes Toward Western Managerial Practices

Questionnaire Statement	Percent of Respondents Who Checked Each Category (N = 128)							
	Strongly Disagree	Moderately Disagree	Neither Agree nor Disagree	Moderately Agree	Strongly Agree	Not Relevant	Insufficient Information for a Response	No Response
27 Soviet negotiators are aware of Western managerial practices	2.3	12.5	9.4	47.7	21.9	0.8	3.9	1.6
28 Soviet negotiators are interested in Western managerial practices	1.6	13.3	6.3	36.7	32.0	1.6	7.0	1.6
29 Soviet firms and/or other economic entities involved in negotiations with Western firms have begun to adopt Western managerial practices	8.6	21.1	24.2	27.3	1.6	0.8	14.8	1.6
30 As a result of their contacts with our company and/or other Western firms, Soviet negotiators have								

become more aware of Western managerial practices	1.6	7.0	0.8	18.0	57.8	10.9	2.3	1.6
31 As a result of their contacts with our company and/or other Western firms, Soviet negotiators have become more interested in Western managerial practices	1.6	14.1	0.8	8.6	39.8	24.2	7.8	3.1
32 As a result of their contacts with our company and/or other Western firms, Soviet firms and/or other economic entities have adopted Western managerial practices	1.6	23.4	2.3	0.0	14.1	22.7	19.5	16.4
33 Western managerial techniques could be applied in the Soviet economy even if it continues to be centrally planned	0.8	7.8	1.6	16.4	39.8	7.0	14.1	12.5

Note: The following information preceded statements 27–33 on the questionnaire: "The remaining statements are related to Soviet attitudes toward managerial practices common in the West. Examples are technical aspects of labor organization, including degree of mechanization, labor location, and job description; determination of organizational structure of firm; internal company planning; internal management control system, including the use of transfer prices; compensation policy; and evaluation of employee performance."

with statement 30. There was less agreement on statement 31: Just under half of the respondents agreed, while about one third either disagreed or were undecided. Nevertheless, the response to statement 31 does suggest that the commercial relationship has stimulated Soviet interest in Western management.

The responses to statement 32 are much less clear-cut. Almost half of the respondents either were undecided or felt that they had insufficient information to respond. Of the 64 respondents willing to state an opinion, 72 percent disagreed with the statement. At present, there is no basis for concluding that the commercial relationship has had much influence on adoption of Western managerial practices in the Soviet Union. Perhaps in a few years the response to this question will be very different.

Statement 33 sought respondents' opinions as to whether Western managerial practices are transferable to the Soviet Union. Here a majority (56.2 percent) agreed with the statement, but there was a significant minority (26.6 percent) who disagreed.

Table 2 shows the relationship between the trade experience of the respondents and their answers to statements 27–32. Trade experience is measured in two ways: first, by the volume of trade with the Soviet Union to date; and, second, by the number of different entities with which the U.S. company has negotiated. U.S. companies are classified as to whether their trade volume to date exceeds or falls short of $15 million. (Many companies did not respond to the question on volume of trade.) The companies are also classified according to whether or not they have had direct contact with Soviet firms (enterprises). In general, companies that have had such contact have been involved in more complex and lengthy negotiations, and thus are in a better position to respond to statement 27–32.

As shown on Table 2, companies having greater trade experience with the Soviet Union were more likely to agree with statements 27–32 and less likely to disagree than other respondents. This result gives somewhat stronger weight to the "moderately agree" and "strongly agree" responses, since many of them are from companies having wide experience in the Soviet Union. The relationship is stronger when trade experience is measured by dollar volume than when it is measured by entities with which the U.S. company has had contact. (There is reason to believe that many respondents misinterpreted the term "firm" in the Soviet context, and thus the responses to that part of the questionnaire are considered less reliable.)

Also of interest is a possible relationship between respondents' perceptions of the rationality of the Soviet negotiating style and their perceptions about the extent to which Western managerial practices have been adopted in the Soviet Union. A cross-tabulation therefore was calculated of the responses to statements 29 (see Table 1) and 26 ("the Soviet negotiating style is highly rational"). A positive, although weak, relationship was found between responses to these two statements. Of those who agreed with statement 26

TABLE 2: Relationship Between Trade Experience of U.S. Firms and Responses to Statements 27–32

		27	28	29	30	31	32
Respondents who were undecided or had insufficient information to respond							
Companies that had direct contact with Soviet firms (enterprises) (N = 48)	Number	8	8	16	8	20	22
	Percent	17	17	33	17	42	46
Companies that did not have direct contact with Soviet firms (enterprises) (N = 75)	Number	8	9	32	15	28	35
	Percent	11	12	43	20	37	47
Companies whose trade volume to date exceeds $15 million (N = 31)	Number	3	5	6	0	11	14
	Percent	10	16	19	0	35	45
Companies whose trade volume to date is less than $15 million (N = 68)	Number	13	11	31	20	27	34
	Percent	19	16	46	29	40	50
Respondents who agreed with the statement							
Companies that had direct contact with Soviet firms (enterprises) (N = 48)	Number	32	33	16	3	25	9
	Percent	67	69	33	81	52	19
Companies that did not have direct contact with Soviet firms (enterprises) (N = 75)	Number	54	51	21	53	34	9
	Percent	72	68	28	71	45	12
Companies whose trade volume to date exceeds $15 million (N = 31)	Number	25	25	14	31	20	8
	Percent	81	81	45	100	64	26
Companies whose trade volume to date is less than $15 million (N = 68)	Number	44	41	15	42	29	5
	Percent	65	60	22	62	43	7
Respondents who disagreed with the statement							
Companies that had direct contact with Soviet firms (enterprises)(N = 48)	Number	8	7	16	1	3	17
	Percent	17	14	33	2	6	35
Companies that did not have direct contact with Soviet firms (enterprises) (N = 75)	Number	11	11	19	4	10	26
	Percent	15	15	25	5	13	35
Companies whose trade volume to date exceeds $15 million (N = 31)	Number	3	0	11	0	0	9
	Percent	10	0	35	0	0	29
Companies whose trade volume to date is less than $15 million (N = 68)	Number	9	13	19	3	9	25
	Percent	13	19	28	4	13	37

Note: Row totals for each statement do not always add to the numbers in the first column (48, 75, 31, 68) because some respondents checked "not relevant" or did not check any response.

165

(40 respondents), 38 percent agreed with statement 29, while only 25 percent disagreed with it. Of those who disagreed with statement 26 (39 respondents), 38 percent disagreed with 29, while only 20 percent agreed with 29. Thus there is some tendency evident for respondents to link Soviet rationality with the use of Western managerial practices.

The statistical results of the survey can be amplified by some of the responses to two of the four open-ended questions at the end of the questionnaire, as well as by further discussion of statements 27–33 in approximately 15 telephone interviews conducted by the author.* Table 3 lists specific areas of management in which Soviet negotiators indicated interest in discussions with U.S. executives. The area of internal company decentralization is especially interesting; several respondents said that Soviet negotiators were impressed by the ability of their U.S. counterparts to make decisions while in the USSR without having to contact their superiors in the United States. Interest in this area of management may reflect a desire on the part of Soviet officials to eliminate bureaucratic delays and to introduce some rationality into the decision-making process. A few of the respondents indicated that their impression of Soviet decision making is that it is highly irrational, that everyone is afraid to make a decision without checking with

TABLE 3: Areas of Soviet Interest in Western Management

Internal company planning	Wage setting
Internal company budgeting	Incentive schemes
Internal company decentralization	Plant organization, flow of work, scheduling,
Western sales methods	breakdown of plant labor force
Corporate structure	

superiors. Soviet interest in decentralization does not necessarily reflect a commitment to decentralization to or within the enterprise; it may simply be interest in avoiding bureaucratic delays at higher levels, for example, ministries or Gosplan.

The Soviet Union is trying to get direct assistance from Western firms by buying management consulting services, and this can be expected to continue. One returned questionnaire was from a company that is now trying to sell consulting services in the Soviet Union. The author learned through a

*The relevant open-ended questions are "(1) Would you attribute any difficulties your company has experienced in negotiating with the Soviet Union to differences between the Soviet and American economic systems, to social and cultural differences, or to other factors? Please elaborate if possible." (2) "Please give other information about your experience which you think might be relevant to my study. I am especially interested in anecdotal accounts of your contacts in the Soviet Union."

telephone interview of a company negotiating with the Soviet Union that had been asked to send a management consultant there. The Soviet negotiators wanted advice on ways to get more productivity out of their people and equipment through incentive plans and better organization.

The responses to statement 27 indicate that respondents have differing impressions about Soviet awareness of Western managerial practices. Telephone interviews suggested that respondents' impressions depend to some extent upon the Soviet negotiators with whom they have had contact. The following organizations and individuals were said to be relatively sophisticated and well informed about Western ways of doing business: Ministry of Foreign Trade, State Committee for Science and Technology, Soviet Ambassador Dobrynin, and Lev Vasiliev, director of the Kama truck plant, whom one respondent described as a "Western-style decision maker." Negotiators from some of the foreign trade organizations and factory representatives who attend some negotiations in order to discuss technical matters are said to be poorly informed about Western management.

Specific details of the negotiating experiences of Western firms shed light on Soviet ignorance of U.S. firms' ways of doing business. Several respondents had the impression that their Soviet counterparts were very well informed on technical matters, but not on economic matters. For example, they often did not provide economic data of great importance to U.S. negotiators, such as cost data. Some Soviet negotiators did not understand U.S. negotiators' concerns about return on investment, obligations to stockholders, establishing a market position, and delivery dates. One respondent said that many of the demands made by Soviet negotiators were illogical and had no rational economic basis, for example, Soviet refusal to incorporate clauses allowing nonperformance of contract due to impossibility (destruction of goods through an "act of God," such as an earthquake).

As Table 1 shows, there is also disparity of opinion on whether Western managerial practices can be used in the centrally planned Soviet economy. One respondent said that autarky and the closed society prevent the free flow of information that is a prerequisite to any reform, including changes in the management system. Excessive secrecy, both as a hindrance to negotiations and as an obstacle to reform, was emphasized by a number of respondents. Another respondent said that the Soviet Union is a prisoner of its Russian cultural heritage, and he therefore considered it doubtful that Western managerial techniques would ever be used effectively there, even though in theory such techniques could be applied in a planned economy. There was a general consensus among respondents who specifically addressed this question that the Soviet system is rigid and stultified, and discourages the kind of creativity, initiative, and imagination needed for genuine economic reform. Undoubtedly many of the respondents who agreed with statement 33 did so in a theoretical sense only: A centrally planned economy can, in principle, use Western management tools, but the Soviet economy is unlikely to do so.

An additional question is whether, with more complex commercial contacts between the United States and Soviet Union—for example, a U.S. firm supervising the construction and equipping of a factory in the Soviet Union—the Americans will insist on changes in Soviet management practices. The Fiat experience described earlier suggests this as a possibility. More specifically, will U.S. companies be reluctant to commit themselves to energy complexes in the Soviet Union if these are to be run as other Soviet enterprises are?

CONCLUSION

There are a number of ways in which knowledge about Western methods of management can be assimilated in the Soviet Union. The simplest and probably still the most important way is for Soviet scholars and practitioners of management to study the Western literature; this transfer of knowledge does not depend on detente except in a most general way. Other avenues of communication—exchange programs and commercial relationships with U.S. companies—depend more directly on detente. This chapter has concentrated on the latter, and has shown that the commercial relationship already has had some impact on Soviet awareness of and interest in Western management, for example, the high degree of Soviet interest in decision processes in U.S. corporations. Whether or not commercial contacts have influenced actual Soviet practice is much more doubtful. Finally, although the study suggests some attitudinal changes as a result of commercial contacts, the impressions of U.S. businessmen do not lend support to the view that the Soviet negotiators have become skeptical of their system in any fundamental way.

This study is a preliminary effort at exploring some domestic implications of expanded U.S.-USSR trade. More work needs to be done, in particular an in-depth study of the trade experiences of a small number of companies having the most extensive contacts with Soviet officials. Especially revealing would be a study of the nature of consulting services sold to the USSR.

Assuming that detente and the associated expansion of the commercial relationship continue, at least two possibilities suggest themselves. First, as Soviet negotiators learn more about Western management, especially through visits to U.S. factories, their awareness of and interest in possible domestic applications may increase. On the other hand, Soviet negotiators, as they see U.S. management practices in action, may become more skeptical about the applicability of these practices in their own country. They may, for example, see the kinds of contradictions pointed out earlier in this chapter in the discussion of transfer pricing.

A resolution of this contradiction between Soviet interest in the use of Western management and the fundamental differences between the two systems can perhaps be found by focusing on the level(s) of the Soviet administrative hierarchy most likely to apply Western management tools. Application of many Western methods in Soviet enterprises depends on decentralization of major decisions to this level, and at present there is no evidence of such reform in the Soviet Union. The economic reform of the 1960s has in reality resulted in very little decentralization. A number of specific provisions have been revoked or even ignored by ministerial authorities. The most important plan indicators continue to be centrally determined. Most prices remain centrally determined and fixed for long periods, and enterprises still have little choice as to customers or suppliers. In other words, most of the terms under which enterprises deal with each other remain centrally determined.

Many Western managerial techniques, however, are applicable at any level of the Soviet hierarchy. One example is employee incentive schemes. Keeping in mind that the typical Soviet enterprise still consists of one plant and has limited decision-making authority, management techniques used by large Western corporations probably have greater applicability at higher levels of the Soviet hierarchy, that is, in ministries and the large industrial associations. It is possible that the Soviet Union is really most interested in those Western methods that facilitate central control (for example, more efficient information systems and improved budgeting techniques) rather than those that are associated with decentralization within the firm (that is, transfer prices). Thus one possibility is that increased knowledge and application of Western managerial techniques will enable the Soviet leaders to postpone meaningful economic reform, and possibly even *increase* the centralization of its economy.

Soviet economist Volkonskiy, representative of those opposed to decentralization, argues that ". . . the decentralistic tendencies in American giant corporations noticeable from the 1920s onwards have been reversed in the 1950s—as a result of the rapid advance in mathematization and computerization.[25]

Although the previous argument seems plausible, it must be remembered that some questionnaire respondents believe strongly that Western managerial techniques cannot be used in the Soviet economy. In this regard, we might pose the questions: As Soviet managers and other officials learn about Western managerial techniques and see them in action, will their attitudes toward the Soviet hierarchical command system change? Will there eventually be a clash between the Soviet leaders' desire to avoid or postpone internal economic reforms and demands for fundamental change— economic, political, and cultural—at lower levels? These are obviously important and difficult economic and political questions, the answers to which we can only speculate on at present.

NOTES

1. V. I. Lenin, *State and Revolution* (New York: International Publishers, 1932), p. 83.

2. Perhaps the Soviet leaders were inspired by Lenin, who advised: "Be able to learn from the capitalists. Adopt whatever they have that is sensible and advantageous." Quoted in Peter B. Maggs, "A Computer Model of the System of Legal Regulation of the Soviet State Industrial Enterprise," in *Contemporary Soviet Law: Essays in Honor of John H. Hazard*, ed. Donald D. Barry, William E. Butler, and George Ginsburgs (The Hague: Martinus Nijhoff, 1974), p. 178.

3. An example of the work done in the Institute for the Study of the USA and Canada is S. Sh. A. Churmanteeva, *Podgotovka rukovodiashchego personala promyshlennykh korporatsii The Training of Managerial Personnel for Industrial Corporations* (Moscow: Nauka, 1975). The major abstract source is *Abstracts of Research on Organization of Management (Referativny sbornik: Organizatsiia upravleniia)* (Moscow: All Union Institute of Scientific and Technical Information). Probably the best Soviet survey of U.S. management theories is D. M. Gvishiani, *Organization and Management (Organizatsiia i upravlenie)*, 2nd ed. (Moscow: Nauka, 1972).

4. U.S., Congress, House of Representatives, *Détente: Hearings Before the Subcommittee on Europe of the Committee on Foreign Affairs*, 93 Cong., 2 Sess., May 8, 15, and 24, 1974; June 10, 12, and 26, 1974; and July 17, 25, and 31, 1974. p. 116.

5. Herbert E. Meyer, "A Plant That Could Change the Shape of Soviet Industry," *Fortune* (November 1974), pp. 150–57, 229–30, and 232.

6. For a detailed analysis of the Soviet merger movement, see Alice C. Gorlin, "The Soviet Economic Associations," *Soviet Studies* 26 (1974): 3–27.

7. A. N. Strel'tsova, "Matrix Structures of Management" ("Matrichnye struktury upravleniia"), *General Branch Questions of the Economics and Organization of Industry (Obshcheotraslevye voprosy ekonomiki i organizatsii promyshlennosti)*, vol. 4 (Moscow: 1975), pp. 82–3.

8. Georgi Arbatov, "Designing the Organization of Large Industrial-Economic Complexes and Their Management" ("Proektirovanie organizatsii krupnykh proizvodstvenno-khoziaistvennykh kompleksov i upravleniia imi"), *Planovoe khoziaistvo*, no. 5 (1975): 20. Arbatov is echoing a concern voiced much earlier by Khrushchev that the same basic organizational structure exists in enterprises of 100 or 1,000 employees. See Barry M. Richman, *Management Development and Education in the Soviet Union* (East Lansing, Mich.: Michigan State University, 1967), p. 198.

9. Barry M. Richman and Melvyn Copen, *International Management and Economic Development* (New York: McGraw-Hill, 1972), Ch. 4.

10. David Granick, "National Differences in the Use of Internal Transfer Prices," *California Management Review* 17 (Summer 1975): 28–40.

11. Leon Smolinski, "East European Influences on Soviet Economic Thought and Reforms," in *The Influence of East Europe and the Soviet West on the USSR*, ed. Roman Szporluk (New York: Praeger, 1975), pp. 68–90.

12. Ibid., p. 87.

13. Richman, *Management Development and Education in the Soviet Union*.

14. Iu. Lavrikov, "Problems of the Five-Year Plan: Formula for Efficiency," *Current Digest of the Soviet Press* 28 (March 10, 1976): 7–8; translated from *Izvestia*, February 10, 1976, p. 2.

15. Ibid.

16. N. G. Kalinin, ed., *The Organization of Management in the Ministerial System (Organizatsiia upravleniia v sisteme ministerstva)* (Moscow: Moscow State University, 1974), pp. 246–48.

17. Ibid., pp. 232–33, 250.

18. Karl W. Ryavec, *Implementation of Soviet Economic Reforms* (New York: Praeger, 1975), p. 76.

19. See *Eastern Europe Report*, no. 25 (June 25, 1976).

20. See Herbert E. Meyer, "The Communist Internationale Has a Capitalist Accent," *Fortune* (February 1977), pp. 134–37, 141–42, 146, and 148.

21. "How Should Economists Be Trained?" *Current Digest of the Soviet Press* 28 (December 1, 1976): 8; translated from *The Economics and Organization of Industrial Production (Ekonomika i organizatsiia promyshlennogo proizvodstva)*, no. 5 (1976): 118–29.

22. "The Making of the Soviet Executive," *Current Digest of the Soviet Press* 28 (August 25, 1976): 7; translated from *Literaturnaya gazeta*, February 1, 1976, p. 12.

23. See David Solomons, *Divisional Performance* (Homewood, Ill.: Irwin, 1965).

24. For a more thorough discussion of Soviet transfer pricing, see Alice C. Gorlin, "Management of Soviet Associations," *Association for Comparative Economic Studies Bulletin* 18 (Spring 1976): 45–66.

25. See Alfred Zauberman, *The Mathematical Revolution in Soviet Economics* (London: Oxford University Press, 1975), p. 35.

7   Detente and the Defense of Europe

Elliot R. Goodman

Despite professions of detente, the Soviet leadership has proceeded with an unabated buildup and improvement of the military forces under its control in the center of Europe. As of the beginning of 1977, the overall force level of the Warsaw Pact was 5.6 million troops, compared with 4.8 million for the North Atlantic Treaty Organization (NATO).[1] Over the last decade, the Soviet Union added more then 800,000 men to its armed forces (not counting border guards and internal security forces), so that the soviet military establishment now amounts to about 4.4 million men, more than twice the number in the U.S. armed forces.[2]

On the crucial central European front, some 962,000 Warsaw Pact ground forces face 791,000 NATO frontline troops.[3] In another measure of comparison, there are 58 Warsaw Pact divisions in central Europe confronting 27 NATO divisions. This latter figure requires some interpretation. A Warsaw Pact division is about three fifths the size of a NATO one, but this difference is accounted for by the smaller proportion of supply and support troops in the East as compared with the structure of a NATO division. If one makes a comparison in terms of firepower and mobility, a Warsaw Pact division is almost equal to a German or U.S. division. Hence the disproportionately large number of Warsaw Pact divisions in central Europe is, indeed, significant. Another 30 Soviet divisions in the western regions of the USSR could be brought into combat in central Europe much more easily than U.S. reinforcements could be transported across the Atlantic.[4] Since the late 1960s, the Soviet Union has increased its troop strength along the central European front by more than 100,00 men.[5]

In terms of weapons deployed in central Europe, Warsaw Pact armor outnumbers NATO's by a ratio of three to one. At the beginning of 1976, there were 19,000 Warsaw Pact tanks facing 6,100 NATO tanks. Since 1970,

This chapter has been adapted from "Reflections on the Shifting East-West Balance of Forces," and from "The Puzzle of European Defense: The Issue of Arms Procurement." Both articles appeared in the 273 Summer-Autumn issue of *Survey*.

this Warsaw Pact tank strength had been increased by 40 percent (from 13,650 to 19,000 tanks in active units). In addition, the 8,000 tanks stationed in the three western military districts of the Soviet Union could quickly be moved into central Europe.[6]

The situation is scarcely better for combat aircraft in central Europe: 2,460 for the Warsaw Pact versus 1,700 for NATO. Again, the Soviet Union could fly in 1,290 additional such aircraft held ready in the western part of the Soviet Union.[7] Warsaw Pact air forces also have undergone dramatic improvements, with substantially improved range and payload, with the result that they can now engage in a variety of offensive missions of which they were previously incapable.

Indicative of the Soviet military buildup in the center of Europe is the tripling of multiple rocket launchers from 1970 to 1976 (from 220 tubes to 700 per Soviet division).[8] Indeed, Warsaw Pact arms now outnumber those of NATO in almost every area of major weaponry, even antitank weapons which had always been considered a NATO strongpoint. In this regard 81 percent of Warsaw Pact antitank weapons are mounted on armored vehicles compared with 43 percent of NATO's, and 83 percent of their antitank weapons can be fired under armored protection compared with only 11 percent of NATO's.[9]

Improvements in the communist force structure, of which the above examples are typical, have added a new dimension to the balance of power in the center of Europe. It is increasingly recognized that the Warsaw Pact has the ability to launch a surprise attack from a standing start.[10] In the past, NATO has assumed that there would be sufficient warning time to bring up reserves and reinforce arms stockpiles. It is now generally conceded that this crucial warning time has been drastically reduced. Soviet doctrine, which emphasizes shock and deception, calls for rapid breakthroughs with armored formations. It is significant that the Soviet army in Germany has now deployed a revolutionary new portable bridge that could be thrown across the Rhine in half an hour. Most Soviet combat vehicles also include a river-crossing capability.[11]

While central Europe is probably where the Soviet leaders would seek to force a military decision, one should note in passing the deployment of forces on the northern and southern fronts. Along the Norwegian border, six Warsaw Pact divisions face a single NATO brigade. Moreover, half of the Soviet submarine fleet is stationed at Murmansk, presenting a grave danger to NATO sealanes in the North Atlantic. Indeed, the Soviet Union has the world's largest attack submarine force, which effectively threatens the essential Atlantic lines of communication, as well as those areas beyond NATO's boundaries, that are vital to the security of Western Europe.

On the southern flank, NATO has 38 divisions, or nearly as many as the Warsaw Pact has stationed in the southern Balkans and the Caucasus. However, the Warsaw Pact has three times the number of combat aircraft in southeastern Europe as does NATO. In the Mediterranean, the U.S. Sixth Fleet still dominates Warsaw Pact naval forces, although the recent rapid expansion of the Soviet naval operations in this area has considerably reduced this advantage.[12]

All of the quantitative and qualitative changes that have strengthened Warsaw Pact forces in Europe have taken place, incidentally, without any drawdown of the more than one million Soviet soldiers standing guard along the Chinese frontier. One can only conclude that in the major confrontation of forces in Europe the accumulated exertions of both sides have resulted increasingly in a significant military advantage for the Warsaw Pact. In the mutual arms reduction negotiations that have been under way in Vienna, the West has tried, in vain, to eliminate the Warsaw Pact superiority in manpower, tanks, and combat aircraft by having both sides agree to reduce their military strength to a common ceiling. But the Kremlin has displayed no interest in this proposition, nor is it likely to do so. If the Soviet leaders hold on to their potentially intimidating position long enough, the willpower of the NATO states will eventually crumble, so they must reason, and their predominant military position can at the very least yield political dividends.

Arms control negotiations have also been under way for strategic weapons in the Strategic Arms Limitations Talks (SALT). Here there is more the impression of a standoff between the superpowers, but again it is the trend of recent developments that must be noted. Between 1965 and 1976, the Soviet intercontinental ballistic missile (ICBM) force increased from 224 to more than 1,500 launchers. The U.S. ICBM force, by way of contrast, following a modest increase in 1966, remained at 1,054 launchers from 1967 through 1976. Similarly in the case of submarine launched ballistic missiles (SLBMs), the Soviet Union increased this force from 29 in 1965 to about 800 launchers in 1976. Again, the U.S. SLBM force, after a modest increase in 1966, remained steady at 656 launchers from 1967 through 1976. In the case of strategic bombers, the U.S. force was cut in half between 1966 and 1976, while the Soviet investment in bombers, always less than that of the United States, began to move upward recently with the development of the Backfire bomber.[13] From 1965 through 1976, the United States developed one new type of ICBM while the Soviet Union developed seven. Soviet missiles generally have held an advantage in throw-weight, while the United States was more advanced in developing multiple independently targetable reentry vehicles (MIRVs). However in the newest generation of Soviet ICBMs, three not only have greater throw-weight, but more and higher yield MIRVs than the newest, comparable U.S. missiles.[14]

The fact that the communist bloc states operate on a command economy makes it possible for them to allocate resources for military purposes in a way that is not possible in the West. Revised intelligence estimates show that since 1970 annual Soviet defense expenditures have absorbed some 11 to 13 percent of the Soviet gross national product, which is roughly three times the average NATO percentage of the gross national product devoted to defense.[15] Despite the fact that the Soviet gross national product is half as large as that of the United States, the Kremlin now spends (in dollar terms) 30 to 40 percent more on defense than does the United States.[16]

In short, the menacing shadow of Soviet military might hanging over Western Europe has scarcely disappeared and NATO is as necessary as ever. Realistically, however, the best that can be expected is only a marginal increase in NATO defense spending. Force improvements therefore must come in some other way.

What is urgently required is a rational arms procurement policy for the NATO forces that will provide much greater value for the money spent. The present irrational use of resources that is the consequence of fragmented and competing national efforts has resulted in an enormous waste of economic resources and manpower in all the NATO countries. At a time when there is increasing pressure on all defense expenditures, there is also a huge, un-economic duplication of effort. This takes the form not only of waste in the procurement of nonstandardized weapons but also of the equally costly expenses for the maintenance of spares and of separate national systems of logistical support. In a careful study by Thomas A. Callaghan, Jr., undertaken for the U.S. State and Defense Departments, it was concluded that the NATO allies annually waste more than $10 billion in their needlessly duplicative defense efforts.[17] A Senate Armed Services Committee study has estimated that as much as $15 billion annually is wasted in this manner.[18] It is finally beginning to dawn upon members of the Atlantic alliance that their existing pattern of arms procurement for the defense of Europe is heading for disaster. The new arrangements that are needed to remedy this situation will necessarily have broad economic, military, and political implications.

In terms of economics, presently nearly a dozen European states are attempting to produce military goods in small or medium-size national markets that are highly protected and highly inefficient. These military markets have continued to receive national subsidies and other forms of protection, and therefore have not been subjected to the healthy erosion of economic barriers that has affected the civilian economies of the European Community. The European arms industries consequently have relatively limited funds for research and development and for the actual production of military equipment. The small scale of their operations means that they lack economy of scale and that they have short production runs and high unit costs.

The United States, on the other hand, has relatively large funds available for research and development (R&D), and it produces on a large scale that permits long production runs and lower unit costs. Moreover, the high quality of U.S. management usually means that U.S. weapons have a shorter development time than comparable European systems. As the late Alastair Buchan noted: "The dilemma that haunts any European government which commits R and D funds to a defense project is that it may get a certain distance, find a broadly equivalent American project being developed at greater speed, and discover that its European neighbors who have not committed R and D funds would rather buy the cheaper American product."[19] Other factors, such as aggressive U.S. sales tactics and the German practice of buying U.S. equipment to offset the U.S. balance of payments on military account in Europe, have aggravated the disparities that exist between the U.S. and European arms industries.

The result of all these factors is an enormous imbalance between the arms Europe purchases from the United States and U.S. purchases from Europe. Strangely, precise data are lacking on this subject, but informed estimates run from a ten-to-one to a fifteen-to-one ratio in favor of the United States. And, in the absence of fundamental structural reforms of the European arms industries, the situation is likely to deteriorate further. Technologically complex, sophisticated equipment tends to become obsolescent at an alarmingly fast pace, and each new generation of sophisticated weapons costs increasingly large, sometimes immensely large, sums. While there will be some exceptions in the development of isolated European weapons, generally speaking, the prospect is for Europe progressively to drop out of the military technology race and to become an industrial backwater, relegated to a position of technological inferiority.

Some observers look hopefully to the new arms technology that promises to provide inexpensive but extremely effective weapons. Their general adoption might make it possible for Europe to avoid being priced out of the weapons market while also reducing the U.S. defense bill. The dramatically increased accuracy of precision guided munitions, operated by radar, electro-optical, laser and infrared homing, and correlation guidance, makes highly probable a one-shot, one-kill ratio. Moreover, their use introduces a new flexibility and control over combat operations that guarantees target destruction at increasingly long ranges while minimizing collateral damage. Thus, even if in some cases the unit cost of "smart" bombs is higher than the old "dumb" bombs, their enhanced accuracy makes them many times more cost-effective. The Yom Kippur War of 1973 left no doubt about the devastating effect of new antiaircraft and antitank guided weapons. Also, the development of remotely piloted vehicles which would replace airplanes with human pilots could realize major savings. The advantage the Warsaw Pact forces have over the NATO forces in central Europe in terms of tanks and strike aircraft might be nullified by the new technology that makes weapons with greatly increased accuracy and firepower available to small defensive units. This also might permit the defense to overwhelm the offense.

While all these substantial advantages are in the offing, one should not look upon the new technology as the panacea for all of NATO's ills. While the new weapons systems will likely be available in abundance and, at low cost, for the shorter range battlefield systems, "both long-range and all-weather precision guided munitions now under development," a weapons specialist testified, "will cost far more than present generation systems."[20] Nor does the new weapons technology basically alter the argument for economy of scale in arms production, so as to provide an efficient return on defense investments. The comparative advantage of producing arms in the United States rather than in the smaller European markets would make it likely that the Europeans would buy much of the new weapons technology from the United States, thereby perpetuating the imbalance in arms trade across the Atlantic. And should the separate European countries supply themselves with these new weapons, there exists the possibility of equipping NATO forces with several incompatible national weapons models. In short, while the new technology is important/ and should be employed where possible, technology alone cannot solve the basic structural problems of the Atlantic alliance, which are both economic and political in nature.

The prospect of a continued lopsided European dependence upon the United States is obviously unhealthy for Europe. It is also unhealthy for the United States as well, since such an unequal relationship can only breed resentment and apathy in Europe and accentuate the divisive factors in the alliance. Moreover, to the extent that Europe continues to fall behind in the production of expensive, high technology equipment, it is by no means certain that the United States can by itself carry the whole NATO burden for sophisticated arms procurement.

While the U.S. defense budget has risen steadily, the increases have been almost entirely dissipated by higher personnel pay in an expensive all-volunteer service and in other operating expenses. As a result, the proportion of the budget spent on R&D and arms procurement has fallen from 48.4 percent of the budget in fiscal year (FY) 1954 to 29.8 percent in FY 1974.[21] During this same period, R&D costs have shot up, with the consequence that the number of weapons systems under development as well as the number of units actually procured has fallen rapidly. On the other hand, the Warsaw Pact, which is still based on conscription, has experienced no such increase in personnel pay. Thus, while the United States now spends over 50 percent of its military budget on personnel pay and less than 30 percent on weapons and equipment R&D and arms procurement, the figures for the Soviet Union are exactly the opposite: over 50 percent for arms R&D procurement and around 30 percent for personnel. Meanwhile, the dramatic rise in the Soviet defense budget meant that by FY 1976 the Soviet Union outspent the United States by 20 percent in R&D and by 25 percent in procurement.[22] In the FY 1978 Defense Department Report, the U.S. secretary of defense recorded that the Soviet

Union was spending 90 percent more than the United States in both R&D and military investment.[23]

It should be obvious that in this competition the United States, and NATO, face a bleak future if the Western nations continue to rely primarily upon the United States, which is already pressing the limits of its resources. It is only by a rational reorganization of the resources of all of the NATO allies that this challenge can be met. And this can only be accomplished by restructuring the arms trade on both sides of the Atlantic.

Beyond an intolerable waste of money, the fragmented national arms programs also have profound military implications for NATO. The Warsaw Pact has the advantage of using almost completely standardized models imposed upon it by the Soviet Union. The NATO forces comprise a collection of nonstandardized, national systems that constitute an intolerable incompatibility in weapons and equipment. On the central European front, for example, the NATO forces are equipped with 23 different types of fighter aircraft, 23 different types of antitank missiles, 8 different types of light tanks, and 7 different types of main battle tanks.[24] Even in the Allied Command—Europe (ACE) Mobile Force, which is the showpiece of allied cooperation in Europe, units of seven NATO countries that constantly train and operate together are prevented from becoming a truly cohesive force because of their lack of standardized equipment. Each of the seven national units must maintain its own logistics personnel and its own separate logistical support system. The commander of this combined force has concluded that if his troops used standardized arms and equipment, he could make them combat ready in half the time and cut the logistical personnel and his airlift requirements in half.[25] Needless to say, these improved forces would also cost much less to maintain.

Not only are NATO logistics a nightmare, but the inability of allied forces to operate effectively side by side could be crucial in an emergency. A recent NATO exercise showed that the lack of common frequencies and codes for data transmission and of standard systems for identification of friend or foe caused the NATO forces to shoot down large numbers of their own aircraft. Of the planes theoretically destroyed, more than half were of NATO origin.[26]

One means of remedying the dependent position of Europe as well as taking a large step toward arms standardization would be the creation of a European Defense Community (EDC) somewhat along the lines of the EDC that met with defeat in 1954. Some European federalists argue that while it is not possible for the defense industries of the European states to survive individually, they could benefit enormously if they would only pool their resources and produce equipment for an assured Europe-wide market. As in the case of the European Economic Community, the European arms market would be protected by a common tariff barrier, both to encourage Europeans to buy from one another and to achieve in large measure a Europe that is self-sufficient in arms.

Second thoughts would suggest major drawbacks to this scheme. Discrimination against defense purchases from the United States might incite U.S. discrimination against European exports, not only in defense equipment but in closely related fields, such as aerospace. Furthermore, this approach, which would aim at European standardization, would not solve the standardization problem on a NATO-wide basis. Instead of drawing the two sides of the Atlantic together, it would drive them apart and conceivably could have a disintegrative impact on NATO. Insofar as an EDC could not, by itself, provide for all of Europe's security needs, and presumably it could not, NATO would still be necessary. Finally, an attempt to create a fully supranational EDC would be too demanding politically in the foreseeable future at any rate. While Europe is taking hesitant steps toward union, full union in defense affairs will doubtless be not one of its next, but one of its last, major achievements.

A more attractive option that could overcome all of these objections would be the creation of a European Arms Procurement Organization operating within the context of an Atlantic Common Arms Market. Such an organization would differ basically in purpose and structure from a complete military union, such as was envisaged by an EDC. Its powers would be limited to planning, financing, and managing the procurement of arms in Europe by aggregating, or joining together, the separate national arms producers in Europe into a single European arms market. This market would not, however, seek to produce arms primarily for European needs, or aim at European self-sufficiency in arms. Rather, it would be the European half of an Atlantic Common Arms Market, which would compete with the United States and Canada on the other side of the ocean, to produce arms on a NATO-wide basis. This would not only provide the necessary economies of scale for producers on both sides of the Atlantic but would also substantially solve the problem of arms standardization for NATO as the arms purchased would be used to supply all NATO forces. Operating under those conditions, a European arms agency would not be divisive but would preserve and indeed strengthen the trans-Atlantic NATO bond. A true interdependence of each side of the Atlantic on the other in the realm of military equipment would unavoidably result in stronger political interdependence.

The details of creating a European Arms Procurement Organization should, of course, be left to the Europeans. In general terms, this should consist of an arrangement whereby the participating states would fund the arms agency, which, in turn, would award contracts and make the actual purchase of equipment on behalf of its members. The basic decision about establishing military requirements, however, should not be left to the European Arms Procurement Organization, any more than it should be left to the

Pentagon. Since both agencies would be purchasing equipment for NATO-wide use, the determination of military requirements should be a NATO function and be entrusted to a NATO body. Perhaps this could be a function of the NATO Military Committee or, in view of the esteem with which the Supreme Allied Commander Europe traditionally has been held, perhaps this determination could be worked up by his staff at Supreme Headquarters Allied Powers Europe (SHAPE). This could be a matter for negotiation among the NATO partners.

Once the decision had been made as to what military equipment is required, the determination of actual specifications and production standards should be worked out between the European Arms Procurement Organization and the Pentagon, in consultation with appropriate Canadian officials. It is only at this point that the two sides of the Atlantic would enter into competition to produce arms and equipment within the agreed upon standardized guidelines. The result would be a more balanced trans-Atlantic trade in military goods that would eliminate the unhealthy dependence of one side on the other.

While the formation of a European arms agency along these lines would not be as politically ambitious as a full-fledged EDC, it would nonetheless represent a significant evolution in the building of European cooperation, and would have latent supranational political and economic implications. Moreover, the participation in the creation of a Atlantic Common Arms Market would represent a significant restructuring of trans-Atlantic arms trade. The question arises as to whether exertions even on this scale are necessary. Is it not possible, instead, to simply search out more piecemeal, cooperative efforts at arms production among the NATO allies and move in a gradual, incremental manner toward more standardization? Essentially, this is a more-of-the-same option, and we already know from past experience that more of the same is not good enough.

For a number of years, various NATO allies have entered into separate coproduction arrangements to create one type or another of military equipment. In each case, the participating European countries realized that the production of the equipment in question would be beyond their financial and technological means if they undertook to "go it alone." While these considerations also applied in some degree to the United States, the U.S. aims in collaborating with different European states in such coproduction schemes also included the desire to transfer to Europe advanced weapons technology and to stimulate wider industrial integration in Europe. Some progress toward these goals was achieved. "By means of these projects," Jack Behrman noted, "Europe was brought through 15 years of technological development in missiles and aircraft within five years, it was provided a base for continuing industrial production, and its aircraft industry was restructured."[27] There was, however, no effective follow-through program to capitalize on such collaborative efforts. Instead of creating a permanent multinational arms procurement organization that could continue to guide joint weapons development, each project became simply an ad hoc effort that expired once the project was completed. It would appear that such coproduction projects, however laudable, simply are not capable of sustaining the progress needed to transform Europe into an equal and independent partner of the United States in the field of arms production.

Moreover, such coproduction projects generally involved no more than two or three partners. While this would standardize equipment for the partners involved, very often it did little more than that, and never did it result in standardization of equipment on a NATO-wide basis. As Callaghan rightly commented: "Standardization is a macro-economic problem." It is "not a problem that will yield to micro-economic methods—to the occasional, ad hoc, project-by-project approach."[28] The popular, presumedly realistic way of attacking the standardization problem has been precisely through the ad hoc, project-by-project approach. But it should be evident that it is anything but realistic. The true dimensions of the standardization problem amount to more than $27 billion a year as a result of the combined NATO expenditures for the development, production, and procurement of conventional weapons and equipment.[29] Occasional collaborative efforts scarcely make a dent in this figure.

One reason that such coproduction efforts will continue to have only a limited impact on the overall allied military budgets is that such production consortia are extremely complicated to set up. Because of the complex nature of their negotiations, they always take a long time to put in motion, and once in operation, progress is often halted by interminable negotiations over which country is to do what. One of the traditional bones of contention revolves around the principle of *juste retour* (just return) under which each country wants to get out of the project exactly as much as it puts in. This involves not only finances but technological and industrial advantages as well. When all of this must be accomplished within the confines of a single project, there is constant juggling and balancing of interests in the name of equity, and without fail this drives up the operating costs so that the efficiency of the project suffers. It is generally conceded that the elaborate arrangements made in the name of *juste retour* cause a coproduction scheme to cost from 20 to 30 percent more than a purely national project.[30]

There is nothing wrong with the concept of *juste retour*, which seeks to be equitable, so long as it does not involve inefficiencies and additional costs; but, as we have seen, this is impossible to avoid when it is applied within the confines of a single project.

If *juste retour* is conceived of as a balancing of inputs and rewards that arises from many transactions over an extended period of years, it then becomes feasible. Such an arrangement is possible within a common arms market. Living proof of this is the common market in arms that has existed between the United States and Canada since World War II. Under the terms of the Hyde Park Agreement signed by President Franklin D. Roosevelt and Prime Minister Mackenzie King on April 20, 1941, economic cooperation between the two countries was extended to a North American common market for defense. As this arrangement worked out in practice, military trade between the two became a genuine two-way street. The figures for the years 1958 through 1974, for example, showed that more than $6 billion of arms and military equipment flowed across the U.S.-Canadian border, with about $3 billion going in each direction. There was no effort to balance out this trade on a project or even on an annual basis, but rather to allow for the normal rise and fall of trade common to ordinary commercial goods, seeking only to arrive at a general balance between the two partners within a long time frame. Even though Canada was economically weaker, Canadian industry was allowed to compete freely with U.S. suppliers for defense contracts on a continuing basis. This production for each other's use also effectively standardized military equipment between the two countries. Moreover, both countries agreed to share R & D projects. The United States also agreed not to duplicate any R & D work undertaken in Canada, unless the Defense Department considered it to be vital for U.S. interests. And even then, it was agreed that both parties would promptly consult with each other before the United States proceeded. The result has been an effective sharing of R & D, almost without any duplication of effort. U.S.-Canadian defense industries operate upon a rational, interdependent basis as a result of being merged in a single common arms market.[31]

This very considerable accomplishment is, strangely, little known or appreciated, even in North America. Wider knowledge and understanding about how it operates would help convince skeptics that a similar arrangement is possible across the Atlantic. The U.S.-Canadian precedent could not, however, serve as an exact model for a U.S.-European arrangement because of the differences in the nature of the Canadian and European markets. The Canadians decided that they would procure their major weapons systems from the United States, where they could be produced more economically than in Canada. For its part, Canada has supplied the United States with smaller systems or weapons components. Europe, however, would certainly not want to be cast in the role of a subcontractor to the United States; this would be neither desirable nor necessary. Once Europe had aggregated its separate, small, national arms markets, it would have the size, strength, and resources to become a supplier of large, sophisticated, high unit cost weapons systems and it could trade with the United States on equal terms. Both regions would be producing for a NATO-wide market, with the consequent standardization of NATO military equipment, and their mutual dependence in military trade would foster greater trans-Atlantic political solidarity.

The obstacles to the realization of these goals are fairly well known. Everywhere there are traditional vested interests in national defense industries that have been carefully protected by national economic barriers. The small, uneconomic arms markets in the separate European states are kept limping along only by such artificial protectionist practices. It is now becoming increasingly apparent that the mounting cost of the arms race is making these high cost, inefficient industries a luxury that the Europeans can no longer afford. It is just conceivable that these extravagant economic costs may finally cause the Europeans to adopt a more rational policy, namely, draw together in a European arms market under the direction of a European Arms Procurement Organization.

Even the vast U.S. market has been artificially sheltered behind the "Buy American Act," which has applied to all U.S. NATO allies except Canada. In October 1975 Congress adopted a "sense of the Congress" resolution sponsored by Senators John Culver and Sam Nunn stating that U.S. forces in Europe should have equipment that is standardized or made interoperable with NATO allies to the maximum extent feasible. But Congress deleted the original language of this legislation, which would have authorized the secretary of defense to procure arms and equipment abroad if this would help achieve standardization. This key operational clause was struck down, leaving the "buy American" principle essentially intact. European allies of the United States naturally have long responded to this policy by requiring that, where possible, their own defense establishments buy at home before buying in the United States. Everyone has paid a high price for these arrangements, but especially the United States. If the United States were to buy on a large scale in Europe, it would help to undermine the defensive rationale of the Europeans for buying only in Europe whenever possible, and it would earn Europeans the money with which to buy in the United States. This would greatly expand the U.S. market, which is strong and highly competitive (especially with its emphasis on technology-intensive products) and which does not need protection in the first place. In sum, both sides of the Atlantic must permit open government procurement policies if an Atlantic Common Arms Market is to be established.

A major step in this direction was finally taken when the Congress passed, and on July 14, 1976 the president signed into law, a revised and strengthened Culver-Nunn Amendment. In place of the previous "sense of the Congress" resolution, the new law specifically holds that NATO standardization is a matter of U.S. government policy. Section 802 of the Department of Defense Appropriation Authorization Act, FY 1977, reads in part:

> It is the policy of the United States that equipment procured for the personnel of the Armed Forces of the United States stationed in Europe under the terms of the North Atlantic Treaty should be standardized or at

least interoperable with equipment of other members of the North Atlantic Treaty Organization. In carrying out such policy the Secretary of Defense shall, to the maximum feasible extent, initiate and carry out procurement procedures that provide for the acquisition of equipment which is standardized or interoperable with equipment of other members of the North Atlantic Treaty Organization whenever such equipment is to be used by personnel of the Armed Forces of the United States stationed in Europe under the terms of the North Atlantic Treaty. . . . Whenever the Secretary of Defense determines that it is necessary . . . to procure equipment manufactured outside of the United States, he is authorized to determine . . . that the acquisition of such equipment manufactured in the United States is inconsistent with the public interest.

As Senator Sam Nunn explained: "This section expressly, in law, authorizes the Secretary of Defense to waive the 'Buy American Act' for purposes of carrying out the policy of NATO standardization." From now on, he continued, "the Defense Department is meant to take NATO standardization seriously. . . . In the day to day procurement and acquisition processes . . . NATO standardization should be a major consideration and not just an afterthought." As to the economic impact of open government procurement policies on both sides of the Atlantic operating within a common arms market, Senator Nunn correctly pointed out that:

> If we can get this "two-way street" working between Europe and the United States, both the United States and Europe will benefit economically in terms of business and jobs, since the total market for military equipment of all the NATO Allies is much greater than the individual market any one of the NATO Allies can offer.[32]

The task, then, is to get on with the business of building an Atlantic Common Arms Market. It has been suggested that it could be established by treaty and, like the Treaty of Rome, have a built-in timetable for the achievement of various stages of integration.[33] A treaty commitment would be required, among other reasons, to provide the Europeans with the certainty that once they had restructured their arms industries they could have free access to the U.S. market by making trans-Atlantic arms trade into a genuine two-way street.

Europeans had long complained about trans-Atlantic arms trade being essentially a one-way street, and argued that it would have to be transformed into a two-way street if this relationship were to be put on a healthy basis. This idea finally found expression in official alliance documents in the spring of 1975. On May 7, the defense ministers of the Eurogroup (the European members of NATO, minus France, Iceland, and Portugal) met in London and issued a communique that emphasized the importance they attach to maintaining a strong European technological and industrial base in the defense field and to increasing the degree of standardization in defense equipment. Ministers also agreed on the need to develop a constructive dialogue between Europe and the United States on these matters; this dialogue will be prepared by very wide consultation between all the countries concerned.[34]

Following the London meeting, the British defense minister, Roy Mason, who was then Eurogroup chairman, wrote to U.S. Secretary of Defense James Schlesinger on behalf of his Eurogroup colleagues. He urged that "arms purchases within the Alliance no longer ... be regarded as a one-way street. In placing its own orders the United States ought to take European output into account." At the subsequent gathering of NATO defense ministers in Brussels on May 22–23, 1975, "Mr. Schlesinger was confronted by closed European ranks on this issue and consented to a mention of cooperation as a two-way street in the communique."[35] Consequently, the NATO ministers, meeting in the Defense Planning Committee, declared:

> Ministers heard with interest a statement by Mr. Roy Mason, this year's Chairman of the Eurogroup Ministers, on current activities in the Eurogroup, and agreed to pursue within the appropriate machinery the establishment of a two-way street between Europe and North America in defense equipment procurement, in order to promote a more cost effective use of resources and increase standardization of weapon systems.[36]

These encouraging developments left to one side the anomalous position of France. If Valery Giscard d'Estaing had been president of France in 1966 instead of Charles de Gaulle, the situation today would doubtless be considerably better. It is unlikely that someone like Giscard would have expelled NATO from France and withdrawn French forces from the NATO-integrated command structure. Similarly, when the Eurogroup was formed in 1968, it is conceivable that France would have responded favorably to the invitation of its European allies and taken part in the work of the Eurogroup. But, alas, de Gaulle was in power, and today Giscard must step carefully in dealing with the Gaullist legacy of antipathy toward any aspect of NATO. This policy is still emotionally defended, not only by the Gaullists on the right but also by the French communist party on the left. Their combined strength sharply circumscribes Giscard's area of maneuver. Even from the French point of view, however, logic points to the association of Paris with the Eurogroup effort, as France is the major European producer of military material, and all Europeans agree that there can be no genuine European arms policy without French participation. The problem, then, was to find some acceptable formula for the association of France with the other members of NATO Europe that would not injure French sensibilities.

When the Eurogroup defense ministers met again—this time in The Hague on November 5, 1975—they sought to develop their May initiatives in a manner that would specifically take France into account. The ministers at first reaffirmed that "it is of the greatest importance to increase the interoperability and standardization of military equipment within the Alliance, while maintaining an effective and viable European defense industry." As a means to this end, they decided to

> explore further the potential for extending cooperation in European armaments collaboration in an independent forum open to all European members of the Alliance. They agree in principle to establish a European Defense Procurement Secretariat. With a view to the longer term, Ministers commissioned a study into the tasks which a European Defense Procurement Organization might undertake.[37]

Formally, France has remained a European member of the Atlantic Alliance, since de Gaulle only withdrew from the NATO–integrated command structure, but not from the North Atlantic Treaty. This distinction permitted the Eurogroup ministers to appeal to France to join "an independent forum open to all European members of the Alliance." It was clear that this body would carry neither a NATO nor a Eurogroup label. The success in establishing this "independent forum" would determine the fate of the European Defense Procurement Secretariat, which would service it. What became of these agencies would also heavily influence the possibility of founding a European Defense Procurement Organization, whose creation had long been urged from many quarters but had never before been promised in an official ministerial communique.

At the semiannual NATO ministerial meeting in Brussels in December 1975, British Defense Minister Roy Mason reported that France had given the Eurogroup offer a noncommittal but generally favorable response. German Defense Minister Georg Leber explained that "France is ready to sit down at one table with the other European countries as long as it is not a NATO table. We will not quarrel about the shape of this table. We are interested in the effectiveness and the success of cooperation." It was evident, however, that the process of negotiating with the French had already affected, at least temporarily, the workings of the Eurogroup. Leber added that while further progress had been made toward weapons standardization, "specific decisions were avoided in order not to prejudice the discussions with Paris."[38] Furthermore, Mason indicated that the creation of a European Defense Procurement Secretariat was not discussed, as it was first necessary to establish the "independent forum" that would include France. For their part, the French asserted that they would refuse to participate in the formation of such a European Secretariat because they thought the "independent forum" would not need such institutional support. If the French do prevent the creation of this Secretariat, it would be much more difficult to lay the foundation for a genuine European Defense Procurement Organization in the future.[39] The French also let it be known that the "independent forum" should ideally consist only of France, Britain, and Germany, and just possibly Italy. The smaller Eurogroup members understandably complained that the only time France put on a European face in military matters was when it was trying to sell them something. France further held that the headquarters for the new organization should be in Paris; the Eurogroup members preferred Brussels.[40]

The foreign ministers of the Atlantic alliance, likewise meeting in Brussels in December 1975, also undertook to engage France in discussions on the arms procurement issue. Since France had always retained its seat on the political forum of the North Atlantic Council, the foreign ministers "agreed to form for a limited time an Ad Hoc Committee under the Council to prepare a specific program of action covering the interoperability of military equipment."[41]

The terms of reference for this committee deserve attention. The committee was to have a limited life (a trial period of one year), and its members were instructed to consider the interoperability, but not the standardization, of military equipment. It was the French who insisted upon drawing this distinction and giving the committee only this more limited task. British Foreign Minister James Callaghan, among others, expressed amazement that standardization should thus be cast aside, but this was necessary in order to obtain French participation.[42] France was determined to retain its own distinctive national arms industry to the maximum extent possible, both for its own use and for Third World sales. Its arms, the French argued, could be made interoperable for use by Atlantic alliance countries through various devices that would permit them to be adapted and then adopted by its allies.

This is surely the hard way to do things. Standardization from the ground up is the simplest and cheapest way to increase the efficiency of allied forces. To make nonstandardized arms and equipment interoperable almost always involves considerable expense to create some new and sometimes cumbersome piece of apparatus. Despite these limitations, it was hoped that this initiative on standardization at the reasonably high level of the North Atlantic Council would help bring France back into the allied fold in the areas of arms procurement.[43]

The Eurogroup initiative, meanwhile, was coming to fruition. On February 2, 1976, the ten Eurogroup countries, plus France, met in Rome and created the European Program Group (EPG).[44] Its mission, at least as initially defined, was to concentrate upon the need to develop a strong European technological and industrial base for arms production. The question of the two-way street in arms procurement was not even put on the agenda. This turn of events was again at French insistence. So long as Gaullist paranoia about U.S. "domination" of Europe continues to permeate French thinking, it will be difficult to discuss a rational trans-Atlantic relationship, as, in this view, any tie with the United States automatically implies U.S. domination. The only meaning the French seem capable of imputing to the two-way street is that Europe will be reduced to the role of subcontractor to U.S. arms industries or that there will be an increase in the production of U.S. weapons in Europe under license.[45]

In the case of the European Program Group, it would seem that the convoy will have to move at the speed of the slowest ship. Moreover, there was the fear in some quarters that this movement might be in an anti-NATO direction. NATO Secretary General Joseph Luns publicly expressed his disquiet over this prospect.[46] It is doubtful if the original Eurogroup ten would allow this to happen, but they may be called upon repeatedly to repel French initiatives along this line.

Some of these fears apparently have been dispelled by the subsequent quiet but substantial work that has been accomplished by the European Program Group. During 1976, the EPG met twice at the political level of secretaries of state and twice at the expert level of national armament directors. In order to expedite its work, the EPG was divided into three panels. Panel I, under U.K. chairmanship, compiled a comprehensive schedule of equipment in service as well as replacement plans. This is essential for the comparison of needs and the formulation of joint plans, and has gone beyond anything hitherto produced. Panel II, chaired by Belgium, which built upon the information provided by Panel I, coordinates the work of ten equipment subgroups seeking to formulate collaboration in specific areas. Panel III, under German chairmanship, concerned with the broad problems of defense economics and procedures, set up five subgroups.[47] (It should also be noted that during 1976 Portugal became a member both of the Eurogroup and the EPG.)

As the countries of the EPG succeed in organizing themselves on the European level, it is inevitable that they will have to deal with the trans-Atlantic aspects of the arms trade. The two processes, of course, are intertwined. Only if the European members of the Alliance effectively organize themselves on an all-European basis can they be in a position to work effectively with their trans-Atlantic alliance partners. Section 803 of the revised 1976 Culver-Nunn amendment specifically recognized this problem when it stated:

> It is the sense of the Congress that standardization of weapons and equipment within the North Atlantic Alliance on the basis of a "two-way street" concept of cooperation in defense procurement between Europe and

North America could only work in a realistic sense if the European nations operated on a united and collective basis. Accordingly, the Congress encourages the governments of Europe to accelerate their present efforts to achieve European armaments collaboration among all European members of the Alliance.[48]

For the moment, the Congress has put the ball back in the European court; the Europeans are now at work seeking what will hopefully be a coherent and adequate response.

The challenge of the arms procurement issue in the Atlantic alliance seems clear enough. The human capacity to meet this challenge, however, must still be judged as in doubt. It will require determined political leadership and goodwill on both sides of the Atlantic. Candor requires us to recognize that long-entrenched parochial national interests must be overcome before a rational NATO-wide arms procurement policy can be fully implemented. But it is only through greater rationality in the use of defense funds that the West can reverse the NATO-Warsaw Pact imbalance, which has increasingly been tilting in favor of the Kremlin.

The NATO states unintentionally have yielded the Soviet bloc other advantages as well. These are of a different character, and come under the rubric of self-inflicted wounds.

The bitter conflicts between Greece and Turkey over Cyprus, as well as over mineral exploration of the continental shelf beneath the Aegean Sea, have injured NATO's ability to operate effectively in the eastern Mediterranean. American diplomacy, or lack of it, at the crucial moment before the Turks invaded Cyprus managed to alienate both the Greeks and the Turks. At the time, Secretary Kissinger was preoccupied with his shuttle diplomacy in the Middle East, among other things, so the Cyprus crisis exploded out of control. Even Britain, which had a treaty obligation to ensure the integrity of Cyprus, remained passive, awaiting some U.S. initiative that never came.

Even though the Soviet Union cannot be said to have caused this interalliance strife, it has certainly been the beneficiary of it. Greece has withdrawn from the NATO-integrated command structure and has circumscribed the availability of U.S. military bases in Greece, while Turkey has expelled U.S. military personnel from a series of bases on Turkish soil that were said to be responsible for about one third of the Western intelligence operations over the Soviet Union. While new agreements with both Greece and Turkey have been prepared by the U.S. administration that would go a long way toward repairing the damage, they must be approved not only by Greece and Turkey but by the U.S. Congress. And Congress demands measurable progress over Cyprus, which at the moment appears most unlikely, before appropriating the military assistance funds involved in these agreements.

The cod war between Britain and Iceland came close to providing the Kremlin with another unearned bonus. As the dispute grew nasty and diplomatic relations were broken between Reykjavik and London, Iceland also threatened to withdraw from NATO. This would have involved the loss of the strategically located Keflavik air base that the United States has long used to track Soviet naval movements in the North Atlantic area. The fact that London gave way finally eased the situation, but the dispute clearly revealed the shallow nature of Iceland's commitment to NATO and suggested the trouble that might still lie ahead.

Neither was the Kremlin responsible for the fall of the Caetano dictatorship in Portugal in April 1974. While the Soviet leadership looked on uncertainly from abroad, the events that almost brought the communists to power in Portugal unfolded largely as a result of the internal dynamics of forces at play inside Portugal. During the summer of 1975, the political situation appeared to deteriorate rapidly, and it was an open secret that Secretary Kissinger was prepared to write off the loss of Portugal as irretrievable. Even when Azevedo replaced the fellow-traveling Gonçalves as premier on August 29, the new government had only a precarious hold on power and a communist takeover still seemed clearly conceivable. It was only after the forceful repression of the attempted leftist coup of November 25, 1975 that the tide of communist power was decisively turned and that a new alignment of forces made possible a noncommunist path of development. Even in retrospect, knowing that Portugal has taken this dramatic turn, it still seems like a miracle that the country managed to escape falling into communist hands.

Not that all is now well in Portugal, of course, for the revolutionary upheaval left the country with staggering economic problems, including the worst inflation rate in Europe. In addition, this small country must absorb some 600,000 destitute refugees who have returned from the lost overseas territories. Nevertheless, the current Portuguese government is determined to make a positive contribution to NATO in a way that was not possible when the country's resources were being siphoned abroad in the fruitless attempt to fight colonial wars. Given time and sympathetic aid from its Western allies, Portugal should be able to take its place as a valued partner in the Western comity of nations, not only in NATO but also in the European Community.

The prospect for participation of the communist parties of Italy and France in their governments is quite another matter. Although the circumstances differ in each country, the probability is high in both cases that within the next few years communist ministers will make their appearance in Rome and Paris. The consequences for NATO will be serious in both countries.

Since 1966, France has not had NATO bases on its territory, nor has it participated in the NATO-integrated command structure or taken part in such sensitive NATO agencies as the Nuclear Planning Group. Neverthe-less, in recent years de facto French cooperation with NATO has been increasingly satisfactory, and close informal arrangements have been worked out with NATO authorities in many areas. By way of contrast, the Common Program of the French communist and socialist parties is so bitterly anti-NATO that it is *plus Gaullist que de Gaulle.* Communist ministers in Paris could unravel France's already delicate NATO ties.

Italy, on the other hand, is host to several important NATO installations and headquarters, and has U.S. forces on its territory. It also fully partici-pates in the NATO-integrated command structure and in bodies like the Nuclear Planning Group. Even though Enrico Berlinguer has promised to keep Italy's NATO ties intact with communist participation in government, questions inevitably arise from the NATO point of view as to how trustwor-thy and secure these contacts might be, the Eurocommunists' declarations of independence from Moscow notwithstanding.

In the past, communist ministers have appeared briefly in Iceland and, more recently, in Portugal without causing a break in their NATO bond. Iceland, of course, has no armed forces, while Portugal in fact did not par-ticipate in a meeting of the Nuclear Planning Group, as it was otherwise scheduled to do, during the period in question. But Italy is not Iceland or Portugal, and major precautions would have to be taken to restrict sensitive materials and to limit Italian participation in various NATO bodies. Exactly how this would affect the performance of the Italian mission to NATO or the operation of NATO agencies in Italy is difficult to anticipate in detail, but generally speaking it could only damage the relationship in both direc-tions.

On the other hand, the Italian Communist party (PCI) is a sword that cuts in two directions. So, to a lesser extent, is the French communist party, which has trailed behind the Italians in adopting revisionist doctrine. The Spanish communists must also be mentioned on this account, although at this point it is too early to tell what impact they may have on the Spanish polity. If these parties demonstrate that they mean what they say about abandoning the Soviet model and accepting the rules of pluralist democracy, then there will be a Eurocommunism that, in time, could help undermine Soviet control over the Warsaw Pact states.

Even though for the moment Soviet control appears secure in Eastern Europe, it must not be forgotten that the Kremlin has found it necessary to resort to armed force in East Germany in 1953, in Hungary in 1956, and in Czechoslovakia in 1968 in order to maintain its control. Berlinguer report-edly has said that one of the reasons he approves of Italy's continued mem-bership in NATO is that this provides protection for the unhindered de-velopment of the PCI, in contrast to the perilous situation in which the Dubcek reformers found themselves where membership in the Warsaw Pact permitted the Soviet army to invade Czechoslovakia with impunity and suppress a communist movement the Soviet leadership did not like.

The subversive influence of a revisionist West European communist party that would be beyond the reach of the Soviet army can already be demonstrated. After the Polish riots of June 25, 1976, in protest against the announced increases in the price of food, the Polish dissident historian and former communist, Jacek Kuron, appealed to the Italian communist party to intervene on behalf of the arrested rioters. Berliguer promptly asked Warsaw to show clemency, and many Poles detected a softening effect on the official Polish reactions as a result of the Italian intervention.

Beyond that, the Italian communist party's concept of political organization held an attraction for the revamping of Polish institutions. Polish officials were quick to admit that they were "walking a razor's edge between growing economic pressures on the one hand and the political force of the population on the other." The Polish leadership generally agreed that "the only solution will be to involve the people to a much greater extent than hitherto in the basic decision-making process of the nation." A prominent party leader was quoted to this effect:

> I cannot say what model of socialism we are going to have to create, but one must look for something new and more effective. Maybe even new institutions will be required. Changes in the press of this country, the trade unions, the Party organizations—many things may be necessary to reestablish essential communication between the people and their leaders. And the need is urgent.[49]

The relative calm that has prevailed in the Soviet block since the invasion of Czechoslovakia is really deceptive, since massive discontents and the desire for liberalizing reforms continue to bubble just below the surface. It is scarcely conceivable that the Kremlin can forever impose its kind of socialism in Eastern Europe. Nor can further colonial revolts be ruled out of the question. The Warsaw Pact rests on a Soviet military imperium and represents the last major empire in the world today. At some point in the future, this empire will go the way of all the others.

Meanwhile, the West cannot afford simply to sit idly by and await what may be a very long-term process of disintegration of Soviet power in the East. The balance of forces in Europe, which is already changing progressively in favor of the Kremlin, could shift irretrievably to the West's disadvantage.

The West has many inherent advantages upon which it can draw in the prolonged struggle ahead. Flanking the North Atlantic—the United States and Canada on one side and Western Europe on the other—are the richest, most technologically advanced industrial economies in the world. Together they have sufficient population, endowed with the most sophisticated skills, to accomplish whatever is required to right the balance of forces over the long haul. What is in doubt is the political will. The question of restructuring the defense economies of the Atlantic alliance is, of course, an economic matter, but the basic requirement for the creation of an Atlantic Common Arms Market is political leadership at the highest levels. Similarly, the resolution of the political difficulties and disputes in the Atlantic Community (which have been referred to above as self-inflicted wounds) is also basically a matter of mobilizing the political will necessary to resolve these seemingly intractable problems.

NOTES

1. Secretary of Defense, Donald H. Rumsfeld, *Annual Defense Department Report, FY 1978*, Executive Summary, 1977, p. 25.

2. Secretary of Defense, Donald H. Rumsfeld, *Annual Defense Department Report, FY 1977*, 1976, p. 113.

3. Lothar Ruehl, "MBFR Talks—Review and Prospects," *Europa Archiv*, no. 13, (1977), reprinted in *The German Tribune* (Political Affairs Review), no. 31 (November 20, 1977). These figures only account for ground force personnel, and only in the limited area in central Europe covered by the mutual force reductions negotiations in progress in Vienna. On the NATO side, this includes the territory of the Federal Republic of Germany and the three Benelux countries. On the Warsaw Pact side, this includes the German Democratic Republic, Poland, and Czechoslovakia, but not Hungary, which the West tried in vain to have included in "central Europe." There are about 100,000 Hungarian and 40,000 Soviet troops in Hungary.

4. *White Paper 1975/1976: The Security of the Federal Republic of Germany and the Development of the Federal Armed Forces* (Bonn, 1976), pp. 33–35.

5. Patrick Wall, rapporteur, *Draft General Report on the Security of the Alliance*, Military Committee, North Atlantic Alliance, May 1977, p. 3.

6. *White Paper 1975/1976*, pp. 33–35.

7. Ibid., p. 33.

8. Ibid., p. 35.

9. Wall, Draft General Report, pp. 3–4.

10. U.S., Congress, Senate, Committee on Armed Services, *NATO and the New Soviet Threat*, Report of Senator Sam Nunn and Senator Dewey F. Bartlett, January 24, 1977, pp. 6–16.

11. Wall, *Draft General Report*, p. 4.

12. *White Paper 1975/1976*, p. 32.

13. *Annual Defense Department Report, FY 1978*, pp. 58, 60.

14. Ibid., p. 10 of Executive Summary.

15. Military briefing given to NATO defense ministers, June 10, 1976, *NATO Review*, August 1976, p. 29.

16. *Annual Defense Department Report, FY 1978*, p. 26. The 40 percent figure is arrived at by excluding U.S. retirement costs. This method of calculating, introduced by Secretary Schlesinger, is thought to be more accurate.

17. Thomas A. Callaghan, Jr., *U.S.-European Economic Cooperation in Military and Civil Technology*, 2nd rev. ed. (Washington, D.C.: The Center for Strategic and International Studies, Georgetown University, September 1975), p. 37. The author gladly acknowledges his indebtedness for the general line of his argument to Mr. Callaghan's excellent monograph.

18. U.S., Congress, Senate, Committee on Armed Services, *Department of Defense Appropriations Authorization, FY 1977*, 94th Cong., 2d sess., Report no. 94–878, May 14, 1976, p. 167.

19. Alastair Buchan, "The Implications of a European System for Defense Technology," in *The United States and Europe: Defense, Technology and the Western Alliance* (London: The Institute for Strategic Studies, 1967), p. 4.

20. Richard Burt, "New Weapons Technologies and European Security," *Orbis* (Summer 1975): 514–32, especially 526, and John H. Morse, "New Weapons Technologies: Implications for NATO," *Orbis* (Summer 1975): 497–513.

21. Callaghan, *U.S.-European Economic Cooperation*, pp. 84–85.

22. Secretary of Defense, James R. Schlesinger, *Annual Defense Department Report, FY 1976*, 1975, p. I-5.

23. *Annual Defense Department Report, FY 1978*, pp. 26, 102. The term "military investment" used here includes procurement and facilities.

24. Report of Senator John Culver to the Senate armed Services Committee, June 1975, quoted in Assembly, Western European Union, Document 689, December 1, 1975, Appendix I, p. 16.

25. Gardiner L. Tucker, "Standardization and the Joint Defense," *NATO Review*, January 1975, pp. 11–12.

26. Ibid., p. 12.

27. Jack N. Behrman, *Multinational Production Consortia: Lessons from NATO Experience*, Department of State Publication 8593 (Washington, D.C., 1971), p. 2.

28. Callaghan, *U.S.-European Economic Cooperation*, p. 64.

29. Ibid., p. 64.

30. Ibid., pp. 53–56, 63. See also the entire Behrman monograph, *Multinational Production Consortia*, for a description of the complexities of coproduction projects.

31. Callaghan, *U.S.-European Economic Cooperation*, pp. 57–63.

32. *Congressional Record*, July 1, 1976, pp. S 11322–23.

33. Callaghan, *U.S.-European Economic Cooperation*, p. 117, has offered the following timetable: "An initial three year goal of $2.0 billion of defense procurement orders from one another. A three year goal for harmonizing all defense basic research. An initial three year goal of $4.0 billion of complementary development projects underway on each side of the Atlantic. A four year goal for common logistic support of all common weapons and equipment. A twelve year goal for achieving complete military-industrial interdependence in the development, production and support of general purpose forces."

34. Eurogroup Communique, May 7, 1975, *NATO Review*, no. 3 (June 1975): 30–31.

35. Carl A. Ehrhardt, "Lessons of the Brussels NATO Summit," *Aussenpolitik* (English ed.), no. 3 (1975): 275.

36. Defense Planning Committee Communique, May 22–23, 1975, *NATO Review*, no. 3 (June 1975): 28. This idea was reaffirmed in the Ministerial Guidance of the same date issued by the same body: "Cooperation in the development and production of military equipment is a particular form of standardization which can exploit the benefits of scale and reduce unit costs. Cooperation between North America and Europe in this field should become a two-way street" (ibid., p. 30).

37. Eurogroup Communique, November 5, 1975, *Atlantic News*, no. 774 (November 7, 1975): 1.

38. *Relay from Bonn*, German Information Center, New York, December 9, 1975, p. 1.

39. *Atlantic News*, no. 782 (December 8, 1975): no. 783 (December 10, 1975): 1; no. 789 (December 24, 1975): 4.

40. "Will France Sneak Back into Europe's Defense Fold?" *The Economist*, December 13, 1975, p. 39.

41. North Atlantic Council Final Communique, December 11–12, 1975, *NATO Review*, no. 1 (February 1976): 24.

42. *Atlantic News*, no. 785 (December 12, 1975): 2.

43. For the composition and tasks of the ad hoc committee, see *Atlantic News*, no. 795 (January 24, 1976): 4; no. 807 (March 5, 1976): 1–2.

44. On the formation of the European Program Group, see *Atlantic News*, no. 798 (February 4, 1976): 1; no. 799 (February 6, 1976): 1–2.

45. *Atlantic News*, no. 789 (December 24, 1975): 4; no. 793 (January 16, 1976): 1.

46. Secretary General Luns was "asked what he thought about the 'independent body' proposed to France by the Eurogroup," following a speech to the Assembly of Western European Union on December 1, 1975. To this Luns replied that "if the honorable member were to reread what I have just said, he would realize that the Secretary General expressed a certain reservation regarding this development" (*Europe Documents*, no. 875 [December 18, 1975]: 1). Luns argued that the deliberations of this proposed group might develop tactical concepts and standardization procedures that would introduce an element of division within NATO, which should remain the principal forum for dealing with political and security matters.

47. Peter Dankert, rapporteur, *A European Armaments Policy*, Committee on Defense Questions and Armaments, Assembly of Western European Union, Document 738, May 10, 1977, p. 5.

48. The key sentence here is taken almost verbatim from the congressional testimony of the West German parliamentarian, Carl Damm, chairman of the Subcommittee on European Defense Cooperation of the Military Committee, North Atlantic Assembly, who said that "the 'two-way street' concept could only work in a realistic sense if the European nations operated on a united and collective basis." U.S., Congress, Senate, *Hearings Before the Subcommittee on Research and Development and the Subcommittee on Manpower and Personnel of the Committee on Armed Services*, 94th Cong., 2d sess., March 31, 1976, p. 9.

49. Malcolm W. Browne, *New York Times*, August 9 and 10, 1976.

8 Detente Politics and the U.S.-USSR Military Balance

Jacob W. Kipp

Beginning in the wake of the Helsinki Conference, and with growing intensity in the early months of 1976, U.S. politicians began to call for a reassessment of detente, as a program and as a policy. Detente became something of an orphan. It was said that detente could not be a "one-way street,"[1] that it must involve more than mere "atmospherics,"[2] that it required a "color of morality."[3] In April 1976, former President Gerald Ford declared the word detente "inoperative," and proclaimed that the United States would pursue a policy of "peace through strength."[4] (Later explanatory statements from the White House left one with the impression that this did not mean a substantive shift in policy, however.[5]) Most analysts agree that Soviet assistance to the Popular Movement for the Liberation of Angola (MPLA) served as the final increment in the disillusionment with detente of a sizable portion of the U.S. political elite. Some have argued that the Soviet leaders grossly miscalculated in the case of Angola, where their "adventurist" policies led to a serious deterioration of relations between the superpowers.[6]

In such a context, the policy of detente and its impact on the U.S.-Soviet military balance takes an added significance. What has been the impact of detente on the U.S.-USSR military balance and arms control negotiations? The purpose of this chapter is to assess and compare Soviet and U.S. views of detente, and to trace the implications of these views for U.S. and Soviet political strategies and arms control negotiations.

From the beginnings of the cold war, and with growing intensity throughout the 1950s and early 1960s, the competition between the United States and the Soviet Union became increasingly militarized. By the mid-1950s, the technological revolution in military affairs had created what statesmen in both nations recognized as a balance of thermonuclear terror. In the last decade, coexistence or detente has served as the foundation for a search by U.S. and Soviet policy makers for an arms control policy that would replace this ominous balance of terror with a more stable, more secure, and less costly strategic weapons posture. The two powers concluded a five-year strategic arms agreement in Moscow in 1972 to further this purpose, and have continued this search through the Vladivostok accords of 1974 and the SALT II negotiations.*

While the 1972 SALT I agreement did not reduce the strategic forces of either power, it did provide a structure for superpower competition in this area and contributed to weapons procurement programs that emphasized technical modernization of existing forces and the exploration of highly sophisticated innovations in research and development. The processes of weapons procurement and research and development in both countries have now reached, or are approaching, a new threshold where the momentum of procurement requirements and the persisting anxiety that technological developments may make strategic superiority a meaningful political instrument coalesce as an imperative for the radical modernization of such strategic systems. This delicate stage, when both powers must decide whether to pursue the objectives of strategic arms control and the demilitarization of their competition or to seek advantage in some form of strategic nuclear superiority, has arrived—just as detente has come under broad and systematic attack in the United States.

Given the importance of detente in defining or delineating a broad range of relations between the superpowers, an assessment and comparison of U.S. and Soviet leaders' definitions of detente deserve our initial attention.

As understood by U.S. policy makers, both opponents and supporters, detente means placing "a lock on the trigger of a weapon." In diplomatic use, it implies a guarded truce between adversaries, in which neither party lays down its arms—for fear of enemy treachery—while attempting to negotiate a resolution of their conflicts. In contemporary use, it has come to mean a "relaxation of tensions" in the context of the mutual possession of weapons of mass destruction. Western statesmen frequently have linked two additional concepts to this basic notion of detente: indivisibility and international stability. Indivisibility implies that detente must apply to *all* aspects of relations between the appropriate powers—military, diplomatic, economic, social, and ideological. International stability implies the maintenance of peace and the status quo. This emphasis on globalism and stability has been a recurring element of U.S. liberal ideology since at least the Wilsonian era. U.S. statesmen have insisted on viewing the world in terms of equilibria as the natural condition of all socioeconomic and politicodiplomatic relations.[7] Threats to peace and stability are assumed to stem from revolutionary chaos and disorder.

---

*With the exception of the limitations on antiballistic missile (ABM) deployment, these agreements have attempted to place ceilings upon strategic delivery vehicles rather than reduce the numbers possessed by either power. Between 1970 and 1977, the stockpile of U.S. strategic weapons increased from 4,000 to 8,500 and from 1,800 to 4,000 for the Soviet Union.

In addition to these elements common to the definition of detente, there is another and very confusing factor. This is the implicit assumption of many U.S. policy makers that the process of detente must, or should, lead to entente (cooperative relations between the superpowers as allied or associated powers pursuing a common goal).[8] *Au fond*, such an interpretation of detente runs directly counter to Soviet views, or at least to one goal of their cooperative: competitive policy of coexistence.

The Soviet leaders rarely use the word detente, preferring instead the three-word Russian phrase *razriadka mezhdunarodnoi napriazhennosti* (relaxation of international tension). They trace the roots of the concept back to Lenin's dicta on the conduct of relations between socialist and nonsocialist states.[9] In the 1950s, N. S. Khrushchev popularized this view under the slogan of "peaceful coexistence." As Khrushchev used the term, it implied a recognition on Moscow's part that thermonuclear war was too destructive to be a catalyst for the world revolutionary process, and that the Soviet Union had to find a more pragmatic and innovative approach to the extension of socialism while protecting the security of the USSR.

Both peaceful coexistence and relaxation of international tensions explicitly postulate "the renunciation of war as an instrument for settling international disputes," yet neither term implies any self-limitation by the USSR of its involvement in other forms of conflict and struggle. Avoidance of nuclear war does not mean an ideological truce or an end of support for wars of national liberation. Long before detente became a household word in the United States, Moscow's official position was that

> Peaceful coexistence does not mean giving up the national liberation movement; on the contrary, it creates the most favorable conditions for it. Moreover, . . . peaceful coexistence is conducted against imperialism—the source of military danger.[10]

Just as the Soviet- and Cuban-supported MPLA forces were gaining control in Angola, General Secretary Leonid Brezhnev reaffirmed this point at the Twenty-fifth Congress of the CPSU, stressing that detente could not be equated with the maintenance of the status quo:

> For it is quite clear that detente and peaceful coexistence are concerned with inter-state relations. This means primarily that quarrels and conflicts between states should not be decided by war, use of force or the threat of force. Relaxation of tensions does not in the slightest abolish, and cannot abolish or change the laws of class struggle.[11]

Unequivocally, the right to give aid to indigenous liberation movements as a means of changing the status quo in the Third World remains an integral part of Soviet doctrine. Hence, in the Soviet view, detente neither precludes aid to revolutionary movements that attack Western interests or undermine Western-backed regimes nor prevents the use of force through wars by proxy. What Western observers consider an irreconcilable contradiction in the Soviet view of detente, the Soviet leaders view as the logical and ideologically correct application of the dialectic to the current correlation of forces in the world arena.[12]

Thus, to the Soviet Union and the United States, detente means two quite different things. Yet there remains a core concept upon which both adversaries are agreed: that all-out nuclear war between the superpowers would entail such destruction as to make it a dubious proposition for either side—attacker or defender, victor or vanquished (if such terms have any meaning in this context).

Any assessment of detente therefore should include consideration of its implications for the military, and especially the strategic, balance between the United States and the Soviet Union. Indeed, Secretary of State Henry Kissinger stressed arms control as the keystone of detente: "We must maintain our military strength. But we have an obligation, in our own interest as well as the world's, to work with other nations to control both the growth and the spread of nuclear weapons."[13]

Soviet spokesmen share this emphasis. Georgi Arbatov, the director of S. Sh. A. (Institute for the Study of the USA and Canada), later echoed Kissinger's sentiments in *Pravda*. Supporting the thesis developed by Brezhnev at the Twenty-fifth Party Congress that detente represented a basic shift in the international balance between the two nations, he stressed the political significance of U.S.-Soviet bilateral agreements such as "The Basic Principles of Relations" and "The Agreement on the Prevention of Nuclear War" of mid-1972:

> Certain progress has been achieved in the practical solution of a number of specific problems of Soviet-American relations. Among them, one should note above all the first steps towards the limitation of strategic arms. Although they have not been able to stop the arms race, one cannot underestimate the importance of the agreements concluded in this field.[14]

Brezhnev himself emphasized "reducing the danger of another world war and in consolidating peace"[15] as the most important fruit of improved U.S.-Soviet relations. Both Soviet and U.S. policy makers see arms control and the prevention of nuclear war as the basic aspects of detente.

During the last decade and a half, the superpowers have concluded a series of formal agreements aimed at structuring their strategic nuclear weapons posture and managing their military competition in a number of areas.[16] Such agreements include the Moscow-Washington hotline and the partial test-ban treaty of 1963, the nuclear nonproliferation treaty of 1969, the strategic arms limitation agreement and lean on biological warfare of 1972, and the Vladivostok Accords of 1974. Negotiations continue on further arms control agreements covering the central European front between NATO and the Warsaw Pact and in the area of strategic arms. The debate accompanying the negotiations of these agreements and attempts to implement the policy of detente have serious implications for U.S. and Soviet policies and future arms control efforts.

Western analyses of these agreements, especially SALT I and Vladivostok, have been almost exclusively technical and primarily concerned with the contribution of such agreements to long-term strategic nuclear stability.[17] Thus, the debate has been over the degree to which these agreements may have enhanced the Soviet posture vis-à-vis the United States, and the extent to which they have made, or will make, possible the achievement by the USSR (in the near or distant future, depending upon the analyst) of a strategic advantage that could, under certain circumstances, be manipulated for political advantage in an area of vital interest to the United States.[18]

While this debate in the United States has been ferocious, it has only tangentially touched the heart of the matter—what one might call the "politics of detente in their domestic setting." The various interpretations of the technical data on the strategic and general military balances reflect their authors' ideological assumptions, not only about Soviet intentions but also about the definition of vital U.S. interests and the role of military power in U.S. relations with the external world. Broadly speaking, these positions break down into three general views: alarmist, realist, and complacent. In U.S. politics, these positions find their most conspicious, if not most articulate, expression in the debates over the U.S. defense budget, particularly about the authorization of new or the expansion of old weapons-procurement programs, that is, the B-1 bomber, cruise missiles, the Trident submarine, or the land mobile launch system (MXICBM).[19]

Each of these positions on the strategic-military balance comes in varying degrees of respectability, hues, and intensities; yet within each position, the similarities of the definitions of vital U.S. interests, the role of military power, and the nature of Soviet intentions are great enough to justify an attribution of commonality. In the case of the alarmists, the assumptions on the role of military power and Soviet intentions go hand-in-hand: Total military superiority is the only security upon which Americans can rely to deter a hostile and adventurist Soviet Union. U.S. interests are assumed to be global, and the national response to any threat should be overwhelming—whether the region in question is Western Europe, the Middle East, Asia, or Africa.[20] The United States cannot, according to this position, be secure until it possesses absolute superiority. Since such strength in conventional forces seems beyond the realm of possibility, the alarmists emphasize the need for overwhelming power in the strategic nuclear field and the will to use it in diplomatic confrontations or even limited nuclear war situations.[21] Former Ambassador Foy Kohler set forth the alarmist position most graphically when he asserted that the present military situation is dangerous because "the U.S. does not have an assured total destruction capability against the Soviet Union."[22]

In every area of the globe where U.S. interests appear to be threatened, whether by indigenous or Soviet-supported movements, the alarmists attribute the primary component of that threat to Soviet military power. The need to counter such threats assumes the dimensions of a crusade demanding the galvanization of U.S. national will.[23] Likewise, the alarmists see the U.S. defense posture as deteriorating vis-à-vis the Soviet Union's, or even as grossly inferior. Whether it be naval forces, civil defense, conventional forces in Europe, the strategic triad (bombers, ICBMs, and SLBMs), the United States is pictured as threatened by growing Soviet military power.[24] The alarmists attribute the "deterioration" of the U.S. defense posture to the "illusions" of detente and call for greater "realism."[25]

The complacent position, using much of the same data on the U.S.-USSR military balance, "proves" with equal conclusiveness that the United States has an overwhelming advantage in each of the above-named areas. Where the alarmists cite throw-weight or the number of launchers to make a case for U.S. inferiority in strategic arms, the complacents look at the total number of warheads and the technical superiorities of U.S. weapons systems to conclude that "the U.S. advantage has been increasing in recent years."[26] In general, the complacent position regards the present concern over the U.S.-Soviet military balance as "an artificial crisis of American security."[27] Such a position narrowly defines U.S. interests, and emphasizes the possibility of mutual agreements with the Soviet Union—particularly those that might contribute to the reduction of defense spending and the investment of resultant savings in domestic social-welfare programs.[28]

The view that mark the realists' position in this debate is their recognition and acceptance of political competition as the underlying characteristic of U.S.-Soviet relations. The realists accept basic asymmetries in the two superpowers' defense postures as historically and socially conditioned. George Kennan asserts that this approach is marked by "a greater steadiness and realism of vision before the phenomenon of Soviet power."[29] While rejecting the immediate prospect of an entente with the Soviet Union, this position calls for a deemphasis of an explicit military threat. Indeed, it makes more effective control of the U.S. military-industrial complex and the lessening of the scope and intensity of the arms race primary national policy objectives.

Unlike either the alarmist or the complacent position, the realists view the military balance in terms of more modest claims with regard to both U.S. military needs and the extent of its vital global interests. This position takes into account both quantitative and qualitative asymmetries in military power, and analyzes these in direct relation to immediate threats to the national interest. This attention to both means and ends brings the realists to a concern for both the domestic consequences of the arms race and to a greater emphasis on the need for improvement of U.S. relations with vital allies.[30] To the realists, three types of threats impinge upon U.S. interests and objectives in ways that relate directly to the U.S.-Soviet military balance: the strategic nuclear threat to the United States, challenges to vital U.S. oceanic communications, and direct confrontations between U.S.-allied and Soviet-allied conventional forces in Europe and northern Asia.[31]

In analyzing these threats, the realist position takes into account not only Soviet capabilities but also intentions. Thus, when evaluating Soviet conventional forces, the problem becomes less one of achieving a bilateral balance between U.S.-NATO and USSR-Warsaw Treaty Organization forces than of achieving a global balance. While alarmists cite the growing strength of such Soviet forces vis-à-vis those of the West, the realists also include the expansion of the Chinese People's Republic's armed forces over the last five years as a potential threat to the USSR.[32] Similar differences in analysis between the alarmist and realist positions can be seen in the areas of naval and strategic forces.[33] Basically, the realists' position rejects out of hand the political acceptability or military feasibility of limited nuclear war, as advocated by former Secretary of Defense James Scheslinger or Paul Nitze.[34] Instead, it emphasizes the political and ideological nature of the Soviet challenge, and suggests that U.S. force postures should reflect this. In this view, military strength is not the end, but only one instrument of national policy.

In practical terms, this emphasis on the military aspects of the Soviet challenge has two noteworthy consequences for the United States. On the one hand, this view calls for greater efficiency in the use of defense allocations to reduce what has been a progressively increasing cost for each unit of force. On the other hand, it points up the need for continuing political initiatives to enhance further and to deepen the process of detente. Barry Blechman and Edward Fried emphasize the need for both agreements and cost-effective U.S. defense allocations:

> A steady U.S. course in maintaining strategic parity with the USSR and in helping to maintain a military balance in Europe and Northeast Asia provides at least the hope of reaching more extensive arms-control agreements with Moscow and of creating an international environment in which military forces can be further reduced at acceptable risk to the general peace. Such additional savings, however, are potential rather than actual; attempting to draw upon them in advance would prevent their realization.
>
> Meanwhile, this wealthy and productive nation can afford the armed forces it needs. To aim at less would be foolhardy. But to spend more, wastefully, could prove to be equally dangerous in the end.[35]

The predominant U.S. views on the U.S.-Soviet military balance—the alarmist, the complacent, and the realist—not only reflect very different assumptions and perceptions of U.S. interest but are as one in their divergence from the Soviet view. Only the realists seem to have any awareness of the political ramifications of detente in a global context, and even they do not explicitly link detente, the military balance, and continuing ideological struggle into a systematic whole as do the Soviet leaders.

The current leadership of the CPSU, the heirs of Lenin, stress the paramount importance of the political element in all forms of struggle. They accept von Clausewitz's dictum that "war is politics continued by other means," and recognize that the most sophisticated use of force lies in its implicit threat as part of a coordinated national strategy.[36] War, the threat of war, or a military presence are only instruments for the achievement of definite political objectives. As Lenin noted in his comments on von Clausewitz's *On War*,

> To subordinate the political point of view to the military is senseless, since politics gave birth to war. Politics are the rationale; war is only the tool and not the reverse. Therefore, it remains only to subordinate the military point of view to the political.[37]

Despite the overwhelming impact of the nuclear-rocket revolution in military and political strategy, both Soviet political and military leaders share this view of military power as a means to a political end. Admiral Sergei Gorshkov's series of articles in *Naval Digest* devoted primary attention to the utility of naval forces in peace as well as war in promoting Soviet state interests, protecting the socialist commonwealth, and in aiding the world revolutionary process.[38] Similarly, Rear Admiral K. A. Stalbo examined the role of Soviet forces in "deterring" imperialistic adventure and thereby imposing upon the United States a series of "zigzags" in the U.S. "grand strategy."[39] The Soviet armed forces serve the USSR's political goals—and detente or relaxation of international tensions is part of that national strategy.

This primacy of political over the military in matters of grand strategy does not mean that the Soviet leaders have imposed *razriadka* unilaterally upon the military, or that such a course has meant any curtailment of the military's claims upon national wealth. Indeed, the available evidence suggests that the military's share of the gross national product has remained in the area of 11 to 13 percent over the last decade.[40] Based upon Soviet weapons procurement trends during this period, it appears that the military leadership and those industrial managers close to them (the USSR's military-industrial complex) seem to have won important budgetary concessions that benefited all services. For example, the number of ICBMs deployed by the Strategic Rocket Forces has risen from 270 in 1965 to 1,527 in 1976.* The

---

*All figures for weapons procurement and deployment used here for the period 1965–76 are taken from *The Military Balance*.

number of submarine launched-ballistic missile systems (SLBMs) increased from 120 to 845 in the same period. Even the Air Defense Command (PVO *strany*), which had to curtail its ABM program, has added new aircraft and SAMs to its inventory. The Soviet army has received more modern equipment, including the new T-72 battle tank.

In addition to these quantitative gains, the pace of Soviet research and development programs has been rapid. The Soviet Union is now well into third- and fourth-generations of intercontinental ballistic missiles (ICBM) and SLBM systems.[41] Soviet commanders and military theorists have made technical modernization the keystone of their defense posture, and demand that "it must be on a level of the advanced achievements of national and world science and technology in order to secure the maximum effectiveness of military production and the adaptation of fighting technology."[42]

For what would appear to be chiefly domestic reasons (relating to the CPSU's intensification of "struggle on the ideological front"), the Soviet leaders have accelerated what William Odom has termed the "militarization of Soviet society," or the increasing mobilization of the population through military and paramilitary institutions, that is, mass conscription; the Voluntary Society for the Assistance to the Army, Air Force, and Navy (DOSAAF); educational institutions, and the All-Union civil defense program. Odom correctly stresses the historical sources of this phenomenon and its relationship to Marxist-Leninist ideology.[43] He does not, however, suggest that this trend has meant that the USSR has become more warlike, aggressive, or adventurist.[44] If Western analysts find such developments troubling, it is not because the Soviet leaders have engaged in a conspiracy to conceal them in broad outline.[45] Neither "the militarization of Soviet society" nor the technical modernization of the Soviet armed forces suddenly appeared during the era of detente, but have their roots in the 1920s.

For those who conclude that the only possible U.S. response to such trends are similar developments at home, especially with regard to the further militarization of civilian society, a reflective reading of Quincy Wright's warnings on a "peace of terror" might be well in order:

> Thus an arms race, if it does not end in nuclear war, will end either in the destruction of free democracies by subversive intervention and propaganda, or in the voluntary abandonment of their institutions by the democracies so that they can compete in power-building on a more even basis.[46]

For the Soviet Union, detente is neither a series of technical agreements about weapons sy tems nor a mere short-range tactic. On the contrary, it is a well-conducted and coordinated political offensive aimed at enhancing both the security and power of the Soviet regime. Ideologically, it serves to strengthen Soviet global prestige by confirming its great power status. At the same time, it increases Soviet security in the nuclear era. The intensity of the U.S. national security debate over detente confirms this advantage as it reveals the political cleavages within U.S. society on the issue and the lack of support for those seeking a more threatening posture or advocating more resolute behavior in general.[47]

The Soviet Union foresees great potential dividends from detente: trade with the United States for the technological modernization of the national economy; greater political stability in Eastern Europe as a result of the West's de jure acceptance of the legitimacy of Soviet-supported regimes and interests in various areas; and the isolation of Moscow's chief ideological rival, the People's Republic of China (PRC). Avoidance of war remains the keystone of its "peace program." General Secretary Brezhnev made this point explicit in his address to the Twenty-fifth Party Congress in February 1976:

> Struggle to consolidate the principles of peaceful coexistence, to assure lasting peace, to reduce, and in a longer term to eliminate, the danger of another world war has been and remains, the main element of our policy towards the capitalist states. It may be noted that considerable progress has been achieved in the past five years. The passage from cold war, from explosive confrontation of the two worlds, to detente was primarily connected with changes in the correlation of world forces. But much effort was required for people—especially those responsible for the policy of states—to become accustomed to the thought that not brinkmanship but negotiation of disputed questions, not confrontation but peaceful cooperation, is the natural state of things.[48]

From the Soviet perspective, detente has given the USSR an instrument to facilitate negotiation of agreements under advantageous conditions with the major capitalist powers while reducing the "danger of nuclear war."[49]

On the subject of the U.S.-USSR military balance, the Soviet leadership has continued its peace offensive. At the strategic level, Brezhnev proposed "coming to terms on banning the development of new, still more destructive weapons systems, in particular the new Trident submarines carrying ballistic missiles and the new strategic B-1 bomber in the United States and similar systems in the USSR."[50] In Europe, the general secretary proposed that the Mutual and Balanced Force Reduction (MBFR) talks in Vienna examine a proposal for a U.S.-Soviet reduction of forces during 1977 in order to break the negotiating deadlock.[51] Both these proposals were presented in a fashion to appeal to Western opinion. In the case of strategic arms, Brezhnev mentioned not only the lowering of the threat of war but potential budgetary savings and the social programs that could be funded with those savings. In discussing the MBFR proposal, he presented his position as one of preserving the equilibrium in central Europe.[52] (In both cases, the Soviet leader addressed his appeal to the realist and complacent elements in Western opinion.)

Brezhnev returned to this theme at the 1976 Conference of European Communist and Workers' Parties in Berlin. Stressing the growing economic, political, and moral crises of capitalism and the favorable (to the USSR) correlation of international forces, he pressed his campaign to "strengthen the peace and security of European nations." For Brezhnev, detente is clearly viewed as a well-defined, long-term strategy that offers great gains with minimum risk:

> The success of the relaxation of international tensions as a policy has advanced and strengthened the forces of peace and progress and has raised their authority and influence among the masses. It has shown that validity of the positions taken by realistic representatives of the ruling circles of bourgeois countries. But it has incited and activated the forces of reaction and militarism who would like to pull Europe and the whole world back into the times of "cold war" and the balancing act on the edge of nuclear catastrophe. It has startled those who profit from the production of weapons of death and destruction, who cannot think up for themselves any other cause except the kindling of "crusades" against the countries of socialism, against communists, or, as the Maoist leaders of China do, to call openly for "preparations for a new war" on the calculation that they will elicit profit for themselves by bringing other states and peoples into conflict.
>
> The opposition of these diverse forces to detente takes different forms. However, the chief is this striving to stimulate even more the arms race that has already reached unprecedented scale.[53]

After a lengthy discourse on the absence of a "Soviet threat" to West European security and the balance of conventional forces on the central European front, Brezhnev reiterated his call for the mutual renunciation of "new and even more destructive types of weapons" by the United States and the Soviet Union.[54] Brezhnev directly related detente and arms control to the advance of progressive and "peace-loving" forces in the West. Indeed, the general secretary of the CPSU wasted no opportunity to try to convince West European communist parties that they were immediate and direct beneficiaries of the Soviet peace offensive.[55]

Soviet assessments of the impact of detente on the U.S. presidential elections and arms control negotiations deserve attention. Moscow clearly recognizes the nature of the foreign policy debate in the United States, and is fully aware that the debate over detente and the military balance is not interparty but intraparty.[56] In 1976, detente became an ideological football reflecting divergent perspectives on the immediate past and future policies within the U.S. "ruling elite," that is, it is viewed either as an explanation for a series of international setbacks in Southeast Asia and Angola or as the basis for a realistic assessment of relations with the Soviet Union in an era when the United States must, and should, renounce its role as global policeman. Since arms control, especially strategic arms limitation, lies at the very heart of detente, it has become the focal point of U.S. debate.[57]

As the U.S. debate about the merits of detente and the appropriate technical response to maintain the strategic-military balance continued, the Soviet leaders conducted their political offensive in a near vacuum. No manifestation of national will emerged during the 1976 election campaign to define national policy. On one hand, detente was not unambiguously declared to be a long-term policy reflecting U.S. interests; on the other hand, no conclusive argument was offered that detente had undermined U.S. military security or that of its allies. Unfortunately, this ambiguous position seriously weakened the U.S. political position, as the national leadership in the midst of an electoral campaign lacked both the will and vision to seize the political initiative and use detente to improve clearly defined U.S. interests and world security.

The Soviet assessment of detente as a political issue in both the primary campaigns and the general election proved rather sophisticated. They understood that during the primaries President Ford underwent a serious challenge from Governor Ronald Reagan, who challenged the wisdom of detente and condemned the administration for its forfeiture of strategic superiority. While President Ford survived this attack, the Republican party's platform included a stinging refutation of the Nixon-Kissinger policy of detente with the USSR and the SALT I agreement. Ford went into the 1976 campaign with an uneasy alliance between the alarmists and realists in his own party. On the Democratic side, candidate Jimmy Carter emerged from the primaries with a united party, but one in which the conflicts over detente and arms control had hardly been addressed or resolved. Senator Henry Jackson, Zbigniew Brzezinski, Barry Blechman, Averell Harriman, and George Ball not only could support the nominee but were considered to be important advisers to the candidate on foreign policy issues. This support of alarmists, realists, and complacents within the Democratic party created a consensus for electoral victory, but it did not bring into focus any clear stand by the president-elect on detente or arms control.

Carter's victory in November made necessary the formation of a definite policy by January 1977. At that time, President Carter announced his first important appointments in the area of national security administration: Cyrus Vance for secretary of state, Harold Brown for secretary of defense, Theodore Sorenson as director of the Central Intelligence Agency, Paul Warnke for director of the Arms Control and Disarmament Agency, and

Zbigniew Brzezinski as national security advisor to the president. Both Vance and Brown used their confirmation hearings before the Senate to affirm that they were realists. Vance stated that the administration would pursue strategic arms control "aggressively."[58] Brown termed the military balance between the United States and the Soviet Union as one of "essential parity."[59] Conflicts over the Sorenson and Warnke nominations underscored the continuing ideological conflicts over detente with which the Carter administration had to deal. While the general thrust of the administration's policies affirmed a realist's assessment of detente and strategic arms control during its first months in office, it had to confront serious challenges from the alarmists.

In addition to opposition to the Warnke and Sorenson appointments, the Carter administration faced pressure from the alarmists over U.S. national intelligence estimates. Responding to charges that the Central Intelligence Agency persistently had underestimated the Soviet military threat, the Ford administration had authorized the formation of "Team B" (under the chairmanship of Richard Pipes) to compose its own estimates on the basis of raw intelligence data. This group concluded that since 1968 the USSR had carried out a modernization of its conventional and nuclear forces that made it possible for the USSR to achieve strategic superiority over the United States.[60] Others joined in the chorus on a nonpartisan basis. The former chief of USAF intelligence, Major General George J. Keegan, Jr. (USAF, Retired), charged that the USSR had achieved superiority, and that the national security estimates that stressed parity were wishful thinking.[61] The Committee on the Present Danger, chaired by Eugene V. Rostow, called for increased defense spending and negotiations with the Soviet leaders from a position of strength. While the Committee on the Present Danger did not explicitly reject attempts to achieve arms control, it did suggest that the United States embark upon weapons development and procurement programs that would counter the Soviet Union's modernization efforts and provide U.S. negotiators with the necessary bargaining leverage to make it possible "to negotiate hardheaded and verifiable agreements to control and reduce armaments."[62] Such comments from the alarmist side did not go unanswered. The realists formed their own organization, the American Committee on U.S.-Soviet Relations, which pressed for the negotiation of an agreement without reference to a cardinal modernization of U.S. arms.[63]

The Carter administration thus began its dealings with the USSR without the backing of any sort of national consensus on detente or SALT agreements. The president apparently made the creation of such support a priority foreign policy objective. From the first days of the new administration, President Carter took the initiative in the ideological struggle with the Soviet Union. His stand on human rights not only engendered broad support for U.S. foreign policy abroad but appealed to diverse groups in the United

States. Alarmists were pleased because such a stance signified Washington's willingness to confront the Soviet Union at one of its weakest and most embarrassing points. Both realists and complacents (primarily in the liberal wing of U.S. politics) found this emphasis upon human dignity well within their own ideological values. Since a moral posture does not involve hard questions of action or immediate costs, the president's stance on human rights satisfied many and gave the administration a brief opportunity to seek its own modus vivendi with the Soviet Union with a domestic consensus and no serious challenges to the overall thrust of its politics.

In the area of arms control, the Carter administration vowed to pursue a SALT II agreement "aggressively."[64] What this meant became apparent during the U.S.-USSR discussions in Moscow. At that time, Secretary of State Cyrus Vance offered two alternative proposals. The first of these, a comprehensive plan, called for substantial reductions in strategic nuclear delivery systems and in the number of MIRV (multiple independently targeted reentry vehicle) ballistic missiles. While the exact figures in the ceilings were negotiable, the administration affirmed that the target levels for delivery vehicles and MIRV strategic ballistic missiles were about 10 percent below those set at Vladivostok in 1974, or 2,400 and 1,320, respectively. In addition, the comprehensive plan called for reductions in the number of large ballistic missiles with MIRV capabilities; a moratorium on ICBM launcher construction; a ban on silo and ICBM modifications; limitations on test firings; a ban on the development, testing, and deployment of new ICBMs and mobile ICBM launchers; a proscription on cruise missiles with a range greater than 300 miles; and a system of checks to guarantee that the Soviet Backfire bomber could not become an effective intercontinental nuclear delivery system.[65] After Washington's long silence on substantive SALT negotiations, the comprehensive proposal represented a strong U.S. initiative, both in its overall terms and in its specific concern for U.S. interests.

Since the Carter administration did not anticipate an immediate Soviet acceptance of the total U.S. package in this round of SALT negotiations, Vance went to Moscow prepared to offer a second plan: a deferral proposal that called for an acceptance of the levels of strategic delivery systems and MIRVed vehicles negotiated at Vladivostok, with no consideration given to the development of either the cruise missile or the Backfire bomber.[66]

Both the comprehensive and deferral proposals were, it seems, rather consciously designed to appeal to a broad spectrum of U.S. domestic opinion. The first gave both realists and complacents the hope that the United States favored real reductions, as opposed to ceilings, in strategic delivery systems, and thus potential long-term savings in the defense budget. The alarmists were offered a program that challenged what they considered to be the most serious Soviet advantages in strategic weapons systems—ICBM

development. Neither proposal called for any U.S. cutback in force modernization—the Trident, B-1, or cruise missile programs. The Soviet Union's
acceptance of the deferral proposal would have given the administration a
quick agreement while allowing existing weapons procurement programs to
continue and even expand. Such a posture appealed to the administration on
three levels. It would, it was hoped, create the climate for an agreement,
which the administration continued to value. It would involve no serious risk
to U.S. security since the United States could continue developments in the
most important strategic areas. And it would serve also to create the domestic consensus that the administration believed to be necessary for both
foreign policy and domestic political reasons. The president and secretary of
state chose to present both packages as a "giant step towards peace." That
the Soviet leadership rejected the proposals out-of-hand as "one-sided"
threw into sharp relief the contradictions in the U.S. position. On the one
hand, the Carter administration had publicized the Moscow talks as an important step toward a new SALT agreement, thereby raising public expectations. On the other hand, proposals made in such a public forum had to
reflect a very firm position to satisfy alarmist fears of unilateral concessions
on vital U.S. interests. The Soviet leadership's cold reception to these proposals left the Carter administration with the task of reducing both frustrated
expectations and public anxiety.

Between January and the Moscow meetings in late March, General
Secretary Brezhnev had, on several occasions, prodded the new administration for responses to Soviet proposals, urging the rapid completion of the
drafting of the SALT II agreement. At Tula he affirmed "that the work of
preparing a strategic arms limitation agreement on the basis of which an
accord was reached in Vladivostok in late 1974 ought to be completed as
early as possible."[67] Noting both the more strident voices of U.S. "hawks"
and the possibility that the strategic arms race might accelerate with a new
generation of nuclear weapons, Brezhnev stressed that there was no time for
delay.[68] Even after the Carter administration had mounted its campaign for
human rights, Brezhnev still affirmed that time was of the essence in
negotiating a new SALT agreement, for example, in his speech to the Six-
teenth Congress of Soviet Trade Unions just prior to Secretary Vance's
arrival in Moscow. At that time, the general secretary noted two developments that were adversely affecting U.S.-Soviet relations: "a slander campaign about a mythical Soviet 'military threat,' " and attempts at "interference in our internal affairs."[69] Articles in both *Pravda* and *Izvestia* reiterated
these themes.[70] S. Kondrashkov warned the Carter administration that
linking political evangelism with diplomatic pragmatism might get out of
hand. Stating that a U.S. campaign for human rights would not force the
Soviet Union to violate its national sovereignty, he warned that enemies of
detente might manipulate this issue to prevent progress in other areas. "To

combine real life and a realistic foreign policy with Sunday sermons is very difficult or simply impossible."[71]

The Soviet leadership clearly anticipated that the Vance visit to Moscow would be a time of testing for both sides. Yet there is every indication that they were unprepared for either the character or the substance of the U.S. proposals. The public mode of stating the U.S. position, and the unilateral U.S. initiatives in revising the Vladivostok ceilings on strategic delivery vehicles, large ICBMs, and MIRV capabilities, came as unwelcome developments. At his press conference on March 31, Soviet Foreign Minister Gromyko rejected both the comprehensive and deferral proposals as nothing short of U.S. efforts to gain unilateral advantage of the USSR.[72] He noted the failure of the proposals to take into account Brezhnev's long-held initiatives to ban both the B-1 and the Trident class submarine ballistic nuclear (SSBN). At the same time, he made his sharpest criticisms of U.S. proposals on the cruise missile (which Washington had attempted to keep out of any arrangement for ceilings on strategic delivery vehicles), saying that cruise missiles were not covered by the Vladivostok accords. While Gromyko noted some progress in the Moscow talks, thanks to the "frank exchange of opinions," and singled out the creation of joint study groups on arms control topics as an important step, the prospects for a new SALT agreement by October 1977 were, to say the least, clouded after the Vance visit.

Prospects for a new SALT agreement have improved slightly since the Moscow talks. Negotiations between Secretary Vance and Foreign Minister Gromyko in May at Geneva underscored a willingness by both parties to continue the search for an agreement. Yet both powers are confronted with difficult choices. While President Carter removed one stumbling block by announcing that the United States would not place the B-1 bomber in production, the decision to go ahead with cruise missile development confronted the Soviet leadership with a weapon system that is relatively inexpensive; that can be launched from land, sea, and air; and in which the United States has a commanding lead in both range and accuracy. On the other hand, the Soviet Union has continued the deployment of both its Backfire bomber and SS-18 heavy missile with a MIRV capability. The response of the Soviet Union to the U.S. commitment to develop the cruise missile [with a range of 2,500 kilometers] has been to raise two new issues in the ongoing negotiations: U.S. forward-basing of nuclear delivery systems and checks upon the transfer of nuclear delivery vehicles to second powers.[73] It seems unlikely that either power will agree to forgo advantages in any of these areas.

President Carter's declaration in early October 1977 that a SALT II agreement was "in sight" suggested that both powers had made some concessions, and that a three-tier agreement would be the basis for further negotiations. It seems likely that such an agreement will include an eight-year treaty setting ceilings on ICBMs and long-range bombers; a three-year protocol limiting deployment of certain strategic systems by both sides, that is, long-range cruise missiles and the SS-18 ICBM; and a statement of principles to guide further negotiations, including a commitment to seek substantial reductions in strategic forces by 1980.[74] Should such an agreement be concluded on these terms, it would not radically affect the technological advantages that either side enjoys. Rather, its objective—and this seems to be the point of the Carter administration's proposals—would be to control the growth of nuclear arsenals, with major reductions to come in the next decade.

Treatment of such technical arms control issues as those presently under negotiation between the United States and the Soviet Union in isolation from the general framework of U.S.-Soviet relations transforms hardware into a fetish, and can lead to either unrealistic hopes or excessive pessimism. No arms control agreement—no matter how low the ceilings or what new weapons of mass destruction are banned—will terminate the ideological and political competition between the two superpowers. No admission that such competition will probably continue for the foreseeable future makes a thermonuclear arms race in search of strategic superiority a sane national policy. The objective of detente and arms control is at once more modest and more important: reducing the incentives to and capabilities of starting a nuclear war.

CONCLUSION

In October 1977, the SALT I agreement between the United States and the Soviet Union expired. On balance, that five-year agreement has contributed to both arms control and detente. Objective evidence suggests that in 1978 the United States does not possess the commanding strategic position that it held throughout the first two decades of the cold war, but this shift has little to do with detente or SALT. Short of a very expensive and unstable expansion of U.S. strategic forces during the last decade, there was little that the United States could have done to counter the rapid modernization of Soviet forces. Detente and the SALT negotiations seem to offer the best hope for a bilateral arrangement to control the arms race.

Unless the Carter administration uses all its negotiating leverage to press Moscow toward a new agreement that will guarantee quantitive and qualitative parity between the two powers' strategic nuclear forces into the 1980s, an escalation in the arms race will almost inevitably follow. Successful negotiations will require that the U.S. government accept as real and permanent continuing ideological struggle with the USSR. They also demand that the administration convince a skeptical and divided public that arms control, rather than a new round of the arms race with the Soviet Union, offers the best hope for U.S. national security and world peace.

NOTES

1. Melvin K. Laird, "Is This *Detente?*" *The Atlantic Community Quarterly* 13 (Fall 1975): 285.

2. Henry Kissinger, "The Moral Foundation of Foreign Policy," *The Atlantic Community Quarterly* 13 (Fall 1975): 277.

3. George Ball, "Capitulation at Helsinki," *The Atlantic Community Quarterly* 13 (Fall 1975) 287.

4. *New York Times*, March 2, 1976, p. 12.

5. *Washington Post*, March 3, 1976, Sec. A, p. 16.

6. *New York Times*, January 22, 1976, p. 7; and March 24, 1976, p. 6.

7. These powerful ideological currents in U.S. foreign policy have been treated by a number of revisionist scholars with whom I am in basic agreement. What seems so tragic about these ideological currents is that they have led to a foreign policy that no longer bears any significant relation to reality. See William Appleman Williams, *The Tragedy of American Diplomacy*, 2nd ed. (New York: Dell, 1962); Arno J. Mayer, *Politics and Diplomacy of Peacemaking: Containment and Counterrevolution at Versailles, 1918–1919* (New York: Knopf, 1967); and Thomas G. Paterson, *Soviet-American Confrontation: Postwar Reconstruction and the Origins of the Cold War* (Baltimore: Johns Hopkins University Press, 1973).

8. Zbigniew Brzezinski, "What Kind of Detente?" *The Atlantic Community Quarterly* 13 (Fall 1975): 289–92. According to Brzezinski, the following factors prevent detente from becoming "more comprehensive and enduring," that is, developing into an entente: Soviet ideological hostility, strategic secrecy, global indifference, distain for human rights, and reciprocity of treatment. For Soviet views on the possibility of detente becoming entente: see V. M. Berezhkov, "Prezidentskie vybory i razriadka," *SShA*, no. 6 (June 1976): 3.

9. V.I. Lenin, *Collected Works*, 4th ed. (Moscow: Progress, 1966), 33, 51–59, Fourth Anniversary of the October Revolution (October 14, 1921).

10. M. Rosenthal and P. Yudin, eds., *A Dictionary of Philosophy* (Moscow: Progress 1967), p. 334.

11. L. I. Brezhnev, *Report of the CPSU Central Committee and the Immediate Task of the Party in Home and Foreign Policy* (Moscow: Novosti, 1976), p. 39.

12. Ibid., pp. 32–35.

13. Kissinger, "The Moral Foundation of Foreign Policy," p. 270.

14. *Pravda*, April 2, 1976, p. 4.

15. Brezhnev, *Report of the CPSV Central Committee*, p. 24.

16. U.S., Congress, Senate, Committee on Armed Services, *United States/Soviet Military Balance: A Frame of Reference for Congress*, 94 Cong., 2d Sess., 1976, pp. 37–39.

17. Donald G. Brennan, "Arms Treaties with Moscow: Unequal Terms Unevenly Applied?" in *Agenda of the National Strategy Information Center* (New York: National Security Information Center, 1975); Paul N. Nitze, "Assuring Strategic Stability in an Era of Detente," *Foreign Affairs* 54 (January 1976): 208–32; and Jan M. Lodat, "Assuring Strategic Stability: An Alternative View," *Foreign Affairs* 54 (April 1976): 462–81. For a cogent discussion of the most common positions taken in such analyses, see Barry M. Blechman, "Handicapping the Arms Race: Are the Soviets Ahead?" *The New Republic*, January 3–10, 1976, pp. 19–21.

18. Nitze, "Assuring Strategic Stability in an Era of Detente." Nitze posits the following alternative postures for the United States in the strategic area: minimum deterrence; massive urban-industrial retaliation; mutual assured destruction; flexible response, including the ability to destroy Soviet counterforce without attacking urban centers; denial of war-winning capability to attack Soviet counterforce and still have strategic reserve to attack urban centers; nuclear war-winning capability to deter attacks and limit Soviet political and military initiatives abroad. Nitze does not explicitly promote the last position as that which the United States should adopt; however, his further comments in the July issue of *Foreign Affairs* (pp. 820–23) leave little

doubt that he assumes the Soviet leaders have accepted such a position.

19. William Schneider, Jr., and Francis P. Hoeber, eds., *Arms, Men and Military Budgets: Issues for Fiscal Year 1977* (New York. Crone, Russak, 1976), p 18 ff. and pp. 215 ff.; "The Artificial Crisis of American Security," *The Defense Monitor* 5, no. 3 (May 1976), and James R. Schlesinger, *Annual Defense Department Report to Congress on the FY 1976 and Transition Budgets, FY Authorization Request and FY 1976–1980 Defense Programs*, 1975. For Soviet analysis of U.S. strategic arms debate, see M. A. Mil'shtein and L. S. Semeiko, "SShA i vopros o novykh vidakh oruzhiia massovogo unichtozheniia" ("The USA and the Question of New Types of Weapons of Mass Destruction"), *SShA*, no. 5 (May 1976): 25–35.

20. Donald H. Rumsfield, *Annual Defense Department Report, FY 1977*, 1976, pp. 5–10.

21. Schlesinger, *Annual Defense Department Report, FY 1976 and FY 1977*, pp. I-12–II-2.

22. Foy D. Kohler, "Forward," in Leon Goure, *War Survival and Soviet Strategy: USSR Civil Defense* (Miami Center for Advanced International Studies of Miami University, 1976), p. xiii.

23. *New York Times*, March 24, 1976, 6; and Paul H. Nitze, "Forward," in Schneider and Hoeber, *Arms, Men and Military Budgets*, p. xiv. Middleton explicitly argues for new strategic weapons systems as a check on Soviet adventurism around the globe, while Nitze attributes a crucial role in galvanizing U.S. opinion to the Middle East crisis of 1973.

24. See John T. Haywood, "The Case for a Modernized U.S. Navy," in George H. Quester, ed., *Sea Power in the 1970's* (Port Washington, N. Y.: Kennikat, 1975), pp. 3–16; Edward Wegener, *The Soviet Naval Offensive* (Annapolis, Md.: U.S. Naval Institute, 1975), pp. 116–18; Robert A. Kilmarx, *Soviet-United States Naval Balance* (Washington: Center for Strategic and International Studies of Georgetown University, 1975); Norman Polmar, *Soviet Naval Power: Challenge for the 1970's*, 2nd ed. (New York: National Strategy for Information Center, 1974), pp. 96–108; Donald G. Brennan, "Arms Treaties with Moscow"; Nitze, "Assuring Strategic Stability in an Era of Detente"; Laird, "Is This Detente?"; and Goure, *War Survival and Soviet Strategy*.

25. Nitze, "Forward"; and Schlesinger, *Annual Defense Department Report, FY 1976 and 1977*, p. I-12.

26. "The Artificial Crisis of American Security," *The Defense Monitor* 5, no. 3 (May 1976: 1.

27. Ibid.

28. *The Defense Monitor* 5, no. 4 (June 1976).

29. George F. Kennan, "The United States and the Soviet Union, 1917–1976," *Foreign Affairs* 54 (July 1976): 689.

30. David N. Schwartz, "The Role of Deterrence in NATO Defense Strategy: Implications for Doctrine and Posture," *World Politics* 28 (October 1975): 128–33.

31. U.S., Congress, Senate, *United States/Soviet Military Balance*, pp. 26–33.

32. *New York Times*, March 8, 1976, p. 11. Comments of Senator William Proxmire and Les Aspin on Soviet force posture and Chinese People's Republic.

33. On naval affairs see Barry M. Blechman, *The Control of Naval Armaments: Prospects and Possibilities* (Washington: Brookings Institution, 1976); George H. Quester, "Naval Arms Races: Functional or Symbolic," in *Sea Power in the 1970's*, pp. 17–42; and M. MccGwirc, K. Booth, and J. McDonnell, eds., *Soviet Naval Policy: Objectives and Constraints* (New York: Praeger, 1974).

34. For a critique of the Schlesinger-Nitze position, see *New York Times*, April 29, 1976, p. 9; and "The New Nuclear Strategy, Battle of the Dead?" *The Defense Monitor* 5, no. 5 (July 1976), pp. 1–8.

35. Barry M. Blechman and Edward R. Fried, "Controlling the Defense Budget," *Foreign Affairs* 54 (January 1976): 248–49.

36. One of the most telling points in support of the realists' position vis-à-vis the alarmists

is their sophisticated grasp of the relationship between Soviet grand strategy and the system of defense *(oborony strany)*, on the one hand, and combat systems of the armed forces and their institutional manifestations, on the other. In this context, declarations by Soviet military commanders about war-winning capabilities and the utility of war in national policy are not treated as overt declarations of national strategic policy, but as manifestations of system capabilities. See James M. McConnell, "The Gorshkov Articles, the New Gorshkov Book and Their Relation to Policy," *Center for Naval Analyses Professional Papers*, no. 159 July 1976, pp. 67–89. For an enlightening treatment of the political factor in Soviet strategic calculations, see Christopher D. Jones, "Just Wars and Limited Wars: Restraints on the Use of the Soviet Armed Forces," *World Politics* 28 (October 1976): 44–68; and Peter Vigor, *The Soviet View of War, Peace, and Neutrality* (London: Routledge & Kegan Paul, 1976), pp. 155–59.

37.   "Posmertnye trudy generala Karla von Klauzevista o voine i vedenii voin" (von Clausewitz on War), *Leninskii sbornik* (Moscow, 1930): 436–37.

38.   Sergei Gorshkov, *Navies in War and Peace* (Annapolis, Md.: U.S. Naval Institute, 1975). On Gorshkov and his views as they relate to Soviet grand strategy, see McConnell, "The Gorshkov Articles."

39.   K. A. Stalbo, "Zigzagi amerikanskoi bol-shoi strategii" ("Zigzags of American Grand Strategy"), *Morskoi sbornik*, no. 8 (August 1971): 93–98. For an analysis of Stalbo's views relating to U.S. naval force postures and U.S. grand strategy, see Kenneth Hagan and Jacob W. Kipp, "US and USSR Naval Strategy," *United States Naval Institute Proceedings* 100 (November 1973): 38–44.

40.   International Institute for Strategic Studies, *The Military Balance, 1976–1977*. If the broadest ranges of Western estimates on Soviet defense spending over the last decade are taken into account, the rates range from 8 to 13 percent. However, within any one particular mode of analysis, the range of difference in percent of annual gross national product devoted to defense would be in the area of 1 percent during the last decade. This range makes no claim to exactness and is derived from CIA estimates for 1976. See U.S. Central Intelligence Agency, *Estimated Soviet Defense Spending in Rubles, 1970–1975* (Washington, D.C., 1976), p. 16.

41.   Doug Richardson, "Soviet Strategic Nuclear Rockets Guide," *Flight International*, December 11, 1976, pp. 1729–33.

42.   F. P. Avramchuk and S. A. Bartenev, "Ekonomicheskoi obosnovanie voennotekhnicheskoi politiki" ("Economic Basis of Military-technological Policy"), *Morskoi sbornik* (March 1969): 24.

43.   William E. Odom, "The 'Militarization' of Soviet Society," *Problems of Communism* September–October 1976, pp. 34–51.

44.   Ibid., pp. 35–49.

45.   Ibid., p. 51. For a penetrating treatment of the Soviet military buildup in historical perspective, see John Erickson, "The Soviet Military Effort in the 1970's: Perspectives and Priorities," *Brassey's Defense Yearbook*, 1976, pp. 84–108.

46.   Quincy Wright, "Maintaining Peaceful Coexistence," in *Preventing World War III: Some Proposals*, ed. Quincy Wright, William Evan, and Morton Deutsch (New York: Simon and Schuster, 1962), p. 411. William Odom, for one, cites Wright's observations on the correlation of socialist trends in societies that engage in modern wars. While his points are well taken from Wright's classic *A Study of War*, especially with regard to the military implications of political organization in Soviet society, one might wish that Odom had recognized the obverse side of this same process with regard to the United States: whether in the competition with the Soviet Union, Americans have not accelerated the process of militarization of their own society deserves serious and dispassionate examination.

47.   *Izvestia*, February 14, 1976, p. 3; *Pravda*, April 2, 1976, p. 4; and Berezhkov, "Prezidentskie vybory i razriadka," p. 14.

48.   Brezhnev, *Report of the CPSU Central Committee*, p. 20.

49.   Ibid., p. 21. For Soviet perceptions on the prospects of an acceleration in the strategic

arms race and its extension into new types of weapons of mass destruction, see Mil'shtein and Semeiko, "SShA i vopros o novykh vidakh oruzhiia massovogo unichtozheniia," pp. 25–35.

50. Brezhnev, *Report of the CPSU Central Committee*, p. 28.
51. Ibid., p. 29.
52. Ibid., pp. 29–30.
53. Izvestiia, July 30, 1976, p. 1.
54. Ibid.
55. Ibid.
56. Berezhkov, "Prezidentskie vybory i razriadka," pp. 12–14.
57. Ibid., pp. 6–7.
58. *New York Times*, January 12, 1977, p. 1.
59. Ibid., p. 12.
60. Ibid.
61. *New York Times*, January 3, 1977, p. 3.
62. *New York Times*, January 11, 1977, p. 33.
63. Ibid.
64. *New York Times*, January 12, 1977, p. 1.
65. *New York Times*, March 31, 1977, p. 12.
66. Ibid.
67. *Pravda*, January 19, 1977, pp. 1–2.
68. Ibid.
69. *Pravda*, March 22, 1977, p. 3.
70. *Pravda*, March 27, 1977, p. 5; and *Izvestiia* March 27, 1977, p. 3.
71. *Izvestiia*, March 27, 1977, p. 3.
72. *Pravda*, April 1, 1977, p. 2.
73. *Pravda*, April 14, 1977, pp. 4–5.
74. *New York Times*, October 11, 1977, pp. 1, 8.

Index

About the Editor and Contributors

DELLA W. SHELDON is Visiting Assistant Professor of Political Science at University of Nebraska, Lincoln, Nebraska. She is a frequent contributor at international, national, and regional international relations, Slavic, and political science conferences and a contributor to *Worldview*.

Dr. Sheldon received her B.A. from Sacramento State University and a Ph.D. in international relations from Claremont Graduate School, Claremont, California.

ELLIOT R. GOODMAN is Professor of Political Science at Brown University, Providence, Rhode Island. Dr. Goodman is the author of *The Soviet Design for a World State*, of *The Fate of the Atlantic Community*, and of numerous articles in U.S. and foreign professional journals. Dr. Goodman received his M.A. and Ph.D. from Columbia University.

ALICE GORLIN is an Assistant Professor of Economics at Oakland University, Rochester, Michigan. A contributor to *The Soviet Economy*, her articles on Soviet economic management have appeared in various journals in her field. She has served on numerous panels at professional conferences. Dr. Gorlin holds an M.A. and Ph.D. in economics from the University of Michigan.

ROBERT O. FREEDMAN is Professor of Political Science and Dean of the School of Graduate Studies at Baltimore Hebrew College, Baltimore, Maryland. Dr. Freedman is the author of *Economic Warfare in the Communist Bloc*, of *Soviet Policy Toward the Middle East Since 1970*, and of numerous articles on Soviet foreign policy and Middle Eastern politics. Dr. Freedman received an M.A. and a Ph.D. in international relations from Columbia University.

JACOB W. KIPP is Associate Professor of History at Kansas State University, Manhattan, Kansas. He coedited *History of the Soviet Air Force and Aviation* and *Acts of the International Commission on Military History* and was a contributor to *Soviet Naval Development*. Dr. Kipp received his M.A. and Ph.D. in history from Pennsylvania State University.

FRED WARNER NEAL is Professor of International Relations and Government and Chairman of the Program in International Relations at Claremont Graduate School, Claremont, California. Dr. Neal is the author of *Titoism in Action, Yugoslavia and the New Communism,* and *The Role of Small States in a Big World.* A contributor to several other books, he has also published widely on Soviet and U.S. foreign policy in both U.S. and international journals. Dr. Neal received his M.A. from Harvard and a Ph.D. in political science from the University of Michigan.

THOMAS W. ROBINSON is a Visiting Fellow at the National War College, Washington, D.C. Dr. Robinson is the co-author and editor of *The Cultural Revolution in China* and *Forecasting in International Relations* and has contributed to several other books and journals on China, the Soviet Union, and Japan. Dr. Robinson received his M.I.A. and Ph.D. from Columbia University.

Related Titles
Published by
Praeger Special Studies